The King is Dead, Long Live the King!

The King is Dead, Long Live the King!

Majesty, Mourning and Modernity in Edwardian Britain

MARTIN WILLIAMS

**HODDER &
STOUGHTON**

First published in Great Britain in 2023 by Hodder & Stoughton
An Hachette UK company

1

Copyright © Martin Williams 2023

A CIP catalogue record for this title is available from the British Library

Hardback ISBN 978 1 529 38331 7
eBook ISBN 978 1 529 38332 4

Typeset in Bembo MT by Hewer Text UK Ltd, Edinburgh
Printed and bound in Great Britain by Clays Ltd, Elcograf S.p.A.

Hodder & Stoughton policy is to use papers that are natural, renewable
and recyclable products and made from wood grown in sustainable forests.
The logging and manufacturing processes are expected to conform
to the environmental regulations of the country of origin.

Hodder & Stoughton Ltd
Carmelite House
50 Victoria Embankment
London EC4Y 0DZ

www.hodder.co.uk

For B,
who knows why

'What will the Future make of the Present?'

C. F. G. Masterman,
The Condition of England, 1909

Contents

Author's Note

The seeds of this book were sown in 2019. The majority of my research having been carried out during 2021, I began to write in January 2022. Work was under way on revisions to the first draft when Queen Elizabeth II died at Balmoral on 8 September 2022. With that event, the chapters pertaining to the death, lying-in-state and funeral of King Edward VII became doubly, and even eerily, poignant.

Edward's reign was short. That of his great-granddaughter was of a length unprecedented in British history. Although the tastes of Her Late Majesty were markedly less opulent than those of her forebear, the two monarchs had several things in common: their love of Sandringham, their passion for horse racing and their unrivalled prestige on the international stage. Prior to 1952, Edward was the most peripatetic sovereign of the twentieth century. Whether he would have relished or balked at the vast distances travelled by Elizabeth over the course of seven decades is a matter of conjecture.

What cannot be doubted is the unswerving devotion to duty that characterised both King and Queen, and the deep-seated affection they inspired in their peoples.

PROLOGUE: 'How sad it is!'

Tuesday, 14 June 1910

The weather on the first day of Ascot was close to perfect. After a morning that had been dull and overcast, the clouds had rolled away to leave a sparkling summer afternoon. In the pretty little garden behind the Grandstand, race-goers basked in glorious sunshine as they listened to the band of the Royal Marines. On the roofs of the coaches drawn up in orderly lines on the Heath, picnic hampers were flung open to reveal pigeon pie, lobster salad and bottles of vintage champagne. In the crowded club tents, tips were exchanged along with the latest gossip from Mayfair and Westminster. Vigilant mamas manoeuvred debutante daughters while journalists scribbled notes on the sartorial triumphs and failures of the Season. Enacted against a backdrop of striped canvas, freshly painted trelliswork and bright rhododendrons, a more decorous scene could hardly be imagined.

Even a cursory glance, however, revealed it to be an Ascot unlike any other. King Edward VII had died five weeks earlier and the nation was deep in mourning. Within the rigorously exclusive confines of the Royal Enclosure, the cream of high society mingled in black garb of the utmost formality. For men, that entailed burnished black silk hats, black coats, black trousers, black ties, black gloves and neatly furled black umbrellas. Instead of their customary florals and pastels, ladies wore narrow-skirted gowns of black silk chiffon, black charmeuse and black mousseline de soie. Fluttering parasols bobbed above feather boas and gigantic hats, all of them dyed the deepest black. The very race-cards had black edges. The effect of so much funereal splendour massed on the manicured lawn was sobering. Again and again, the same remark was heard: 'How sad it is!'[1] Even the bookies in their designated corner were less raucous than usual.

The contrast with the Epsom Derby of 1909 was stark. On that damp occasion, the royal horse Minoru had passed the post to ecstatic cheers. Descending to the paddock, the King had been mobbed by well-wishers. Even the policemen assembled for his protection had tossed their helmets into the air. In the crush, somebody had begun to sing the National Anthem. Gradually, it was picked up by the crowd until the downs thundered with its patriotic strains. Queen Alexandra was observed to be quite overcome by her husband's reception. That night, the members of the Jockey Club convened at Buckingham Palace. After a sumptuous banquet of devilled whitebait, salmon mousse, quail cutlets, venison, ortolans and *chartreuse de fraises à la Léopold* washed down with Château Lafite 1875, toasts of loyalty and congratulation were proposed by the Prince d'Arenberg and the Earl of Coventry. It was a fitting end to an unforgettable day.

Only a monarch as popular as Edward could have elicited such demonstrations of jubilation and sorrow. He reigned for less than a decade yet left an indelible impression on the retina of his age. In his person, the English saw their aspirations reassuringly – indeed, joyfully – affirmed. His love of sport, rich food, fine wine and beautiful women was proverbial. Neither abstemious nor hypocritical, his easy charm and pleasant vices made him seem infinitely relatable.

Gregarious, charismatic and cosmopolitan, the King relished his role as a roving goodwill ambassador. More peripatetic than any of his predecessors, his flair for diplomacy proved extremely beneficial. Under his genial auspices, relations with France and Russia improved by leaps and bounds. Those with Germany remained problematic, but the threat of war was, for the time being, contained. In the minds of many of his subjects, the emollient Edward was personally responsible for the maintenance of peace in Europe.

In a climate of energy and optimism, Britain dilated. The pace of progress was staggering. Electricity and wireless, automobiles and aeroplanes: cutting-edge technology augured a future that would be bright, fast and safe. The capital of the greatest empire in history, London rose to dizzy heights of architectural magnificence. For its theatres, restaurants, department stores and grand hotels, they were golden years. Decorators, dressmakers and jewellers amassed fame and fortune in the service of the upper class. The elegance was extreme, the luxury overwhelming. Above all, there was faith in the immutability of those values – imperial, patriarchal, hierarchical – that had been imported wholesale from the nineteenth century. Looking back in later life, Violet Bonham Carter, whose father was Prime Minister from 1908, could only marvel at the blithe self-assurance of the world of her youth. The established order was, she recalled, 'as firmly fixed on earth as the signs of the Zodiac in the sky'.[2]

Except, of course, it wasn't.

Away from the rose-tinted milieu of palm courts, garden parties and race meetings, millions lived in abject poverty. From 1906, the Liberals moved to eliminate, or at least to mitigate, the worst inequalities by setting in motion a vigorous programme of reforms. The initiative sparked an acrimonious stand-off as the House of Commons went head-to-head with the Tory-dominated House of Lords. The long-running battle between elected government and hereditary privilege tested Edward so sorely that he flirted with the idea of abdication.

Parliament was under assault from without as well as within. No matter how highly educated or financially independent, women were ineligible for the vote. Polite activism having failed, militant suffragettes went on the offensive. Under the leadership of the messianic Emmeline Pankhurst, they adopted ever more disruptive tactics to achieve their goal.

Culture, too, was in a state of ferment. In the squares of Bloomsbury, brilliant and iconoclastic painters, writers and critics were evolving modes of thought, perception and behaviour that prized individuality over conformity and self-expression over inhibition. In the early months of 1910, they were gestating an art exhibition that would baffle, appal and astound, but would fundamentally redefine Britain's relationship with modernism.

Long considered unassailable, the status quo was under severe pressure. Slow to germinate, the seeds of the twentieth century were poised to flower in full.

There was little sign of these tensions in the funeral rites of Edward VII. From the lying-in-state in Westminster Hall to the Royal Enclosure at Ascot, his obsequies – sober, dignified and, for the most part, well-choreographed – provided an opportunity for a fractured and fractious nation to come together. Yet even in the depths of grief, thoughts turned uneasily to the future. Clearly felt, if imperfectly understood, the significance of the moment was lost upon nobody. Surveying the febrile landscape all around, G. K. Chesterton articulated the prevailing sense of apprehension in a tribute published on 14 May. 'We can all feel that England is in a crisis, and that England is taking a turn,' he wrote. 'We all know that the King mattered mightily to the turn that it took; and we all know that the King is dead.'[3] The obvious question – what will happen now? – was left hanging.

Unlike Chesterton and his readers, we know the answer. That doesn't make the story of the Edwardian era any less compelling. On the contrary: it is more relevant today than it has ever been. Surfeited with material comforts, our society is once again riven by dissent and disaffection. The gaps between rich and poor, conservative and progressive yawn wider by the year. In thrall to hitherto unimaginable forms of technology, we have no inkling of their long-term consequences. We are the beneficiaries of an unprecedented period of peace yet are increasingly beset by fears of war. In 2022, just as in

1910, political differences were temporarily forgotten while the country bade farewell to a beloved monarch. On both occasions, recollection was swift.

A fortnight after Edward's death, Princess Daisy of Pless reflected on the tragic turn of events. 'The shock I may say has passed, but the feeling of a sudden dark cloud and great change will remain for very long, I am sure,' she confided to her diary; 'in fact, for me, the whole face of England seems changed.'[4] In the coming months and years, that cloud would swell in size and menace. Far from blotting out the setting sun, it only accentuated the weird and discordant hues suffusing the skies above Britain. In their glow, the lineaments of a new age – our age – could be traced.

1: 'He went everywhere, saw everyone, and *listened*'

SOCIETY'S IDOL, 1891.

Early on the evening of 22 January 1901, Queen Victoria died at Osborne House, her overblown Italianate villa on the Isle of Wight. In recent months, her health had given increasing cause for concern. Her eyesight had deteriorated, she had required assistance when she walked and a deepening depression had manifested itself in bouts of insomnia and indigestion. Her passing at the age of eighty-one was nevertheless a shock. Since her accession sixty-three years earlier, she had been a reassuringly constant presence in an ever-changing world. A dignified but unglamorous figure barely five feet tall, she was a creature of habit with an aversion to show. More comfortable wearing a bonnet than a crown, she personified the values – solidity, sobriety, propriety – of the era to which she gave her name. The majority of her subjects could remember no other monarch.

A mother of nine, Victoria had outlived three of her children. Of the remaining six, those who were able hastened to Osborne when it became clear she was failing. Seated at her bedside, her eldest son, Edward, was present when she drew her last breath. At that moment, he stepped seamlessly, as was the royal custom, into the role she had occupied for so long. The transition took some getting used to. When Victoria's coffin was carried aboard the royal yacht *Alberta* for transportation to the mainland, Edward, who followed on the *Victoria and Albert*, noticed the Royal Standard was flying at half-mast. In a message to the captain, he demanded an explanation. 'The Queen is dead, Sir,' he was told.

'The King of England lives!' he replied. The Standard was promptly hoisted to full-mast.[1]

In an age in which life expectancy hovered around fifty, Edward VII, at fifty-nine, was considered old. It was not at all certain he was wise. The American novelist Henry James was stricken when he learnt of Victoria's demise, and apprehensive about the future. 'I feel as if her death will have consequences in and for this country that no man can foresee,' he wrote from the Reform Club. 'The Queen's magnificent duration had held things magnificently – beneficently – together and prevented all sorts of accidents. Her death, in short, will let loose incalculable forces for possible ill. I am very pessimistic.'[2] He was not reassured by the reputation of the man he derided as 'Fat Edward – E. the Caresser'.[3] The King's infidelities were, he considered, a bad omen. For James, Victoria had been 'a sustaining symbol – and the wild waters are upon us now'.[4]

Such extravagant misgivings may have been premature, but they were not isolated. In a pompous editorial, *The Times* alluded to Edward's chequered history, which had, on more than one occasion, brought him close to disaster. 'We shall not pretend that there is nothing in his long career which those who respect and admire him could not wish otherwise,' it sighed.[5] Clearly, the new king had big shoes to fill. Many doubted he was up to the job.

In the event, the most entrenched sceptics were forced to admit they were wrong about Edward. Not many years elapsed before he proved himself to be one of the most able and, moreover, popular monarchs Britain had ever known. Contrary to expectation, his marathon stint as Prince of Wales had equipped him with the tools to be an exemplary ruler.

Born at Buckingham Palace on 9 November 1841, Albert Edward – known to his relatives as 'Bertie' – was the second child of Queen Victoria and her German husband, Prince Albert of Saxe-Coburg and Gotha. Although secure in their love for each other, his parents were haunted by recollections of Victoria's predecessors: her grandfather, George III, who had died blind and senile, and her paternal uncles, the dissolute George IV and the bluff but uninspiring William IV. Now, with the nineteenth century well under way, and the demand for democracy growing ever more clamorous, the survival of the dynasty was felt to be vested in the virtue of the sovereign – and of her heir.

When scarcely out of his cradle, Edward became the subject of a remorseless programme of education designed by his father to mould him into the 'perfect man' and, in time, the perfect king. It was an experiment doomed to failure. Every waking hour was crammed with lessons. Holidays were few and far between. Worse, the naturally gregarious prince was segregated from boys of his own age, and particularly from the sprigs of an aristocracy his parents believed to be decadent and corrupt. The punishing regime might have suited the serious and compulsively industrious Albert. It didn't suit his son. Wrung out by the impossible pace, Edward was prone to ungovernable tantrums in which he screamed, shouted and threw things. It was obvious he had inherited the Hanoverian temper of his mother. The Prince of Wales was, Victoria admitted, her 'caricature', every bit as stubborn and wilful as she was herself. Not that she found the similarity endearing. On the contrary, courtiers believed that history was repeating itself. 'The hereditary and unfailing antipathy of our Sovereigns to their Heir Apparent seems . . . early to be taking root, and the Queen does not much like the child,' noted the diarist Charles Greville.[6]

Given the strenuousness of his education, it was remarkable just how little, when he finally came of age, Edward was given to *do*. Prince Albert, who loved but never really understood his son, died of typhoid in December 1861. Thereafter Victoria, who had come to depend on her husband utterly, guarded her prerogatives jealously. Whatever skills Edward possessed were not to be deployed in her service. The Queen asserted her wish that he should be kept out of government and public affairs. 'Her Majesty is very much opposed to the system of putting the Prince of Wales forward as the representative of the Sovereign,' the Home Secretary was informed in 1864. It was her considered opinion that it would be 'most undesirable' to give him any kind of official role that might 'bring him forward too frequently before the people'.[7] Mired in funereal seclusion at Windsor, Osborne and Balmoral, Victoria was virtually invisible to her subjects, but she was not about to cede her rightful place in their affections. For almost forty years, Edward was without any particular responsibilities. He had to wait until April 1898, when he was fifty-six, to be granted permission to deputise for his mother at a meeting of the Privy Council.

The Prince of Wales found his enforced inactivity intensely frustrating. To his Private Secretary, Francis Knollys, he complained that 'he is not of the slightest use to the Queen; that everything he says or suggests is pooh-poohed'.[8] His exclusion from affairs of state compelled him to seek other means of occupation. Averse to books, Edward excelled in an area that was to prove indispensable to the modern conception of royalty. He was marvellous with people. With time hanging heavy, he immersed himself in two activities, travel and social life, that stood him in excellent stead when at last he ascended the throne.

Edward grew up in an era when, thanks to advances in technology and transportation, the world was shrinking. Railways and steam ships enabled him to roam further afield than any Prince of Wales had before. He relished the excursions to France, Switzerland, Germany, Italy, Spain and Portugal he undertook while still in his teens. In 1860, he was despatched to Canada and the United States on a tour that saw him feted in Halifax, Toronto, Montreal, Washington, Cincinnati, Pittsburgh, Chicago, St Louis, Philadelphia and Baltimore. In New York, immense crowds cheered him down Broadway as he rode in a carriage at the side of the mayor. Three thousand guests were invited to a ball in his honour at the Academy of Music. Five thousand turned up; so many, in fact, that the floor collapsed beneath their weight and carpenters had to be summoned to repair it as the bejewelled and crinolined throng palpitated in the presence of the handsome young heir. The tour marked the beginning of a mutually appreciative relationship between Edward and the American people that would last for the rest of his life. More than that: it inaugurated the American obsession with the British Royal Family that endures to this day.

Over the next two decades, the Prince of Wales travelled all over the globe: to Palestine and the Middle East in 1862, to Egypt in 1869, to Russia in 1866 and 1874 and to India in 1875-6. Everywhere he went, his curiosity and innate charm endeared him to his hosts. In Oxford, where he spent a spell as a student at Christ Church, Dean Liddell found Edward to be 'the nicest fellow possible, so simple, naïve, ingenuous and modest, and moreover with extremely good wits; possessing also the Royal faculty of never forgetting a face'.[9] They were attributes the Prince put to excellent use on his tours, enhancing the profile of the Crown and broadening his own horizons. By the standards of the age, he was remarkably free of racial prejudice. He deplored as 'disgraceful' the callous disdain shown towards the native population by the British in India, expressing his belief that just 'because a man has a black face and a different religion from our own, there is no reason why he should be treated as a brute'.[10] Early in his reign, he severed all but the most formal ties with his cousin King Leopold II of the Belgians, because of atrocities in the Belgian Congo. Through his complicity in the barbarous acts committed in his name, Leopold had, Edward considered, 'neglected his duty towards Humanity'.[11]

Even as he unfurled on the international stage, the Prince of Wales put down roots at home. On 10 March 1863, he married Princess Alexandra of Denmark in St George's Chapel at Windsor. It was less of an occasion than it might have been. Prince Albert had died fifteen months earlier. Queen Victoria remained in such deep mourning that she refused to mingle with the congregation, preferring to view the ceremony from Catherine of Aragon's closet high above the Quire. She could at least console herself that her late husband would have approved of the proceedings. One of Albert's final projects had been to earmark Alexandra as a prospective bride. Now he was dead, his every word was law. In carrying out his father's wishes, Edward was merely fulfilling what Victoria held to be his 'sacred duty'.[12]

Never passionate, the match was reasonably successful. Alexandra, or 'Alix' as she was known within the family, won all hearts with her beauty, grace and charm. Even the hard-to-please Queen adored her. 'This jewel!' Victoria raved, after one of their first meetings. 'She is one of those sweet creatures who seem to come from the skies to help and bless poor mortals and lighten for a time their path!'[13] Born and raised in sleepy Copenhagen where her father, Prince Christian, was Heir Presumptive, Alexandra was touchingly devoid of pretension. 'You perhaps think that I like marrying your Brother for his position,' she told one of her in-laws, 'but if he was a cowboy I would love him just the same and would marry no one else.'[14]

Although the sentiment was undoubtedly sincere, Alexandra revelled in her new-found eminence. Together, she and Edward rocketed to the head of London Society. In town, they lived at Marlborough House, designed in the early years of the eighteenth century by Sir Christopher Wren, but now splendidly remodelled at great expense. Their country estate, Sandringham in Norfolk, was undistinguished, if not downright ugly. 'No fine trees, no water, no hills, in fact no attraction of any sort or kind,' moaned the Countess of Macclesfield, who, as Alexandra's Lady of the Bedchamber, was compelled to spend a considerable amount of time there. 'As there was all England wherein to choose, I do wish they had had a finer house in a more picturesque and cheerful situation.'[15] Sandringham's charms were debatable, but it was greatly loved by its master and mistress. In any case, nobody ever refused an invitation. For four decades, membership of the so-called Marlborough House Set denoted the ultimate in elegance and exclusivity.

At the time of their marriage, Queen Victoria had attempted to lay some ground rules for the Prince and Princess of Wales. She recommended they eschew festivities during the Season and limit their circle to only the most irreproachable members of Society: two or three Cabinet ministers, say, and perhaps a 'very few' high-ranking and elderly peers. To stray beyond those narrow perimeters would be to court disaster. Decrying the 'love of pleasure, self-indulgence, luxury and idleness' of the elite, Victoria evoked the spectre of the French Revolution as a warning to her son and his cronies.

'The Aristocracy and the Higher Classes must take *great care*, or their position may become *very* dangerous,' she wrote in 1868. 'I shall do what I can in this direction, but as you mix much with the gay and the fashionable, you can do more, and so can dear Alix, to whom I wish you to show this letter.'[16] Edward and Alexandra paid no heed. Young, attractive and energetic, they were soon to be seen at every lighted candle. To Victoria's dismay, they became 'nothing but puppets, running about for show all day and all night'.[17] The Queen foresaw calamity in the hedonism of a couple so addicted to fun.

Sure enough, Edward would sail perilously close to the wind on at least two highly publicised and embarrassing occasions. In 1869, Sir Charles Mordaunt, a member of the Marlborough House Set, sued his wife for divorce. Letters were produced, which suggested the Prince of Wales might have been among her lovers. Although their contents were in fact fairly innocuous, Edward was summoned as a witness by Lady Mordaunt's counsel. In the course of his seven-minute testimony, he categorically refuted the allegation of impropriety. Sir Charles's petition was dismissed, but not before real, if only temporary, harm was done to the Prince's reputation.

The second incident, which unfolded between 1890 and 1891, was more compromising still. During a stay at Tranby Croft, the Yorkshire home of the shipping magnate Arthur Wilson, Sir William Gordon-Cumming was observed to be cheating at baccarat. It was a serious breach of the rules of gentlemanly conduct. In exchange for their silence on the matter, Gordon-Cumming's accusers made him sign a pledge that he would never again play cards for money. Edward, who was among the party, was one of the witnesses, adding his own signature alongside those of the other male guests.

In spite of the promise of secrecy, the debacle was soon the talk of fashionable London. His good name in jeopardy, Gordon-Cumming resorted to legal action. Once again, the Prince of Wales was required to testify in court. After a trial that attracted immense interest, the jury returned a verdict against the plaintiff, who was expelled from his regiment and clubs, and never again received in Society. Nevertheless, the case shone an unwelcome light into the workings of the Marlborough House Set. Republicans, Nonconformists and middle-class moralists fell over each other to express their outrage over the tawdry revelations of illegal gambling and questionable ethics.

Edward became so unpopular he was even booed at Ascot. Although the furore eventually died down, the memory of it lingered. What became known as 'the Royal Baccarat Scandal' was uppermost in the minds of those who, like Henry James, expressed doubts about the character of the King upon his accession. Edward's track record was littered with indiscretions. His talents had yet to reveal themselves.

Between the incessant dinners, balls and race meetings, the nursery at Marlborough House filled with children. Albert Victor was born in 1864, followed by George in 1865, Louise in 1867, Victoria in 1868 and Maud in 1869. A third son, Alexander, lived for just one day in 1871. The quick-fire succession of pregnancies undermined Alexandra's increasingly fragile health. A bout of chronic arthritis caused her agonising pain and left her permanently lame in one leg. Worse, her hearing, which had never been good, degenerated to the point that she was no longer able to follow conversations or enjoy music. For one who loved company, this was a cruel blow.

Over time, her well-concealed afflictions pushed the Princess of Wales into the wings of her husband's frenetic social life. By the mid-1870s, their relationship had settled into a comfortable groove. They were undoubtedly fond of each other. Alexandra's loyalty to Edward was absolute. Grateful for her devotion, he was careful to ensure she would never be slighted or disrespected. Still, he remained a man of prodigious appetites with too much leisure and a tendency towards boredom. With his wife indisposed, he embarked upon a wandering quest that would see him linked to any number of women. Some of his dalliances were transitory. Others were more serious. During the final quarter of the nineteenth century, he had a succession of mistresses tacitly recognised by Society at large. The first was the celebrated beauty and actress Lillie Langtry. The second was the pretty but indiscreet Lady Brooke, subsequently Countess of Warwick. The third, from 1898 until the end of his life, was Alice Keppel, the attractive wife of a younger son of the 7th Earl of Albemarle.

Although there was a great deal of gossip about his liaisons, Edward was never flagrant. There were no exposés or kiss-and-tells. In any case, as long as appearances were maintained, adultery in the upper class was taken for granted. Worldly hostesses took pains to keep abreast of the extra-marital activities of their guests and allocated bedrooms accordingly. It was one of the ironies of the era that single girls were considered untouchable. No self-respecting gentleman would have dared seduce a debutante. Once wed, however, and provided she had furnished her husband with a couple of children indisputably his own, a lady was permitted to take a lover. All of Edward's 'official' mistresses were safely married.

There is no evidence Alexandra ever tried to even the score with her errant spouse. She did possess one admirer, the Honourable Oliver Montagu, who was a younger son of the 7th Earl of Sandwich. A confirmed bachelor, he worshipped the ground she walked on. At every ball, the Princess of Wales – who, in the words of the Countess of Antrim, 'remained marvellously circumspect' – danced the first after-supper waltz with her besotted 'cavalier'.[18] Edward rejected the suggestion of impropriety out of hand. It would be an insult to his wife, he told one busybody, to ask her to see less of her friend. After Montagu's death from cancer in 1893, Alexandra applied herself, with every sign of contentment, to her children, her charities and her family in Denmark to whom she was devoted. Adored by all, she was an icon of royal glamour. The jewelled chokers she wore to conceal a scar on her throat became high fashion. Even her limp was slavishly emulated by those who aspired to her allure. But compared with that of her husband, her influence in Society was slight.

For, despite his mother's misgivings, real advantages had accrued from Edward's relentless pleasure-seeking. It was an age in which the levers of power were, for the most part, in the hands of the aristocracy. Statesmanship and high-level diplomacy were transacted not just in Westminster and Whitehall but in the embassies and country houses he frequented so assiduously. Conversations over billiards and brandy could reverberate across Europe. The Prince of Wales was able to hone his skills and knowledge of world affairs in the company of ministers and ambassadors as well as Guards officers and racehorse owners. He gathered around him a cabal of well-placed friends and advisers who kept him abreast of the latest developments, and through whom he could communicate his opinions and wishes. Politically conservative but socially ecumenical, he forged a new elite defined as much by pragmatism as by his insatiable appetite for amusement. Edward's commitment to the status quo was instinctive and unswerving – he was adamantly opposed to the suffragette movement and regarded with distaste the Labour Party, which emerged at the turn of the twentieth century – but so was his belief that enjoyment could be found in company that was neither male nor patrician.

Between 1870 and 1914, dozens of American women married into the British aristocracy: a cohort so numerous that, in time, 17 per cent of the peerage and 12 per cent of the baronetage could claim transatlantic connections. 'At the present day, so close has the union between ourselves and the United States become that Americans are hardly looked upon as foreigners at all, so many people having American relatives,' marvelled the octogenarian Lady Dorothy Nevill in 1907.[19]

From this sequence of high-profile matches, a number of stereotypes – of mercenary toffs, hapless heiresses and pushy parents – emerged. In 1893, Cornelia Martin brought a million dollars to her husband, the 4th Earl of Craven. When Consuelo Vanderbilt was coerced by her mother into marriage with the 9th Duke of Marlborough two years later, her dowry included $2.5 million in preferred railway stock. May Goelet, who wed the 8th Duke of Roxburghe in 1903, was so amply funded that her settlement permitted Floors Castle, up in the draughty Scottish Borders, to break out in a rash of Gobelins tapestries and state-of-the-art plumbing. The 'cash for coronets' phenomenon was real enough. Yet the so-called 'Dollar Princesses' were appreciated for their own sakes too. Sophisticated, self-confident and, above all, fun, the Americans introduced fresh air and vitality into an aristocracy sorely in need of ventilation. The high-spirited Consuelo Yznaga, who married Viscount Mandeville, later 8th Duke of Manchester, in 1876, was one of Edward's closest friends. When she died in late 1909, *The Times* paid tribute to her 'high intelligence, sunny nature and uncommon personal charm', traits she shared with many of her compatriots and which, her anonymous obituarist believed, had had 'a profound physiological influence upon a certain stratum of the upper classes'.[20]

It was an influence that worked in both directions. Many of the Americans came to feel a passionate devotion to their adopted land. 'There is only one place and one great society in the world & that is London & the English,' declared Belle Wilson, who married a younger brother of the 13th Earl of Pembroke in 1888.[21] Even Consuelo Vanderbilt, whose union with Marlborough was notoriously

you good night, for I must set to work,' he said, pointing to a stack of boxes containing official papers.

Redesdale was astonished. 'Surely,' he exclaimed, 'Your Majesty is not going to tackle all that work tonight!'

Edward merely beamed. 'Yes, I must!" he replied. 'Besides, it is all so interesting.'[29]

Somehow, his responsibilities were made to fit around an itinerary that saw him constantly on the move. Christmas and New Year were spent at Sandringham. Dipping into London at intervals throughout January, the King was in residence at Buckingham Palace for the whole of February. In March, he departed for the Continent, invariably passing through Paris on his way to Biarritz. The Season found him back in London during the week, and at various country houses at the weekends. Windsor was his base for Ascot in June, followed by Goodwood in July and Cowes Regatta in early August. After taking the waters at Marienbad in the present-day Czech Republic, Edward returned to London in early September before departing for the races at Doncaster. Balmoral was visited in October, with break-out trips to Newmarket. During the late autumn and winter, he rotated between Buckingham Palace, Windsor and Sandringham, when the cycle would begin all over again. Not since the fabled progresses of Elizabeth I had a British monarch been so mobile, or so visible. Yet, frenetic as it was, the unvaried routine introduced stability into the once rackety royal lifestyle. 'Far behind now is the *Sturm und Drang* period,' wrote a commentator of the Edwardian Court in 1903. 'The fierce light is lowered; only a mellow lustre illuminates the scene. Pleasure was formerly a passion; it has been transfigured into an art.'[30] Having learnt from past mistakes, the King had at last acquired dignity.

Edward's outreach was more than merely national. Thanks to an intricately woven tapestry that saw him related by blood or marriage to most of the crowned heads of Europe, he enjoyed unrivalled access in any number of capitals. His father-in-law was the King of Denmark, while his brother-in-law was the King of Greece. Various nieces and nephews either occupied or were set to occupy the thrones of Germany, Russia, Sweden, Spain and Romania. In 1905, his youngest daughter, Maud, became the Queen of Norway. As comfortable in Vienna and Lisbon as he was in Paris and St Petersburg, Edward was almost uniquely versed in Continental as well as domestic affairs. He actively encouraged his ambassadors to supplement their official reports with off-the-record accounts of their private impressions and opinions. The British-born Princess Daisy of Pless was succinct in her analysis of his influence: 'He went everywhere, saw everyone, and *listened*.'[31] His last foreign secretary, Sir Edward Grey, admitted that 'the King's own knowledge and judgement is much superior' to that of any of his ministers.[32]

Slow to be appreciated by his mother, Edward's gifts were given free rein after her death. His accession coincided with a shift in government thinking that saw him, over the next nine years, burnish a reputation as an extra-mural diplomat, whose travels were seen as indivisible from the maintenance of peace in an increasingly fractious Europe. It was a heavy burden, but one he experienced, at least at first, as a source of pleasure and satisfaction – and never more so than during his epoch-defining visit to France in the spring of 1903.

2: 'A perfect master of his métier!'

ÉDOUARD VII. — Hein! je vous l'avais bien dit : Chamberlain ne veut que votre bien.
LE PRÉSIDENT. — C'est justement là ce qui m'inquiète.   Dessin de CAVAL et lini.

Edward had long been an ardent Francophile. In August 1855, at the impressionable age of thirteen, he accompanied his parents on a state visit to Emperor Napoleon III in Paris. Dressed by Worth and set to music by Offenbach and Waldteufel, the glamour of the French Court went straight to his head. As a model, it provided a shimmering alternative to the dowdy domesticity of Osborne and Balmoral. On the day of his departure, Edward begged the elegant Empress Eugénie to let him and his elder sister remain a while longer. When she tactfully suggested that Victoria and Albert would not be able to do without them, he was swift to disabuse her. 'I don't fancy that,' he scoffed, 'for there are six more of us at home, and they don't want us.'[1]

Since that intoxicating initiation, Edward had returned on numerous occasions. Eugénie obligingly arranged introductions to the most beautiful and sophisticated women at the Tuileries and Compiègne. 'You are going to enjoy yourself for once,' she told him, 'and don't worry about your keeper. I know he has orders to get you off to bed at eleven, but I'll corner him and keep him talking.'[2] The ladies of Paris Society proved hospitable in more ways than one. It was rumoured that the abrupt reconciliation of the Prince and Princesse de Sagan, who had been estranged for several years, was the result of an unforeseen pregnancy, and that their second son had in fact been sired by the heir to the British throne. The Austrian ambassador in London liked to regale guests with the story of Edward's supposedly anonymous arrival at the Moulin Rouge. Known to her fans as 'La Goulue', the can-can dancer Louise Weber had mischievously shattered his incognito. *'Ullo, Wales!'* she shouted. *'Est-ce que tu vas payer mon champagne?'* That the prince *had* paid for it, and then ordered bottles for the orchestra too, was taken as proof of his impeccable *savoir faire*.[3]

In a very real sense, France was Edward's spiritual home. During a speech he delivered at the opening of the Paris Exhibition in 1878, he described his involvement in the organisation of the British section as 'the best way of showing sympathy for the French people to whom I owe so much'.[4] Léon Gambetta, the statesman who personally proclaimed the Third Republic in 1870, remarked that 'he loves France both in a gay and a serious sense, and his dream of the future is an entente with us'.[5]

By the turn of the century, that dream appeared far-fetched. Competing colonial ambitions in Africa had placed the European neighbours on a collision course. In 1898, a tense stand-off between French and British forces at Fashoda in present-day South Sudan brought the countries close to war. The French Foreign Minister Théophile Delcassé pushed for a peaceful resolution that saw France withdraw its troops, but not before popular sentiment had been whipped up by a mutually antagonistic press. In Britain, righteous indignation over the French handling of the Dreyfus Affair, in which a Jewish officer in the French Army was falsely accused and wrong-fully convicted of passing military secrets to the Germans, was trumped by outrage in France over the abysmal treatment of Boer women and children in British internment camps during the war in South Africa. The Queen and the Prince of Wales were lampooned in cartoons of astonishing vulgarity. Animosity reached such a pitch that, in 1900, the aged Victoria was forced to give up her annual holi-day on the Riviera in favour of a trip to Ireland. Conditions for an alliance had seldom been less propitious.

Behind the scenes, however, the ground was shifting. Delcassé was keen that Britain and France should reach an understanding. The French ambassador in London, Paul Cambon, was soon planting words in increasingly receptive ears. From 1895, the Conservative Government under the premiership of the 3rd Marquess of Salisbury had adhered to the policy of so-called 'Splendid Isolation', which saw Britain hold itself aloof from Continental entanglements. Brilliant but cautious, Salisbury had done double duty as Foreign Secretary until late 1900, when he ceded the office to the more flexible 5th Marquess of Lansdowne. By then, most of the major European nations had forged alliances: the Triple Alliance between Germany, Austria-Hungary and Italy and the Dual Alliance between France and Russia. Britain, on the other hand, stood friendless and was therefore danger-ously exposed in the event of conflict.

From the earliest weeks of Edward's reign, Lord Lansdowne had been scouting the possibility of an alliance with Germany. When that scheme foundered, influential minds turned to France. Via his contacts in Paris, Edward learnt that President Émile Loubet was favourably disposed. The French people were less enthusiastic. In the wake of Fashoda and the Boer War, public opinion was decidedly anti-British. The most dexterous – moreover, charismatic – diplo-macy would be required to melt the *froideur*.

When Edward descended upon Paris in the spring of 1903, he did so on his own initiative, and in defiance of the wary Lansdowne. The Foreign Secretary made clear the British Government was not about to strike terms over Morocco, where the influence of the French was a bone of contention, and that cross-Channel relations were unlikely to improve until the issue was resolved. Edward went anyway. Loubet had signalled his willingness to host him; and the King, when he was asked how he wished to be received, replied, 'As officially as possible, and the more honours that are paid, the better.' Far from being 'quite an informal affair', as Lansdowne recommended to Cambon, the enterprise assumed the character of a full-blown state occasion.[6]

Having leapfrogged the Foreign Secretary at the planning stage, Edward dispensed with him altogether on the ground. The Foreign Office was to be represented by Charles Hardinge, a junior if extremely able under-secretary, who basked in the royal favour and whose wife was a lady-in-waiting to Queen Alexandra. To this unorthodox arrangement, the affronted Lansdowne consented 'very unwillingly'.[7] It was clear the King intended to act as his *own* Foreign Secretary while he conducted diplomacy at the highest level, and for the highest stakes. Presented with a *fait accompli*, the dubious Cabinet could only hope for the best.

On the day of Edward's arrival, 1 May 1903, the weather in Paris was flawless. The sun sparkled on the waters of the fountains in the Place de la Concorde as a gentle breeze tossed the white blossoms and fresh green leaves of the chestnut trees on the Champs-Élysées. The colourful display of banners and bunting was belied by the atmosphere on the crowded boulevards. The welcome extended to the British as they drove down the avenue du Bois de Boulogne lacked warmth, and in some instances courtesy. Stray cries of '*Vive Fashoda!*' and '*Vivent les Boers!*' prompted a disheartened member of the royal suite to remark, 'The French don't like us.'

'Why should they?' Edward replied.[8]

The reticence of the Parisians persisted into the evening, when the King, accompanied by his host, President Loubet, went to the Comédie Française for a performance of Maurice Donnay's *L'Autre danger*. Largely devoid of representatives of *haute société*, the audience was perceptibly cool. During the interval, Edward left his box to mingle with the crowds in the foyer. Spying the celebrated soprano Jeanne Granier in the middle of a circle of admirers, he approached, kissed her hand, and saluted her in impeccable French. 'Mademoiselle,' he said, 'I remember applauding you in London, where you represented all the grace, all the *esprit*, of France.'[9] It was the turning point. Over the next three days, throughout a packed programme of events, the King's charisma captured all hearts. A brief and impromptu speech he delivered at the Hôtel de Ville provided a platform to make his private sentiments known. 'I shall never forget my visit to your charming city,' he said, 'and I do assure you that it is with the greatest pleasure that I find myself among you here, where I always feel just as though I am at home.'¹⁰ The only sticky moment came at Longchamps where, again in radiant sunshine, the smart set treated Edward to an afternoon of racing. Alas, etiquette meant that he was seated in the presidential box, not with two ravishing *élégantes*, but between the decidedly unprepossessing Madame Loubet and the equally frumpy wife of the Governor of Paris. Unable to converse with them about a sport he loved but about which they clearly knew nothing, the King grew restive. Beckoning a member of his suite, he discreetly secured his own extrication by arranging for three members of the Jockey Club to come across to invite him to inspect their new stand. For the duration of one race, at least, Edward was able to enjoy himself in the kind of company he relished.¹¹

By the time he took his leave, the mood towards him, and by extension Britain and the British, had changed to one of appreciation, and even affection. With his 'ease, frankness and simple pleasure in the beautiful city of which he is a cosmopolitan freeman', wrote the *Illustrated London News*, the King had ensured the good humour of Paris. 'See what an impression is made,' it continued, 'by a Sovereign who . . . is tranquil, genial, a perfect master of his *métier*!'¹² The French papers marvelled at the revolution in the spirit of cross-Channel relations. 'One's imagination was formerly haunted with the possibility, and perhaps the imminence, of conflict with . . . Great Britain,' observed the *Journal des débats*. 'How times have changed! But it was not enough that they were so for diplomatists. It was necessary that they should be so for the people and for those who believe only what they see. Their convictions are formed by their eyes; what they see today consecrates, as it were, the abolition of a past of apprehension and disquietude, and shows them Europe in a new light.'¹³

Edward reciprocated the hospitality he had enjoyed in Paris when Loubet came to London in early July. That visit, too, was a remarkable success. The King was cast as the embodiment of goodwill, this time on home soil. Edward Linley Sambourne captured the mood in a cartoon in *Punch*. Immaculate in breeches and decorations, a beaming Edward presents the British lion, sportingly bedecked with a tricolour rosette, to the timid President. The caption reads,

'See, M. Loubet, he offers you his paw!' The metaphor may have been fanciful, but the sentiment was real. So was the very active role the King played in the transformation of Anglo-French relations ahead of the signing, in April 1904, of the diplomatic agreement known as the Entente Cordiale.

Edward's stake in the actual negotiations was nil. That responsibility fell to Lansdowne and Cambon. What Edward *did* do was decisively alter the climate in which those negotiations could unfold. In January 1907, Sir Eyre Crowe, a senior clerk in the Foreign Office, gave credit where credit was due in a memorandum he authored for Sir Edward Grey, who succeeded Lansdowne as Foreign Secretary under the Liberal Prime Minister Sir Henry Campbell-Bannerman at the end of 1905. Surveying the developments of the last few years, Eyre explained that:

> The French nation, having come to look upon the King as personally attached to their country, saw in His Majesty's words and actions a guarantee that the adjustment of political differences might well prepare the way for bringing about a genuine and lasting friendship, to be built upon a community of interests and aspirations.[14]

The spirit of the Entente captured the popular imagination on both sides of the Channel. In his diary, the blue-blooded anti-imperialist Wilfrid Scawen Blunt described how Edward was hailed as 'the greatest diplomatist of the day, and how French opinion has been quite converted by him to friendliness with England'. An English acquaintance who had grown accustomed to the cold shoulders he encountered at his club in Paris told Blunt of his astonishment when, overnight, he was greeted 'almost with demonstrations' of goodwill by his fellow members.[15] Yet even while this new-found amity was being celebrated, its precise vocabulary proved, to some, elusive. At a reception for a party of French officers hosted in an English town hall, the mayor, in the middle of his speech of welcome, suddenly paused. 'Quick!' he whispered urgently to his neighbour. 'What is the French for Entente Cordiale?'[16]

In the collaboration of the architects Charles Mewès and Arthur Davis, the Entente found its purest expression. That the learned

Mewès, who was French, and the urbane Davis, who was British, had each trained at the École des Beaux-Arts equipped them with the skills to design buildings that reflected the social as well as the diplomatic aspirations of their age. Together they transformed the visual identity of Edwardian London in a way highly agreeable to the Francophile King.

Entering into partnership in 1900, Mewès and Davis were exponents of the Paris school of the mid- to late eighteenth century. In just a handful of years, they brought its refined aesthetic to bear on a series of country-house refurbishments for members of Edward's inner circle: for Queen Alexandra's Treasurer Lord de Grey at Coombe Court; for the brewing heiress Mrs Ronald Greville at Polesden Lacey; and for the South African mining millionaire Sir Julius Wernher, whose seat, Luton Hoo, was one of the most sumptuous in southern England. But it was their work in the capital that won the duo the greatest acclaim. The premises of the *Morning Post* on Aldwych could have been lifted lock, stock and barrel from the 8th *arrondissement*. Under construction from 1908, the Royal Automobile Club on Pall Mall owed a sizeable debt to Ange-Jacques Gabriel's work on the Place de la Concorde. Its elaborate décor was executed by a team of French craftsmen who were seen going about their business 'dressed in their smocks, many wearing sabots and invariably smoking'.[17] Outside, the neoclassical façade soared upwards to a pediment in which allegorical figures decorously lolled. Only the sharpest eyes could descry that one of the sculpted putti was riding in an open-topped motor. There was, too, a Mayfair townhouse for the Honourable Henry Coventry, a younger son of Edward's racing crony Lord Coventry, who was feeling flush after his marriage to a Dollar Princess in 1907.

Most symbolic of all was the Ritz Hotel. Opened in May 1906, it was completely, unapologetically Parisian. At street level, an arcade ran along Piccadilly for over two hundred feet. Dubbed 'the shortest rue de Rivoli in the world', it was no less evocative for that. The exterior walls, of pale grey Norwegian granite and Portland stone capped with a steeply raked mansard roof, were deceptive, being nothing more than a veneer grafted onto a steel frame, one of the first and largest of its kind in Britain. Within, the interiors were Louis XVI down to the smallest detail. From the Arlington Street entrance,

Mewès and Davis contrived a Grand Gallery, which terminated in a frescoed and chandelier-hung restaurant overlooking Green Park. Midway, a ravishingly pretty Palm Court was lined with panelled mirrors and ornamented with a tinkling fountain of gilded lead and Échaillon marble. The materials were of the richest, but the effect, far from being ponderous, was of grace, delicacy and even frivolity. The very lampshades, of apricot pink silk, were specially selected to flatter the complexions of the female guests. Edward adored everything about it. Not only did he dine in the aptly named Marie Antoinette Suite with Mrs Keppel and Sir Ernest Cassel on a regular basis, he also, upon occasion, had *pâtisserie* sent from the hotel kitchen to Buckingham Palace on the grounds it was better than anything the royal chefs could confect.[18]

'A small house to which I am proud to see my name attached,' was how this sybarites' paradise was summed up by its advising manager, César Ritz.[19] It was a wry piece of self-deprecation from a man who, over the course of the previous two decades, had become synony-mous with hospitality at the most exalted level.

Ritz's origins could not have been more unpromising. The thir-teenth child of an Alpine shepherd, he had laid the foundations of his stellar career in Paris. Working his way up from waitering jobs in lowly bistros to the stewardship of top hotels in Switzerland and on the Riviera, he evolved sophisticated ideas about hygiene and effi-ciency, as well as an intuitive understanding of the lifestyles of his elite clientele.

In 1889, he was wooed across to London by the impresario Richard D'Oyly Carte, who installed him as manager of the Savoy on the Strand. Introducing the English to unprecedented standards of comfort, the magnificent new establishment enticed them out of their homes and persuaded them to begin socialising in public. Until then, no 'respectable' woman would have been seen in a restaurant at any time of day or night. That dining out now became extremely chic was due in no small measure to the genius of Ritz's close friend and long-time associate, the chef Auguste Escoffier.

A consummate professional and visionary, Escoffier knew his diners as intimately as Ritz knew his guests. Endlessly experimental, he honoured the most favoured with one-of-a-kind dishes of his own creation. *Pêches Melba* was first served at the Savoy in the early 1890s, when the Australian soprano Nellie Melba was performing in *Lohengrin* at Covent Garden. *Cuisses de Nymphes à l'Aurore* had a lyrical ring, but its ingredients were something of a mystery. It was only after they had tucked in with gusto that the members of the party for whom it had been concocted were informed that the succulent 'thighs of nymphs at dawn' were in fact frogs' legs poached in bouillon, then served chilled with a *chaud-froid* sauce.[20]

In the spring of 1898, there was an acrimonious falling-out with D'Oyly Carte, which saw Ritz and Escoffier depart the Savoy in high dudgeon. Nothing daunted, they trained their sights on Paris where, with the backing of a syndicate of wealthy investors, they inaugurated the first hotel to bear Ritz's name. Located on the Place Vendôme, it opened to instant and universal acclaim. Flushed with triumph, Ritz shuttled back to London to apply his expertise to yet another new hotel, the Carlton, which was about to launch on Haymarket. Besides boasting a plethora of modern conveniences – central heating, electric lighting, en-suite bathrooms – it was to be extremely glamorous. On the threshold of the Edwardian era, consumption had never been more conspicuous, and long-held notions of reticence and modesty were crumbling fast. Attuned to the mood of an ever more performative clientele, Ritz and Mewès devised a simple but dazzlingly effective *coup de théâtre*. At the Carlton, a sweeping staircase ascended from the Palm Court to the Escoffier-run restaurant above. Providing elegantly dressed diners with the opportunity to stage dramatic exits and entrances in full view of the assembled throng, it was a masterful arrangement that did much to make the hotel the most fashionable in town.

Throughout those years of frenzied activity, Ritz kept uppermost in his mind the tastes of one man in particular. First in Europe, and then in London, he strove to anticipate the Prince of Wales's legendary love of luxury. Over time, he became a touchstone, trusted implicitly and followed devoutly. Upon learning of the severance of Ritz's connection with the Savoy, Edward immediately cancelled a party he had planned there. 'Where Ritz goes, I go,' he declared, and he meant it.[21] When the Ritz in Paris opened its doors, he forsook the venerable Hôtel Bristol, his haunt of more than three decades. Ritz's motto, 'The best is not too good', might very well have been his own.

Then again, Edward would have been content in any establishment in which the cuisine was so certain to be superb. Few monarchs have enjoyed food more, or eaten quite so much of it. As early as 1860, the abstemious Prince Albert had counselled his son, then just eighteen, against over-indulgence in rich dishes, which 'an experienced and prudent liver will carefully avoid'.[22] As he did to so many of his parents' strictures, Edward turned a deaf ear. The effects were soon clearly visible. In his youth, he had been boyishly handsome. Queen Victoria was swift to lament his 'true Coburg nose' and total 'want of chin', but those defects were mitigated by his good figure, fresh complexion, and clear, if heavy-lidded, Hanoverian eyes.[23] By the close of the 1860s, he was definitely and terminally stout. For a man who cared about his appearance, it was a sore point – the more so as he was uncomfortably aware that his girth was one of the factors that defined his public image. On one notorious evening at Sandringham, Sir Frederick Johnstone was observed to be inebriated. Placing an avuncular arm around his shoulders, his host gently admonished him with the words, 'Freddy, Freddy, you're very drunk.'

Slurring his *r* in the German fashion, the impudent baronet retorted, 'Tum Tum, you're verrrry fat!'

For once, Edward's good humour deserted him. Summoning an equerry, he gave orders that Johnstone should be shown the door the following morning.[24]

The heaviness of late Victorian and Edwardian cooking was not conducive to slimming. 'They ate excessively and competitively,' recalled Harold Nicolson of the members of the Marlborough House Set. 'No age since that of Nero can show such unlimited addiction to food.'[25] Even so, Edward's appetite was remarkable. So insatiable was his hunger that he frequently forgot to chew, bolting whole platefuls in a matter of minutes. Alexandra confessed that she found her husband's greed to be 'appalling', but she could do nothing to check it. By the time of his accession, Edward was so large his waist, at forty-eight inches, was the same size as his chest, and his clothes no longer met in the middle. Given the richness and frequency of the meals he consumed, that was not surprising. His tastes veered indiscriminately between the relatively simple – roast beef and Yorkshire pudding were served every Sunday without fail – and the extremely opulent. He adored caviar, oysters and quails stuffed with truffles. Game of all varieties was relished, and he derived enormous pleasure from foods he associated with his favourite social occasions. Pigeon pie was a perennial feature at Ascot, while the menus of the Derby Day dinners he hosted for the Jockey Club invariably included whitebait.

When the King stayed with friends, he and his fellow guests gorged themselves from morning to night. Nicolson's evocation of the Edwardian country-house breakfast, 'in no sense a hurried proceeding', is by far the best:

> Rows of little spirit lamps warmed rows of large silver dishes. On a table to the right between the windows were grouped hams, tongues, galantines, cold grouse, ditto pheasant, ditto partridge, ditto ptarmigan. No Edwardian meal was complete without ptarmigan. Hot or cold. Just ptarmigan. There would also be a little delicate rectangle of pressed beef from the shop of M. Benoist. On a further table, to the left between the doors, stood fruits of different calibre, and jugs of cold water, and jugs of lemonade. A fourth table contained porridge utensils. A fifth coffee, and pots of Indian and China tea. The latter were differentiated from each other by little ribbons of yellow (indicating China) and of red (indicating without *arrière pensée* our Indian Empire). The centre table, which was prepared for twenty-three people, would be bright with Malmaisons and toast-racks. No newspapers were, at that stage, allowed.[26]

After lunch – 'strained and bright', in Nicolson's account, with the hostess doing her best to encourage cross-table chatter – the house party would reconvene around four o'clock for afternoon tea. Escoffier, who considered it an aberration that blunted the appetite ahead of the climactic evening meal, thoroughly disapproved of this English custom. Laid out by the butler and footmen, who then discreetly retired, the spread comprised an infinite number of sandwiches, scones, jams, cakes and pastries, as well as such improbable but mouth-watering additions as lobster salad, which was known to be one of the King's favourites. In 1902, Edward called in for tea at Tyninghame, the East Lothian home of the 11th Earl of Haddington. 'They had to provide *pâté de foie* sandwiches and

Curaçao,' reported a neighbour, Lady Frances Balfour. 'If he reigns long, it will be surprising!'[27]

The menu at dinner was always extensive. At a minimum, there would be a hot and a cold soup, a hot and a cold fish (each with a suitable sauce), an entrée, a sorbet, a roast, a sweet, a savoury, and fruit. Like tea, the fiddly little savouries, of bacon, cheese or anchovies on toast, were indigenous to England. At Balmoral, something called 'deer pudding' was served as often as four times a week. Interspersed with lavish displays of hot-house flowers and trailing greenery, artfully constructed pyramids of peaches, nectarines, grapes and pineapples, all home-grown, were sure to be much admired.

Certain foods were peculiar to the era. Ortolans were one. Considered the greatest of delicacies, the tiny birds were drowned in Armagnac, roasted, then eaten whole, bones and all. Highly prized for their rarity and flavour, they were also extremely pricey – something the Duchess of Marlborough discovered to her cost when she scheduled one too many house parties in rapid succession. 'The chef quite rightly claimed that he was overworked,' she wrote, 'and he certainly made us pay for it by ordering quails at five shillings each and ortolans, which were even more expensive, and then serving them at breakfast, an extravagance so *nouveau riche* that I blushed with shame as well as annoyance.'[28]

Queen Alexandra, who never lost her svelte figure, found culinary marathons tedious, and attempted to curtail the length of time the parties over which she presided lingered at table. With anything from eight to twelve courses to gallop through, that presented challenges of its own. The Marchioness of Londonderry whittled *her* dinners down to just one hour, which required her guests to eat against the clock. On one occasion, Consuelo Marlborough watched with amusement 'the silent but no less furious battle between a reputed gourmet who wished to enjoy every morsel of his large helping and a footman equally determined to remove his plate'.[29]

Inevitably, what Vita Sackville-West described as 'those endless, extravagant meals' took their toll. At the end of each summer, the members of Society trundled across the Channel to purge themselves at one of the fashionable spas. Until 1903, Homburg near Frankfurt was Edward's resort of choice. Thereafter, he transferred his allegiance to Marienbad. Thanks to a regime of relative, if strictly temporary, abstinence, he would contrive to lose a few pounds ahead of the shooting season. 'Really,' commented Sackville-West, 'there was very little difference, essentially, between Marienbad and the vomitorium of the Romans.'[30]

It was a cruel irony that Edward, who as Prince of Wales had done so much to further César Ritz's reputation as the greatest hotelier in Europe, should, as King, inadvertently help to bring it to a close.

In the summer of 1902, London was excitedly preparing for the Coronation, due to take place on 26 June. Acres of flags had been hoisted and miles of bunting strung. Tickets for the best seats in the specially constructed stands along the processional route were changing hands for vast sums. Every available window and rooftop would be crammed with sightseers.

At the fully booked Carlton, Ritz and Escoffier planned the dinner to end all dinners. From caviar to bird's nest soup, and from sole mousse with lobster and truffles to ortolans in pineapple juice, they envisaged a truly royal repast. The King and Queen would be honoured by the inclusion of *Poularde Édouard VII* (poached chicken in curry sauce) and *Pêches Alexandra* (a particularly festive variation on Escoffier's signature *Pêches Melba*). Neither effort nor expense would be spared to make it a meal to remember.[31]

And then – disaster.

For some days, Edward had felt increasingly unwell. At first, he stubbornly refused to admit that anything was wrong. He had waited sixty years to be crowned. Under no circumstance whatsoever would he countenance further delay. By 23 June, the pain caused by an abdominal abscess was so acute his doctors, fearing for his life, urged him to undergo emergency surgery. In spite of the King's violent protestations – 'I will go to the Abbey on Thursday if I die there!' – he was forced to submit to the scalpel. The Coronation was indefinitely postponed.[32]

On the verge of hosting the greatest banquet of his life, it was too much for Ritz to bear. Anxiety over the condition of his most illustrious patron was outweighed by the stress of dealing with the blizzard of cancellations that now engulfed him. Undermined by the cross-Channel exertions of the last four years, his health gave way. Although he was not to die until 1918, he was much reduced by the after-effects of a complete nervous breakdown. Responsibility for the construction and decoration of the new hotel on Piccadilly largely devolved to its architects, Mewès and Davis. 'Do what you like,' Ritz told them wearily. 'You know by now what my ideas are. Incorporate them.'[33] It was a dismal end to what had been a glorious career.

Edward, on the other hand, bounced back surprisingly quickly. He spent the next few weeks convalescing at Buckingham Palace and aboard the royal yacht. When, on 9 August, the Coronation at last took place, the massed peers and peeresses in their decorations, jewels and robes of velvet and ermine compensated for the absence of the foreign delegations, which had long since departed for home. Beady eyes were swift to note a special box filled with the King's glamorous lady friends, who would not otherwise have been eligible for invitations. In the chilly Crypt, peckish courtiers popped champagne corks and munched chicken and ham sandwiches. Tanned and cheerful, Edward had never looked better. His waist, it was said, had shrunk by as many as six inches.

3: 'For the peace of the world'

In Edward's triumphant visit to Paris in the spring of 1903, Russia scented opportunity. 'We have the right to hope that the Anglo-French *rapprochement* will react favourably upon Anglo-Russian relations,' speculated the St Petersburg newspaper *Novosti*, 'and that in general the *rapprochement* between the Powers of the Dual Alliance and Great Britain will serve as a basis for the renewed strengthening of the political equilibrium in Europe, and for the maintenance of peace.'[1] The King was to spare no effort to attain that objective. It proved to be an uphill struggle.

If, in Edward's eyes, France represented 'Fun', Russia represented 'Family'. Queen Victoria may have disparaged Tsar Alexander III as a 'sovereign whom she does not look upon as a gentleman',[2] but she had been unable to prevent two of her granddaughters from marrying into the bosom of the Romanovs. In 1884, Princess Elisabeth of Hesse, the daughter of Edward's favourite sister, Alice, wed Alexander's brother, Grand Duke Serge Alexandrovich. Ten years later, her younger sister, Alix, married Alexander's son and successor, Tsar Nicholas II. To further complicate matters, Nicholas was the nephew of Edward's wife, Alexandra, by her own favourite sister, the Dowager Empress Marie Feodorovna. Edward was therefore an uncle twice over.

Handsome, charming and modest, Nicholas was easy to like. He was also, Edward judged, 'weak as water'[3] – and weakness in the autocratic monarch of a vast empire did not bode well. Worse, the premature death of his father had left him ill-equipped to shoulder responsibilities of such overwhelming magnitude. 'I know nothing of the business of ruling,' he wailed upon his accession at the age of twenty-six. 'I have no idea of even how to talk to the ministers.'[4] In dealing with one so diffident, Edward realised that charm would yield greater dividends than pugnacity. It was he who persuaded Queen Victoria to appoint the young Tsar Colonel-in-Chief of the Royal Scots Greys: a purely honorary role, but a symbolic gesture of goodwill from one crowned head to another. Nicholas was so appreciative that he was twice painted in the regiment's scarlet tunic, which flattered his athletic physique. The shaggy uniform he bestowed upon his uncle in return was somewhat less becoming. In it, observed an embarrassed member of his suite, the rotund Prince of Wales resembled nothing so much as a giant polar bear.[5]

In 1894, Edward travelled to Russia for the funeral of Alexander III and the wedding, just days later, of Nicholas and Alix (who, upon her conversion to the Orthodox faith, took the name Alexandra Feodorovna). The trip was an opportunity for him to woo his impressionable nephew, and to seed the ground for a cordial – and, he hoped, co-operative – relationship. His initiative paid off. Seven years later, Nicholas sent a letter to Edward upon his own accession. In it, he expressed his desire to build upon the foundations of their earlier understanding. 'I am quite sure that with your help, dear Bertie, the friendly relations between our two countries shall become still closer than in the past,' he wrote. 'May the new century bring England and Russia together for their mutual interests and for the general peace of the world.'[6]

Would that matters could be so easily arranged. Since Britain and France had declared victory over Russia in the Crimean War of 1853-6, Anglo-Russian relations had been characterised by simmering mistrust. In Westminster and Whitehall, successive governments worried about the threat Russia posed to India, as well as its creeping influence in China. Culturally, the exchange between the nations was distinctly lopsided. In St Petersburg, a sizeable community of expatriate Britons had taken root. Mills and manufactories were run by English and Scottish owners and managers. There was the Anglican Church, the New English Club, and an English Shop (confusingly known as the 'Magasin Anglais') in which British-made goods could be purchased in an atmosphere redolent of 'the High Street in Chester, or Leicester, or Truro, or Canterbury'.[7] Sophisticated members of the Russian aristocracy had what Vladimir Nabokov described as 'a traditional leaning towards the comfortable products of Anglo-Saxon civilisation . . . fruitcakes, smelling-salts, playing cards, picture puzzles, striped blazers, talcum-white tennis balls'.[8] English governesses were highly sought-after, and English came to rival French as the language of choice among the elite.

In 1903, the Imperial Court jeweller, Peter Carl Fabergé, opened a branch of his store in London. Inspired by the patronage of Edward and Alexandra, the cream of Society came flocking. Beyond its threshold, however, Russia continued to be regarded with a blend of incomprehension and indignation. In October 1904, popular opinion was outraged by an episode in which the Russian fleet, steaming through the North Sea, mistook a flotilla of British fishing smacks for the torpedo boats of its enemy, Japan, and opened fire, killing or injuring several sailors. Russia eventually shelled out £65,000 as compensation for what the *Daily Telegraph* called its 'heartless, cowardly murder',[9] but the incident left a bitter aftertaste.

Three months later, in January 1905, sentiment was again inflamed by the events of so-called 'Bloody Sunday'. 'Two thousand Russians . . . have been shot down in the streets while on their way to the Winter Palace to ask for the rights which every human being in a civilised country has enjoyed for the last 200 years,' raged Violet Asquith, the teenage daughter of the Liberal MP Herbert Henry Asquith. 'I cannot think of it without tears.'[10] The massacre sparked civil unrest across Russia. 'What are the workmen fighting for?' asked the *Daily Mirror*. 'That is lost sight of. Their object was to gain peaceful audience of the Tsar. Now their hearts are filled with wild rage against their Sovereign and all who advised him to butcher his subjects in the public street.'[11] In a letter to Charles Hardinge, Edward's protégé in the Foreign Office, Sir Arthur Nicolson, the British ambassador in St Petersburg, warned that, sooner or later, a successful revolution would 'sweep away dynasty, Government, and much else'.[12] Until then, Russian dissidents hunkered down in the safe haven of London. Free speech, freedom of the press and minimal police interference attracted Leon Trotsky, Maxim Gorky, Vladimir Lenin and Joseph Stalin to the British capital. Disapproval of the conditions under which so many Russians suffered even seeped into polite Edwardian nurseries. Into *The Railway Children* of 1906, E. Nesbit wrote the character of 'the Russian gentleman', Mr Szezcpansky, who escapes to England from Siberia, to which he had been exiled for writing 'a beautiful book about poor people and how to help them'.[13]

Diplomatically, the outlook improved in August 1907 with the signing of the Anglo-Russian Convention. In the months beforehand, Edward had launched a man-to-man charm offensive against the Russian Foreign Minister, Count Izvolsky, who was then in Paris. The King made it known that he hoped to welcome the deeply flattered count to London as well. In Hardinge's opinion, his overture 'helped materially to smooth the path of the negotiations then in progress for an agreement with Russia'.[14] The terms of the Convention, which resolved colonial disputes in Persia, Tibet and Afghanistan, sent a clear signal that the nations were embarking upon a new phase of co-operation. Plans could at last be made for a long-overdue state visit to the Tsar.

When the scheme was announced, there was a storm of protest in Parliament. Keir Hardie and Ramsay MacDonald, two of the leading lights in the newly founded Labour Party, were especially vitriolic. In the wake of 'Bloody Sunday', MacDonald went so far as to denounce Nicholas as nothing more than a 'common murderer'.[15] Edward was furious. Instinctively conservative, he nevertheless looked askance at the repressive Russian regime. In the autumn of 1905, he had instructed Hardinge to convey personally to his nephew 'my hope that he may find himself able to grant a more liberal form of Government to his Country'.[16] Even so, nothing could excuse such an insult to a foreign sovereign who was also a close relation. Three of the MPs who had caused him particular offence were duly scratched from the guest list of a garden party to be held at Windsor Castle.

The *Daily Telegraph* dismissed the dissenting voices out-of-hand. 'All countries have their busybodies of this particularly vexatious type,' it sniffed, 'forever placing fresh obstacles in the path of diplomatic conciliation.'[17] Yet public opinion could not be discounted altogether. It was stressed that at no point would the King or any member of his party set foot on Russian soil. Instead, the royal yacht, the *Victoria and Albert*, would sail to the Baltic, where it would be greeted by the Russian imperial yacht, the *Standart*, off the coast of Reval in present-day Estonia. It was an elegant solution, which served to offset the criticism levelled against the King on the one hand while allaying the security concerns of the Tsar on the other.

After weeks of intensive planning, and multiple exasperating changes of personnel, the rendezvous was set for 9 and 10 June 1908. The Tsar, Tsarina and all five of their children, as well as the Dowager Empress Marie, turned out to greet their relatives. The cheerful tone was set when Nicholas, in a surprise departure from protocol, boarded the *Victoria and Albert* to welcome them in person. Politics were relegated to the side-lines in a flurry of affectionate greetings. The King and Queen then transferred to the *Standart*, where the love-in continued. Habitually stiff and reserved, the Tsarina was visibly pleased to see her uncle. Contrary to hostile rumours at home, she had always identified more closely with her English than her German ancestry. A member of the Russian suite was surprised to see her treated by the British 'as if she were ONE OF THEM'.[18]

The genial atmosphere persisted as the families shuttled back and forth between their yachts. Edward was at his avuncular best, making his nephew feel 'gay and at his ease'.[19] At the first banquet aboard the *Standart*, his off-the-cuff reply to the Tsar's speech of welcome paid tribute to the recent signing of the Convention:

I believe it will serve to knit more closely the bonds that unite the people of our two countries, and I am certain it will conduce to the satisfactory settlement in an amicable manner of some momentous questions in the future. I am convinced that it will not only draw our two countries more closely together but will help very greatly towards the maintenance of the general peace of the world.[20]

Edward's bonhomie eventually ran away with him entirely. The mood after lunch on the second day was so expansive that, on the spur of the moment, he created Nicholas an Admiral of the Fleet. When he learnt of the gesture, the Prime Minister, Herbert Henry Asquith, who was not on the trip, and who had not been consulted, was seriously put out.*

A year later, in August 1909, the Romanovs descended upon Cowes. Once again, the visit was deplored by left-wing politicians and journalists. Once again, stringent security measures were implemented to ensure the safety of the Tsar. The Reval format was reprised, but this time on a grander scale. A naval review elicited a pang in the breasts of the Russians, their own fleet having been decimated by the Japanese at the Battle of Tsushima in 1905. After sunset the ships were magically illuminated against the inky sea and sky. As a girl, the Tsarina had spent many happy holidays on the Isle of Wight, and it was the remembrance of them that encouraged the family to put aside their fears of assassination to venture ashore. There was an outing to Queen Victoria's former residence at Osborne, and the children collected shells on the beach. The two elder grand duchesses, Olga and Tatiana, even managed to slip away on an impromptu shopping excursion, although they were soon forced to beat a retreat when they were almost mobbed by curious onlookers.

The exchange of visits by the King and the Tsar was preceded, not followed, by a signed agreement. Diplomats were keen to point out that they were essentially reunions, with neither agendas nor fixed

---

* On the other hand, the First Sea Lord, Sir John 'Jackie' Fisher, who *was* on the trip, applauded Edward's initiative. 'It's a jolly good thing we have a King who knows how to act,' he exclaimed, 'as cabinet ministers seem always to me like frightened rabbits!' (Lee, Vol. II, p.594)

objectives. Nevertheless, the symbolism was widely trumpeted. The *Tatler* hailed the meeting at Reval as 'the crowning stone of the magnificent structure of ententes and understandings which more than anything else has made this reign memorable in all history'. With a nod to the encouragement of the French, it concluded that the 'Entente Cordiale between England, France and Russia . . . seems to ensure the peace of the world for at least our generation.'[21]

Between February 1907 and August 1908, Edward was absent from home for a combined total of three months. During that time, he visited France, Spain, Italy, Malta, Germany, Austria, Denmark, Sweden and Norway, besides sailing up to the Baltic for his rendez-vous with the Tsar. On Fleet Street, the Court correspondents struggled to keep up. Lord Northcliffe, the proprietor of the *Daily Mail*, wrote in some exasperation to Francis Knollys that 'The King has become such an immense personality in England that, as you may have noticed, the space devoted to the movements of Royalty has quintupled since His Majesty came to the Throne, and our diffi-culties have increased likewise.'[22] In an era in which the crowned heads of Europe were more mobile than ever before, the frequency and scope of the King's travels immeasurably enhanced his interna-tional profile. Only one of his relatives loomed as large in the popu-lar consciousness. Unfortunately, it was the relative Edward liked least.

In 1891, the Liberal MP John Morley scrutinised Kaiser Wilhelm II of Germany during one of his frequent trips to London. His account conveys some sense of the impression created by a character who, in spite of his diminutive stature and withered arm, seemed somehow larger than life:

He is rather short; pale but sunburnt; carries himself well; walks into the room with the stiff stride of the Prussian soldier; speaks with a good deal of intense and energetic gesture, not like a Frenchman, but staccato; his voice strong but pleasant; his eye bright, clear and full; mouth resolute; the cast of face grave or almost stern in repose, but as he sat between two pretty women he lighted up with gaiety, and a genial laugh. Energy, rapidity, restlessness in every movement from his short, quick inclinations of the head to the planting of the foot.[23]

While conceding Wilhelm's charm, Morley detected more worrying tendencies. 'I should be disposed strongly,' he summed up, 'to doubt whether it is all sound, steady, and the result of a . . . rightly co-ordinated organisation.' Over the next two decades, the Kaiser's volatility dismayed countless statesmen, diplomats and journalists. He was not a figure the British – least of all the King – contemplated with equanimity.

From boyhood, Wilhelm had defined himself against his parents. Crown Prince Frederick of Prussia had married Edward's elder sister, Victoria, in 1858. The match had promised to usher in a new age of Anglo-German solidarity. The peaceable Frederick was a liberal and an Anglophile. Taking after her progressive father, Prince Albert, Victoria had been steeped in similar ideals of democracy and religious toleration – ideals her son, as well as an influential faction within the Prussian ruling class, rejected entirely. Wilhelm conflated his complicated emotions about his brilliant but domineering mother with an inferiority complex about the country of her birth. Nationalist sentiment, combined with rapid industrial growth and a surge in militarisation after German Unification in 1871, saw his hostility play out in a series of collisions with his English family. These took on greater significance in 1888, when Frederick died of throat cancer after a reign of just ninety-nine days. His untimely death robbed Edward of a brother-in-law he had respected and left him to contend with a nephew he did not.

Wilhelm wasn't always disagreeable. On the contrary, he frequently professed warm feelings towards Britain. His descent from Queen Victoria was a source of particular pride. Whenever their relationship showed signs of strain, he was apt to remind his uncle of the vigil they had shared at her deathbed in 1901. On that occasion, the Kaiser's solicitude impressed all who witnessed it. Lord Esher, the Court mandarin who was to become one of Edward's closest advisers, remarked that 'His tenderness and firmness were extraordinary, so unlike what was expected of him.'[24] Edward himself was so pleased he conferred upon his nephew the rank of field marshal in the British Army, simultaneously investing his son and heir, 'Little Willy', as a Knight of the Order of the Garter.[25]

Alas, the goodwill never endured. Where Edward was suave, Wilhelm was bombastic. Where Edward charmed, Wilhelm bullied.

Princess Daisy of Pless, who knew both men well, was frustrated by the Kaiser's tendency to undermine his own advantages. From promising beginnings, he left Germany isolated and friendless. 'While the King of England in the estimation even of his enemies is acknowledged to be the greatest diplomat in Europe,' she wrote in her diary, 'the Emperor has . . . played his cards badly. He is so terribly tactless, loud and theatrical.'[26]

Almost as addicted to travel as his uncle, Wilhelm descended upon Tangier in North Africa in the spring of 1905. He used the visit, which lasted a few hours at most, to pledge German support for Moroccan independence. It was tantamount to a repudiation of the terms of the Entente Cordiale, which had recognised French claims in Morocco in exchange for British claims in Egypt. As one of the chief facilitators of the Entente, Edward was incensed. In a letter to Lord Lansdowne, he described the episode as 'a political-theatrical fiasco' and 'the most mischievous and uncalled for event which the German Emperor has ever been engaged in since he came to the Throne'. The Kaiser, the King raged, was 'no more nor less than a political *enfant terrible* and one can have no faith in any of his assurances'.[27] For his part, Wilhelm cast Edward as an arch-intriguer, whose trips around Europe were part of a scheme to weave a web of alliances that would leave Germany encircled. At a dinner in Berlin, he talked excitedly of what he supposed to be his uncle's machinations. He didn't mince his words. Edward was, Wilhelm claimed, 'a Satan; you can hardly believe what a Satan he is'.[28]

The mutual antipathy of the King and the Kaiser was reflected in a deterioration of relations between their peoples. Culturally, Britain and Germany were tightly knit. London was home to tens of thousands of expatriate Germans. German financiers were prominent in the City – Sir Ernest Cassel, for example, had been born in Cologne – and German governesses could be found in many aristocratic households. There was a German hospital, a brace of German-language newspapers and as many as a dozen German churches. Lined with German-owned cafés, restaurants and clubs, Charlotte Street, parallel to Tottenham Court Road, was dubbed 'Charlottenstrasse' by locals. Conversely, Germany was irresistible to the high-minded British. Violet Asquith was one of innumerable girls despatched to be 'finished' in Dresden prior to her debut. The annual festival at Bayreuth was unmissable for fans of Wagner, while Richard Haldane, the Secretary of State for War between 1905 and 1912, had earlier in his career won acclaim for his translation of Arthur Schopenhauer's *The World as Will and Representation*.

Despite these affinities, Germany was increasingly perceived by the British as a rival and, worse, a threat. In 1909, Robert Graves entered Charterhouse, the prestigious public school in Surrey. There, he was struck by his classmates' hatred of all things German. The very word, used interchangeably with 'dirty German', denoted 'cheap, shoddy goods competing with our sterling industries'. More broadly, it signified 'military menace, Prussianism, useless philosophy, tedious scholarship, loving music and sabre-rattling'. The French, on the other hand, were unusually popular. 'King Edward VII,' Graves recalled in later life, 'had done his Entente Cordiale work thoroughly.'[29]

Popular authors stoked the fire with contributions to the burgeoning genre of 'Invasion Literature'. In *The Riddle of the Sands* of 1903, Erskine Childers described a pair of British yachtsmen foiling plans for a German invasion to be launched from the Frisian Islands. Still more sensational was a 1906 story by William Le Queux in which, in the very near future, German troops swept inland from beachheads in East Anglia to occupy half of London. First serialised in the *Daily Mail*, it was published as a book under the title *The Invasion of 1910*. Then there was *An Englishman's Home*, which opened at Wyndham's Theatre in January 1909. Written by Guy du Maurier under the nom de plume 'A Patriot', it depicted an invasion by a foreign power euphemistically dubbed 'Nearland'. Sold out for weeks on end, the play was credited with bringing about a surge in recruitment in the Territorial Army.

In military circles, belligerence ran rife. In 1904, the peppery Admiral Sir John 'Jackie' Fisher was appointed First Sea Lord. Enjoying privileged access to the King, he almost immediately proposed that the Royal Navy should 'Copenhagen' its German counterpart at Kiel, just as Admiral Gambier had forced the surrender of the Danish fleet in 1807, thereby neutralising a potential threat without the formality of a declaration of war. Edward was swift to scotch this outrageous suggestion, but it did nothing to ease the Kaiser's paranoia when he learnt of it. Nor was Edward entirely free from paranoia himself. In his diary, Wilfrid Scawen Blunt described a crackpot scheme rumoured to have been hatched in Berlin whereby the Kaiser 'will throw a *corps d'armee* or two into England, making proclamation that he has come, not as an enemy to the King, but as grandson of Queen Victoria' to deliver his uncle from the 'socialistic' Liberal Government. Edward would then be instated as an autocrat, albeit one owing allegiance to the German Empire. 'Such is the programme,' Blunt wrote, 'and the King believes in it as true.'[30] In each nation, the rate at which cutting-edge battleships were commissioned and built accelerated alarmingly, with neither side prepared to slacken the pace lest they found themselves outmanned and outgunned in the conflict many were convinced was inevitable.

Into this charged atmosphere, Wilhelm lobbed a grenade in October 1908 when the *Daily Telegraph* published, as if taken down in an interview, his views on world affairs. Speaking with what was described as 'impulsive and unusual frankness', Wilhelm vented his frustration with the chronic mistrust of the British Government and people. He was, he complained, 'sorely tried', 'continually misrepresented', and had 'so often experienced the mortification of finding that any momentary improvement of relations is followed by renewed outbursts of prejudice'. Lambasting the English as 'mad, mad, mad as March hares', he insisted that German activities in Morocco were in no way contrary to his desire for peace, and that the German naval build-up was not made with Britain in mind, but for use against the Japanese and Chinese in the Pacific. Most intemperate of all, he looked back to the Boer War when, he alleged, France and Russia (both of which had since become allies of Britain) had approached Germany with a proposal to simultaneously 'save the Boer Republics' and 'humiliate England to the dust'. Not only had the Kaiser refused to participate in any such scheme, he claimed he had responded by drawing up and submitting a plan for a campaign that, when implemented, had enabled Lord Roberts, the British Commander-in-Chief, to attain victory.[31]

The interview sent ripples of unease across Europe. Wilhelm's indiscretions appeared to confirm the widespread belief that he was a dangerous loose cannon. Chancellor Bernhard von Bülow, who had carelessly passed the text before publication, and who was to resign the following summer, described the 'dark foreboding [that] ran through many Germans that such clumsy, incautious, over-hasty – such stupid, even puerile – speech and action on the part of the Supreme Head of State could lead to only one thing – catastrophe'.[32] When it became known that a second, even more damaging, interview had taken place with an American newspaper – one in which Edward himself was castigated as corrupt and an Anglo-German war cited as a foregone conclusion – the King moved to prevent its publication in England. A fortnight later, Margot Asquith, the wife of the Prime Minister, was at a party at Windsor Castle for the King and Queen of Sweden. Wilhelm's gaffe was much discussed. 'I am glad his poor Mother is dead. It would have broken her heart,' exclaimed Queen Alexandra, who had a visceral detestation of the Kaiser, and had never forgiven Germany for its defeat of her beloved Denmark in the Second Schleswig War of 1864. '*Such* a man! Such *things!*' she went on. 'The newspapers shocking!!' Edward echoed her sentiments. 'Oh! It is very serious – he is most unwise and unbalanced & this ought to be a severe lesson to him,' he said. 'My poor sister, it would have been a great grief to her – in fact it would have killed her I think.'[33]

To mitigate the damage done to the Kaiser's self-esteem by the criticism he received in the wake of the *Telegraph* affair, and to offset the impression created by his own meeting with the Tsar at Reval, Edward reluctantly undertook a state visit to Berlin in February 1909. It was to be the last and least auspicious of his reign. During the carriage procession into the German capital, uncooperative horses caused havoc. From the guest list of the banquet of welcome, the prettiest and most amusing women in Society were unaccountably omitted. The King was bored stiff. Vigilant eyes searched for and found symptoms of his malaise. It was observed that he was so stout that he was often short of breath and that he had a disconcerting habit of nodding off in company. There was an alarming incident when, after an official lunch at the British Embassy, he had a seizure while chatting with Princess Daisy of Pless:

> Suddenly he coughed and fell back against the back of the sofa and his cigar dropped out of his fingers, his eyes stared, he became pale, and he could not breathe. I thought, 'My God, he is dying; oh! Why not in his own country?' I tried to undo the collar of his uniform (which

was too tight), then the Queen rushed up and we both tried; at last he came to – and undid it himself. I then made him sit on a higher seat, but he would not let me move from him.[34]

Edward pulled himself together and the incident was hushed up, but the princess was left fearful for the future. 'Please God this dear, kind, able Monarch is not in for a serious illness!' she confided to her diary.

Outwardly cordial, the visit did little to ameliorate the growing tensions. Edward was demoralised and depressed. 'It is strange,' he wrote to Charles Hardinge, 'that ever since my visit to Berlin the German Government has done *nothing* but thwart and annoy us in every way . . . If we can only ensure peace, it is worth giving way, as long as we do so with honour and dignity.' He admitted that 'We may safely look upon Germany as our greatest foe, as she hardly attempts to conceal it.'[35] By the early months of 1910, he had shed his residual illusions about the Kaiser. Passing through Paris that spring, Edward called on his friend the Comtesse de Greffulhe. Usually upbeat in the city that had witnessed his greatest diplomatic triumph, he was uncharacteristically morose. Over tea, he confided his worry: 'I have not long to live. And then my nephew will make war.'[36]

4: 'Conditions so altered'

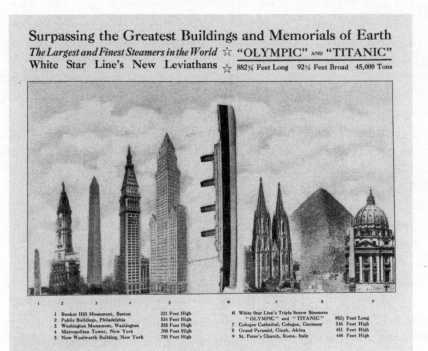

Surpassing the Greatest Buildings and Memorials of Earth
The Largest and Finest Steamers in the World ☆ **"OLYMPIC" AND "TITANIC"**
White Star Line's New Leviathans ☆ 882½ Feet Long   92½ Feet Broad   45,000 Tons

1 Bunker Hill Monument, Boston	221 Feet High
2 Public Buildings, Philadelphia	534 Feet High
3 Washington Monument, Washington	555 Feet High
4 Metropolitan Tower, New York	700 Feet High
5 New Woolworth Building, New York	750 Feet High
6 White Star Line's Triple Screw Steamers "OLYMPIC" and "TITANIC"	882½ Feet Long
7 Cologne Cathedral, Cologne, Germany	516 Feet High
8 Grand Pyramid, Gizeh, Africa	451 Feet High
9 St. Peter's Church, Rome, Italy	448 Feet High

Edward's diplomatic activities had a significance out of all proportion
to the size of the country over which he reigned. Compared to
France, Russia and Germany, Great Britain was small. Its imperial
outreach was vast. Canada, Australia, New Zealand, India and Ceylon
were among the constituent parts of its far-flung empire. Vast swathes
of Africa had been colonised, including present-day Kenya, Nigeria,
Uganda and Sudan. Egypt was effectively a British protectorate. The
messy war in South Africa had been wound up with the signing of
the Treaty of Vereeniging in 1902, when the Boer Republics had

come under British control. In September 1909, the South Africa Act proclaimed a Union to be established the following May. On the maps pinned to countless classroom walls, British territories were splashed pink or red. In total, they covered eleven million square miles, or one-fifth of the habitable surface of the globe. One-quarter of the human race owed allegiance to Great Britain and its sovereign.*

Dominion over the high seas had enabled a diminutive nation on the outskirts of Europe to attain unrivalled – indeed, unprecedented – influence. Since the days of Raleigh and Drake, the British had plumed themselves on a supremacy that could not, under any circumstances, be ceded to another power. A combination of patriotic pride and gnawing anxiety propelled the naval arms race that became a hot topic in Westminster in 1908. That spring, Germany introduced a new Navy Law, which would, it was projected, see it accrue more vessels than Britain by 1914. To an electorate consumed by fears of invasion, it was an intolerable prospect. The Conservative Opposition didn't scruple to capitalise on the prevailing paranoia. Coined by a Tory MP, the refrain 'We want eight and we won't wait!' was parroted by those who felt the Liberal Government should spend less on welfare reforms and more on the construction of battleships.[1]

Technologically, Britain had a head start. Under the auspices of First Sea Lord Admiral Sir John 'Jackie' Fisher, HMS *Dreadnought* was laid down in Portsmouth in the autumn of 1905. Built at breakneck speed, she was ready for launch in early 1906. Edward, who was keenly interested in everything pertaining to the Royal Navy, did the honours when he shattered a bottle of Australian wine on her bulbous bow. He and the other dignitaries were intensely gratified by what they saw on the slipway. Powered by revolutionary steam turbines, the *Dreadnought* could outstrip any of her contemporaries. Bristling with state-of-the-art weaponry, her twin-funnelled silhouette projected majesty and menace in roughly equal measure. She was so synonymous with British naval might that her name was used as shorthand

---

* Unlike his mother Queen Victoria and his son George V, Edward VII took relatively little interest in the Empire and its affairs. His preferred sphere of influence and activity was Continental Europe.

for the entire generation of ships commissioned after her. Her well-scrubbed decks were not an obvious staging ground for one of the twentieth century's most imaginatively conceived, carefully planned and flawlessly executed practical jokes. Yet on one notorious afternoon in February 1910, that is precisely what they became.

That winter, an uninitiated eavesdropper on the talk at 46 Gordon Square would probably have been shocked, and certainly astonished, by its frankness. Behind its brick and stucco façade lived Vanessa Bell, the thirty-year-old daughter of the late Sir Leslie Stephen, the eminent man of letters. Predeceased by his second wife, Julia, Sir Leslie's death in 1904 had prompted his orphaned children – two girls and two boys – to leave Kensington and migrate to Bloomsbury, the prosperous but unfashionable district north of High Holborn and east of Tottenham Court Road.

At first, the siblings had shared the capacious house in Gordon Square. In 1907, Vanessa wed Clive Bell, the younger son of a wealthy coal magnate, who was busy pursuing his interests in history and, latterly, modern art. With the marriage, which was followed in short order by the birth of a child, Julian, the family splintered. Vanessa's younger brother, Thoby, had died of typhoid in November 1906: a source of enduring grief to all who had loved him. That left Virginia and Adrian, who decamped to 29 Fitzroy Square, where they lived without the supervision of relatives or chaperones. It was an unorthodox arrangement, which permitted Virginia, who turned twenty-eight in January 1910, an unusual degree of liberty at a time when the lives of most single women were constrained by the obligation to be – or at least appear to be – 'respectable'.

Then again, little about the Stephen sisters was ordinary. Born into the heart of the late Victorian intelligentsia, they had each embarked upon careers: Vanessa as a painter and Virginia as a writer. For both, it was early days. Nevertheless, Vanessa's work had already attracted favourable notice in public exhibitions, while Virginia had begun her first novel, *Melymbrosia*, to which she would return at intervals until it was finally published, under its new title *The Voyage Out*, in 1915.

The women were encouraged in their creative endeavours by a lively social circle. In 1899, Thoby had entered Trinity College,

Cambridge, where his contemporaries included Lytton Strachey, Leonard Woolf and Clive Bell. From 1902, John Maynard Keynes was at nearby King's. It was Thoby who introduced his fellow students – all clever, sophisticated and solidly middle to upper-middle class – to his sisters. After his death, the bonds he had forged had strengthened. These were to be the founder members of the Bloomsbury Group.

Almost from the outset, the friends played with an illicit vocabulary with adolescent glee. 'Sex,' Virginia wrote later, 'permeated our conversation. The word "bugger" was never far from our lips. We discussed copulation with the same excitement and openness that we had discussed the nature of good.'[2] Their talk was probing as well as uninhibited. Ideas were welcomed, opinions were invited and honesty was obligatory. 'What exactly do you mean?' was a frequently asked question. In an era when modes of address tended to be formal, kisses were exchanged instead of handshakes and Christian names were freely used. 'Manners were to depend on feelings rather than conventions,' recalled Clive.[3] When, in 1911, Leonard Woolf returned to London from a Civil Service posting in Ceylon, he was struck by the atmosphere of 'greater intimacy' promoted by this 'sweeping away of formalities and barriers, which I found so new and so exhilarating'.[4] As yet largely unknown in the wider world, the embryonic Group was self-regarding, and even hermetic. Strachey, who was establishing a reputation as a critic and reviewer, was in love with his cousin, the emerging artist Duncan Grant, who lived a few doors down from Virginia and Adrian in Fitzroy Square. Grant was also loved by the budding economist Maynard Keynes but would eventually father a child by Vanessa. Young Bloomsbury's preoccupation with sex was perhaps an attempt to make sense of its complicated terrain.

In this company of chattering bohemians, Horace de Vere Cole was the odd man out. Extravagantly rich and handsome, he was the product of a union between English trade and the Irish gentry. Educated at Eton, he had served as a cavalryman in the war in South Africa while still in his teens. Since then, he had flirted with Radical politics, dabbled with poetry, travelled luxuriously around Europe and embarked upon a passionate but abortive affair with an American heiress married to an Italian count. In Cole, a boisterous temperament was blended with a hyperactive imagination, which found expression in a sequence of elaborate hoaxes. Adrian, who had got to know him at Trinity, duly introduced him to his sisters. Their reactions were mixed. Vanessa considered him flashy, vulgar and a bit of a bore. Virginia liked him but found him disconcerting. He was, in her estimation, 'rather a dangerous friend to have'.[5]

Her misgivings were justified. In want of occupation in the early weeks of 1910, Cole and Adrian hatched an audacious, if to our way of thinking racially insensitive, plot. In it, they would reprise an exploit from their student days when they had blackened their faces and masqueraded as the Sultan of Zanzibar's uncle and his suite. They had quite taken in the mayor of Cambridge who, with great ceremony, had personally escorted them around the sights of the city. The prank had attracted considerable attention, especially when it made the *Daily Mail*, and the mischievous young men decided to repeat it now. They and a handful of co-conspirators would dress up as potentates from a far-off land and avail themselves of a second round of official hospitality. This time, however, their target would be infinitely more high-profile than a provincial mayor and his corporation. It would be nothing less than a national icon.

That February, the much-vaunted and fiercely protected *Dreadnought* lay at anchor off the coast of Dorset. Adrian and Cole planned to deceive their way aboard for a tour of inspection. In order to do so, they would have to adopt suitably convincing disguises. Building upon the 'Sultan of Zanzibar', they would, on this occasion, pretend to be Abyssinian royalty: not, as was subsequently claimed, the real-life Emperor, but his fictitious cousin, 'Prince Makalen', and a party of his attendants. Given that Abyssinia (present-day Ethiopia) was a bulwark against the expansion of the German Empire in East Africa, its representatives were likely to receive a warm – and, it was hoped, credulous – welcome.

For Adrian, the risk, and therefore the flavour, would have a personal dimension. Since childhood, the Stephen siblings had regarded with distaste and derision the self-satisfied offspring of their maternal aunt Mary. One in particular was singled out for scorn: the priggish William Fisher, who was, at that very moment, serving as one of the *Dreadnought*'s senior officers. Just as Bloomsbury would enjoy pulling the wool over the eyes of the Royal Navy, so Adrian would delight in tricking his irritatingly conventional cousin.

For the hoax to succeed, more than two participants would be required. Therein lay a difficulty. Aside from Guy Ridley, the son of a High Court judge, and the splendidly named Tudor Castle, who had also been at Trinity, none of Cole's other friends could commit. For a time, the venture was in jeopardy. Then, at the eleventh hour, Anthony Buxton, the son of a former Liberal MP, agreed to join. He was followed by Adrian's neighbour Duncan Grant, who was something of an experienced practical joker.

The seventh hoaxer was the last to enlist. In a matter-of-fact memoir penned decades later, Adrian wrote that he had 'got hold' of Virginia to swell their ranks.[6] On the other hand, Willie Clarkson, the theatrical costumier who furnished robes and make-up, described how she had begged, pleaded and wheedled until her 'Portia-like' arguments carried the day.[7] Virginia herself recalled that she simply said, 'I'm quite ready to come, I should like nothing better.'[8] Whatever the circumstances, she was soon every bit as invested as her brother.

Vanessa, who was not involved, made her disapproval plain. She was particularly apprehensive about the treatment that might be meted out to the hoaxers should their plan fall apart. In 1910, Virginia's mental health was precarious. Her first breakdown had occurred upon the death of their mother in 1895. Their father's death nine years later had triggered a relapse, during which she was convinced the birds were singing in Greek and a foul-mouthed King Edward was lurking among the azaleas. Back then, she had attempted suicide. Complete rest had been prescribed and she eventually recovered, but her underlying fragility remained. The protective Vanessa worried that her sister would not be able to withstand rough handling by a pack of indignant sailors.

Early on the morning of Monday, 7 February, Willie Clarkson and his assistants arrived in Fitzroy Square to help the group prepare. Not all of them were to be Abyssinians. Cole would assume the persona of 'Herbert Cholmondeley' of the Foreign Office. As such, he would be smartly but unremarkably attired in the dress of an Edwardian official, silk hat, wing collar and all. The exceptionally tall Adrian was to be the interpreter, 'George Kauffmann'. In an oversized coat and undersized bowler, he resembled, in his own words, a 'seedy commercial traveller'.[9] The rest of the pranksters were provided with slippers, baggy trousers and richly coloured draperies. With his own hands,

Clarkson wound their turbans and made up their faces with darkening paints. Virginia's high-boned and extremely feminine looks defied his first attempt. Piqued, he tried again. Second time round, the result was gratifying in the extreme. 'The beautiful girl had vanished,' Clarkson recalled with pride, 'and in her place was a slim, dignified, dusky nobleman with a sombre countenance and a flowing regal beard.'[10] When everybody was ready, the group travelled by car to the Bond Street studio of the fashionable firm of Lafayette to be photographed for posterity.

As yet, Admiral May, the Commander-in-Chief of the Home Fleet, had no inkling of the imminent arrival of the 'royal' delegation. The first he heard was at 3.45 p.m., when he received a telegram, sent by Tudor Castle from a post office on St James's Street, which informed him that 'Prince Makalen of Abyssinia and suite' would arrive at 4.20 p.m. and that they wished to tour the *Dreadnought*. Regrets were tendered for the very short notice. In a flourish of verisimilitude, the telegram purported to be from Charles Hardinge, who had accompanied the King to Paris in 1903, and who would be appointed Viceroy of India at the end of the year.

With half an hour to spare, May swung into action. Alighting from the train at Weymouth, the group were welcomed onto a red carpet by an officer in full dress uniform. A smart launch conveyed them to the flag-bedecked battleship where they were met with every courtesy. On the journey down, they had wondered if they had overreached themselves. Surely, they feared, somebody – not least William Fisher – would see through their disguises? Apparently not. Greeted with a rendition of the National Anthem of Zanzibar (the bandmaster had not been able to find sheet music for the National Anthem of Abyssinia, so had substituted what he considered to be the next best thing), they were shown over the *Dreadnought* from stem to stern. It helped that they were now inhabiting their roles with ease, and even insouciance. In his memoir, Adrian wrote that 'It was hardly a question any longer of a hoax. We were almost acting the truth. Everyone was expecting us to act as the Emperor [sic] and his suite, and it would have been extremely difficult not to . . . We almost, I think, believed in the hoax ourselves.'[11]

Resourcefulness, though, remained essential. The cramming in Swahili Adrian had done on the train, from a dictionary procured from the Society for the Propagation of the Gospel, proved to be woefully insufficient and so, as the designated interpreter, he was forced to interpolate scraps of Virgil and Homer he had learnt at school. Thankfully, Buxton, as 'Prince Makalen', swiftly cottoned on, and was able to reply in kind. There was a frightening moment, too, when Grant's moustache almost blew off and had to be furtively reapplied. Otherwise, everything went like clockwork, to the point that the hoaxers began to feel guilty about the warmth and generosity of their reception. They graciously declined a gun salute, lest it cause additional trouble to the sailors who would have to clean the weaponry afterwards. By the time they took their leave, Virginia confessed to feeling 'rather on the side of the *Dreadnought*'.[12]

When the prank was made public, it was a nine-day wonder. Although its participants had agreed between themselves not to brag about it, an extremely satisfied Cole, no doubt wishing to prolong his high, informed the Foreign Office, which in turn informed the Admiralty. From there, the story, possibly leaked by Clarkson, made the papers: the *Globe* and the *Express* on 12 February, the *Daily Telegraph* and, most colourfully, the *Daily Mirror* two days later. On 16 February, the *Mirror* published one of the photographs taken at Lafayette's studio on its front page, noting in the caption that 'all England is laughing' along with the perpetrators.[13] The *Globe* was frankly admiring, praising the escapade as 'so well planned and carried out that it will probably go down in history as one of the smartest [hoaxes] on record'.[14] Questions were asked in Parliament of the First Lord of the Admiralty, Reginald McKenna. Cole was the recipient of bags of fan mail. The phrase 'Bunga Bunga!', which had allegedly been used by the pseudo-Abyssinians to denote approval of every-thing they had been shown aboard the *Dreadnought*, was briefly on every lip. Schoolboys shouted it after sailors on shore leave and it even worked its way into a music-hall song.

William Fisher was one of the few not to see the funny side. Incandescent, he called on Adrian (sensibly, Virginia remained upstairs) and castigated him in no uncertain terms: 'Did we realise we owed our lives to the British Navy? Did we realise we were impertinent, idiotic? Did we realise that we ought to be whipped through the streets?'[15] Fisher stopped short of demanding satisfaction of his cousin, but he and his fellow officers did mete out retribution of a schoolboy kind to Cole and Grant. Cole was visited at home and threatened with a caning. He declined to fight, so it was finally agreed, in gentlemanly fashion, that he would receive six strokes if he could then administer the same number back. Meanwhile, Grant was abducted at breakfast-time, bundled into a cab in his slippers, and driven to Hendon. There he received two strokes with a cane before being turned loose – although not before his captors politely offered to give him a lift back to his parents' house. Ironically, the only one of the conspirators who might have got into real trouble was Tudor Castle, who hadn't even been aboard the *Dreadnought*. By sending the telegram under Hardinge's name, he had likely caused an offence under the Post Office Protection Act. After much discussion along the corridors of power, it was decided not to embarrass the Navy any further by bringing charges against him.

That the Navy *had* been embarrassed was something an indignant correspondent to the *Express* was certain of. The whole thing had been, he blustered, 'a contemptuous fraud on His Majesty's authori-ties'. There was no saying where future jokes might end. 'If such tricks as these may be performed with impunity,' he went on, 'I can imagine that in the guise of a prank a more diabolical piece of mischief might be accomplished.'[16] He would have been relieved – or possibly aghast – had he known of the scheme Adrian had proposed to Cole before they had settled on the Zanzibar stunt, which had led them on to the *Dreadnought*. 'Of all the institutions in the world that offered a leg for everyone's pulling,' Adrian remem-bered, 'the most obvious was the German Army.'[17] Why shouldn't they, he suggested, acquire the uniforms of German officers, commandeer a troop of soldiers in Alsace-Lorraine, and march them over the border into France? Of course, they wouldn't get very far without being apprehended. In the meantime, the hilarity would be intense. With any luck, the Kaiser would get excited, and an international incident would ensue.

Had it not been for Virginia's subsequent fame as a writer, the *Dreadnought* hoax would likely have been forgotten. Conceived in a spirit of mischief by two amply funded but under-employed young men, it was, for them, an afternoon's diversion that just happened to generate an unusual amount of coverage.*

With hindsight, however, the hoax acquired its own significance. Essentially frivolous, it was nevertheless one of Bloomsbury's first sallies against the status quo. In the eyes of those destined to have a transformative impact on British art and literature, the *Dreadnought* embodied three of the preoccupations of the age that were ripe for skewering. The military and the Empire were two, but it was the third, modern technology, that opened up a realm of hitherto unimagined and potentially limitless possibilities for Edwardians of every class and political persuasion.

An enthusiast for everything conducive to greater comfort and efficiency, the King worked the latest inventions into his daily routine whenever and wherever he could. In October 1909, while staying at West Dean, the up-to-the-minute country house of Mr and Mrs Willie James, he inaugurated the Royal Edward Institute for Tuberculosis in Montreal by remote control. At the touch of what looked like a bell-push, he transmitted an 'electric spark', which raced four thousand miles under the North Atlantic to open the Institute's doors, turn on its lights and break the Union Flag on its flagstaff. 'By the marvellous power of science,' wrote the author of a commemorative booklet, Edward was 'brought virtually into the midst of his loyal subjects', causing 'a wave of patriotic emotion . . . to pass over the entire assembly'.[18] The *Daily Telegraph* was no less impressed. The episode had, it observed, 'demonstrated in the most dramatic manner how electrical science . . . had annihilated both time and space'.[19] The Jameses were so in awe of the miracle that had been wrought under their roof that they erected a commemorative niche containing an allegorical statuette in their hallway.

On that occasion, Edward had not been required to venture beyond West Sussex. In every other respect, he was a monarch on the move. During his reign, the number of motorised vehicles in Great Britain quadrupled, from 23,000 in 1904 to 100,000 in 1910. Every day, fewer

---

* Virginia evidently retained a vivid recollection of her involvement in the *Dreadnought* hoax. In July 1940, it was the subject of a light-hearted talk she delivered to her local chapter of the Women's Institute.

and fewer carriages were to be seen on the streets, and those that remained appeared increasingly anachronistic. The demise of the hansom cab, one of the most potent symbols of Victorian London, elicited a pang in the hearts of traditionalists. Veteran cabbies fretted over their livelihoods, as well as the fate of the animals under their care. 'I'm that fond of the little 'oss there,' one told reporter Charlotte Humphry. 'I don't like the thought of partin'. An' what'll become of he?'[20] But few others were inclined to melancholy. Wealthy Edwardians were in thrall to the almost god-like powers motoring conferred upon them. Riding in an automobile was like flying to the moon. Lady Cynthia Asquith feared her new-found velocity was 'almost impious'.[21] Hurtling along in an open car, Osbert Sitwell felt himself to be 'heir of all the ages'.[22]

The King had been an early adopter, acquiring his first Daimler as far back as 1900. Thanks to his lead, motoring became ultra-fashionable. 'Whether in town or country,' wrote a Society commentator, 'the motor has become as much a part of a courtier's baggage as is the cigarette case.' Edward expected his friends to discourse on the internal combustion engine with the same authority 'that they once possessed or affected of the pedigree of the royal thoroughbreds'.[23] Yet he didn't forsake his carriages entirely. In the winter of 1905, he drove out in a fog so dense his brougham had to be preceded and followed by running footmen brandishing flaming torches.

Given the spirit of the times, it was almost inevitable that European rivalries would play out in the fields of transportation and technology as surely as they did in politics and diplomacy. The battle between Britain and Germany for maritime supremacy was waged as fiercely in the commercial sector as it was in the military. In the summer of 1889, the Kaiser had been the guest of honour at a naval review at Spithead. During his visit, he was conducted by his uncle, the Prince of Wales, on a tour of the brand-new White Star liner *Teutonic*. Wilhelm was so impressed by its magnificence that he turned to an aide and remarked, 'We must have some of these.'[24] By 1902, the coveted Blue Riband, claimed by the North Atlantic liner with the highest speed, was firmly in German hands. The *Deutschland* of the Hamburg America Line and the *Kaiser Wilhelm der Grosse* and *Kronprinz Wilhelm* of Norddeutscher Lloyd trumpeted Germany's sea-going achievements as blatantly as they flattered the ego of its ambitious sovereign.

Dented but not chastened, the pride of the British reasserted itself in 1907 with the advent of two stupendous sisters, the *Lusitania* and the *Mauretania*. The Cunard Line received government subsidies to build and operate the pair on the condition they could, in the event of war, be requisitioned by the Admiralty and converted into armed merchant cruisers. Almost eight hundred feet long, the four-funnelled flagships carried over two thousand passengers in conditions that ranged from the clean and comfortable in third class to the frankly luxurious in first. Moreover, they were extremely fast. The *Lusitania* snatched the Blue Riband from the Germans in her second month of service with an Atlantic crossing of four days and nineteen hours. When she lost it, it was to the *Mauretania*, which would end up holding the east- and westbound speed records for two decades.

Yet in no way did the Cunard sisters mark the last word in transatlantic travel. On the contrary, they would soon be eclipsed. In 1908, the American-owned but British-managed White Star Line gave the go-ahead for a brace of liners to be constructed by Harland & Wolff in Belfast. They were not intended for speed, but for immense size and extreme opulence. The *Olympic* was laid down that December. Work began on her identical twin, the *Titanic*, the following March. The publicity department went into overdrive. Whereas Cunard had set out to woo prospective passengers by photographing motor-cars passing through the *Mauretania*'s yet-to-be-fitted funnels, White Star depicted their new giants dwarfing a selection of the world's greatest buildings. With their electrically operated watertight doors, they would be so safe that in due course a leading industry publication would blithely proclaim them to be 'practically unsinkable'.[25]

Danger on the high seas had abated for another reason. More and more ships were now equipped with wireless. It was with particular pride that the crew of the *Dreadnought* had shown the pseudo-Abyssinians its own set, which was, Virginia noted, 'of the newest and the most efficient kind'.[26] The Italian inventor and electrical engineer Guglielmo Marconi had been experimenting with wireless telegraphy since the 1890s, gradually increasing the range of signals that could be transmitted and received. By 1909, his pioneering efforts had earned him sufficient recognition to see him awarded, jointly with the German Karl Ferdinand Braun, the Nobel Prize in Physics.

Marconi's technology had proved its efficacy in the most newsworthy sense at the beginning of that year when the White Star liner *Republic* was involved in a collision with the *Florida* in thick fog off the coast of Nantucket. The *Republic*'s wireless operator, twenty-four-year-old Jack Binns, put out a distress call, which was intercepted by other ships in the vicinity. Her passengers were ferried to the rallying rescue craft in orderly fashion and with minimal loss of life. Binns became a celebrity. His heroic exploit was dramatised in a motion picture (which he did not enjoy) and he was mobbed by chorus girls in New York (which he did). Overall, the episode appeared to confirm the increasingly prevalent belief that technology would eventually eliminate danger altogether. Captain Ranson of the *Baltic*, one of the ships that had assisted the evacuation of the *Republic*, could declare that, thanks to wireless, 'the passenger on a well-equipped transatlantic liner is safer than he could be anywhere else in the world'.[27]

Ocean travel was, then, increasingly free of risk. Aviation was not, but it had a grip on the Edwardian imagination that not even the forthcoming wonders of the *Olympic* and *Titanic* could rival. On 17 December 1903, the Wright brothers, Orville and Wilbur, made a number of flights at Kitty Hawk, North Carolina, in history's first powered, manned and controlled aeroplane. That the ground they covered was minimal was immaterial. The fact that they had flown at all demonstrated that it could be done. Never one to miss a scoop, Lord Northcliffe somehow overlooked that one. His paper, the *Daily Mail*, accorded the Wrights little coverage. Three years later, when the Brazilian Alberto Santos-Dumont took to the sky in Paris, Northcliffe belatedly realised what the feat portended. 'In a year's time, mark my words, that fellow will be flying over here from France,' he told his staff. 'Britain is no longer an island. Nothing so important has happened for a very long time.'[28]

Northcliffe's fierce, even chauvinistic, patriotism was combined with an infallible nose for headline-generating material. In the service of both, he offered a prize of a thousand pounds to the first aviator to fly the Channel. If he hoped it would be claimed by an Englishman, he was to be disappointed. The winner was the thirty-seven-year-old Frenchman Louis Blériot, who took off in his monoplane from Les Barraques near Calais at dawn on 25 July 1909, touching down in Dover just over thirty-five minutes later. An outsider in the field of competitors, Blériot's actual arrival in a gently sloping meadow passed almost unnoticed. His welcoming committee consisted of a solitary police constable who had seen 'the flying man' go over while making his early-morning rounds. But when the press – led, of course, by the *Mail* – got wind of his achievement, he was hailed as a hero. After a fleeting return to France, this time aboard a destroyer, he made a triumphant entry into London, where he was greeted by immense crowds at Victoria station. With forty-eight hours' notice, Northcliffe had organised a celebratory lunch and award ceremony at the Savoy in the presence of the French ambassador. In a flowery speech of congratulation, he paid tribute to the spirit of the Entente Cordiale. Blériot replied in kind: 'Hitherto France and England had been united by the right hand across the sea; now they are united also by the left hand across the air.'[29]

In both countries, the official line was that this great stride forward in aviation would assist the cause of peace. Nevertheless, it was telling that chief among the dignitaries who welcomed Blériot to the Savoy was Richard Haldane, the Secretary of State for War, who assured him his achievement 'marked the beginning of a new era'.[30] A French paper, *Le Siècle*, could scarcely keep from gloating: 'Great Britain is no longer the impregnable fortress of which the garrison could intervene without uneasiness in foreign wars. She constituted at will a European or an extra-European Power. Very soon she will no longer have the opportunity of choosing. She will be vulnerable like her allies.'[31] H. G. Wells, the prophet of the age, had already written of great cities laid waste by flying machines in his 1908 novel, *The War in the Air*. Suddenly, that alarming prospect crept closer.

That the world had been revolutionised in the space of half an hour was the theme of an editorial in the *Tatler* in the first week of 1910. Aeroplanes, it predicted, would soon become as ubiquitous as automobiles, ocean liners and dreadnoughts. Blériot's feat 'brings in its train conditions so altered that no one can truly prognosticate what will arise out of them, but one thing is certain, that with this conquest of the air, this island is one only in name, and great energy, patriotism and expenditure will be needed if our supremacy over the highways of the world are [*sic*] to be maintained'.[32] Like many of his subjects, the King, who granted the prefix 'Royal' to the Aero Club that February, was fascinated by flight. During his annual holiday in

Biarritz in the spring of 1909, he had made an excursion to nearby Pau to witness a demonstration by the Wright brothers. Now he met Blériot, watching with avid attention as he landed his plane. The effect was, he observed, 'very pretty'.[33]

Not everyone was so sanguine. Already an author of note, E. M. Forster would drift into the orbit of the Bloomsbury Group towards the end of 1910. In the meantime, he was hard at work on *Howards End*, a novel that would speak for all those alienated by the newly motorised and clamorous Britain. He described roads that, month by month, 'smelt more strongly of petrol, and were more difficult to cross, and human beings heard each other speak with greater difficulty, breathed less of the air, and saw less of the sky'.[34] The best-selling Marie Corelli embroidered on the theme in *The Devil's Motor*. In it, Satan, 'clothed in black and crowned with fire',[35] drives the wheels of his diabolical car 'over all beauty, all tenderness, all truth'.[36] Part fantasy fiction, part environmental polemic, the pages of her sinister tome were begrimed with soot and impregnated with the stench of oil to ram the message home.

Written by P. H. Ditchfield and illustrated by Fred Roe, *Vanishing England* was an exercise in pure nostalgia that masqueraded as a guide-book. A lament for a lost idyll of thatched roofs and half-timbering, maypoles and coaching inns, it took aim at 'a busy, bustling world that knows no rest or peace'. The automobile was characterised as a 'hideous monster' roaring through village centres, 'startling and killing old, slow-footed rustics and scampering children, dogs and hens, and clouds of dust strive in very mercy to hide the view of the terrible rushing demon'. 'In a few years' time,' Ditchfield concluded, 'the air will be conquered, and aeroplanes, balloons, flying-machines and airships will drop down upon us from the skies and add a new terror to life'.[37]

For his part, the caricaturist Max Beerbohm, who lampooned the King and other Edwardian notables in his wickedly funny drawings, was positively dyspeptic. Setting his face against the brash modernity of the age, he foresaw only dislocation and destruction. He fumed:

When penny stamps and steam-engines were vouchsafed to the world it was honestly thought that thereby a great deal of time and trouble would be saved for us.

When, furthermore, motor cars and telephones and 'tubes' were shaken out of the cornucopia, you scrambled for them eagerly, not having learned your lesson. You have learned it now. There is not one thinking person among you who would not, for the sake of the happiness of the human race, be glad to have these 'tyrannous toys' smashed up and swept away and forgotten . . .

Nobody – except perhaps a fourth-form boy here and there – wants to possess an airship. But every nation will have to possess as many of them as it can – until airships be superseded by some subtler and swifter vehicle, for use in the very-soon-by-some-inspired-idiot-to-be-discovered fourth dimension of space. In course of time, thanks to science, the human race will collapse and cease.[38]

5: 'We shall all be in our graves before it is finished!'

The apocalyptic fiction of H. G. Wells notwithstanding, few Edwardians entered into Max Beerbohm's fears about the over-enthusiastic embrace of technology. On the contrary: buoyed by the rhetoric of empire and dazzled by the wonders of science, they surrendered themselves to the current of ever-accelerating change, confident it would bring them, and the nation, nothing but good. Britain was booming. Since the turn of the century, its population had burgeoned by three million each year. By 1910, it was nearing forty-five million. During the same period, the population of Greater London had increased by nearly seventy thousand each year until it reached, and would soon surpass, seven million. Not only was it the largest city in the country, it was the largest in Europe. Twice the size of Berlin, the number of its inhabitants exceeded those of Paris, Vienna and St Petersburg combined.[1]

Swollen with riches and crackling with energy, London seemed to the novelist Stephen McKenna to be a 'new imperial Rome in a new silver age'.[2] Developers were never busier. In *Howards End*, E. M. Forster wrote of 'bricks and mortar rising and falling with the restlessness of the water in a fountain',[3] of the transformation of Whitehall and Regent Street as the capital 'rose and fell in a continual flux'.[4] Victorian architects had favoured styles that recalled bygone civilisations: the dignified Greek Revival, the sacerdotal Gothic. Edwardian architects also drew upon the past, but to quite different ends. Now the seventeenth and eighteenth centuries were rifled for inspiration. Columns, domes and pediments loaded with swags, garlands and allegorical statuary rioted in indiscriminate abundance. At the time, it was known as 'English Renaissance'. A later appellation, 'High Edwardian Baroque', was nearer the mark, denoting all that was exuberant and bombastic.

Just as they vied with each other at sea, the White Star and Hamburg America Lines competed on land with the construction of massive new headquarters on Cockspur Street. To profit from the moneyed visitors pouring in from abroad, grand hotels sprang up like mushrooms. The Carlton and the Ritz were joined by the Piccadilly in 1905 and the Waldorf in 1908. Not to be outdone, the Savoy expanded between 1903 and 1904. On Oxford Street, consumers were wowed by a new department store, Selfridges, which threw open its doors with tremendous fanfare in March 1909. The greatest achievement of the American magnate Harry Gordon Selfridge, it was saturated in modernity. Six acres of floor space necessitated a sales team of twelve hundred. There were telephones, electric lifts, a post office, a restaurant, a smoking room and a rooftop tea garden.

Prior to its launch, Selfridges had been at pains to assure its competitors that its Goliath presence would only enhance their operations by confirming London as the undisputed 'Market of the World'. Even so, the nearby store of Debenham & Freebody, which had remodelled its own lavish premises just two years earlier, was quite eclipsed. Harry Selfridge was as adept at generating publicity as Lord Northcliffe was at capturing headlines. Within days of Louis Blériot's cross-Channel flight, his aeroplane was on display in the Motor Accessories and Sports department. Customers flocked in their thousands to see the latest technological wonder in the most advanced retail space in the country.

At the heart of this vibrant metropolis was the effulgent figure of the King. Unlike his mother, he believed it was the business of the monarch to be visible. Queen Victoria had come to loathe London, preferring to seclude herself in what Lord Esher described as an atmosphere of 'hushed reverence ... deep memories ... queenly pity ... of personal sorrows, and of duties simply performed through long years'. In her elderly presence, statesmen were 'half afraid to speak above a whisper'.[5] Quite apart from finding it desperately dull, Edward had judged such remoteness to be politically inexpedient. 'The people – not only Londoners – cannot bear seeing Buckingham Palace always unoccupied,'[6] he had urged Victoria in 1869. 'We live in radical times, and the more the *People see the Sovereign*, the better it is for the *People* and the *Country*.'[7]

With his accession, the Crown returned to the capital. After decades of neglect, the Palace was spectacularly revitalised. Forsaking Marlborough House, his home of nearly forty years, the King wasted little time in purging what he referred to as the 'sepulchre'.[8] In the words of his grandson the Duke of Windsor, it was 'as if a Viennese hussar had suddenly burst into an English vicarage.'[9] Cases of knick-knacks and family mementoes vanished into storage, Prince Albert's library of valuable first editions was dissolved with almost indecent haste and museum-quality paintings were cleaned and rehung. Under the direction of C. H. Bessant of Bertram & Son, the Grand Staircase and Marble Hall were enveloped in glittering white and gold. The vast ballroom was turned over to Frank Verity, whose training in Paris revealed itself in a Louis Revival scheme redolent of pre-revolutionary France (and, indeed, the Ritz). No detail of the overhaul was too small for Edward. Lionel Cust, the newly appointed Surveyor of the King's Pictures and Works of Art, remembered that he 'liked to supervise everything himself, enjoying nothing so much in the intervals of leisure as sitting in a roomful of workmen and giving directions in person'.[10] He did not, in Cust's opinion, possess much imagination, but he did have an infallible eye for effect. 'I do not know much about Arrrt,' Edward was fond of saying with a characteristic roll of his *r*, 'but I think I know something about Arrrangement.'[11]

The King understood his role to be a performative one, and it was as a giant stage that Buckingham Palace was now conceived. 'Like a highly trained actor,' Cust recalled, he had 'studied and learnt the importance of mien and deportment, of entrance and exit, of clear and regulated diction and other details, which he absorbed quite modestly and without any ostentation into his own actions'.[12] Edward emitted a 'curious electric element'[13], which galvanised all who came into contact with it. The rental value of houses in Pimlico and Belgravia shot up, owing to their proximity to the rejuvenated Court. Foreign visitors were dazzled by its panache. 'Everything is so tastefully and artistically arranged, it makes one's mouth water to see all this magnificence,' wrote the Dowager Empress of Russia during a visit to Windsor Castle in 1907.[14]

Outside, Edward involved himself in a comprehensive redesign of The Mall and its environs which would transform the Palace into the locus of a processional route of the utmost grandeur. Stretching from the monumental Admiralty Arch, built from 1908 to a design by Sir Ashton Webb, it terminated in an immense memorial to Queen Victoria. Funded by public donation, plans for the latter had been in train from the first weeks of the new reign. Even the Kaiser had been allowed his say. By the early months of 1910, the fountains, pools and sculpted reliefs around its base were largely complete, but the wedding-cake-like plinth of solid marble had still to be garnished with florid bronze statuary by Thomas Brock. To Edward, the plodding pace was something of a joke. On a visit to the Franco-British Exhibition in White City with President Armand Fallières of France, he caught sight of a picture of the memorial, then in the seventh year of its construction. 'We shall all be in our graves before it is finished!' he scoffed.

Hilldrop Crescent in Islington, North London, might have existed on a different plane from intellectual Bloomsbury and the fashionable West End. The clattering traffic of the adjacent Caledonian and Holloway Roads bypassed it as surely as cultural subversion and Society sophistication. Its semi-detached houses – square, solid, entirely unremarkable – sheltered the kind of middle-class residents they had been built for. There, anonymity was not considered a mark of failure so much as a badge of respectability.

Murmurs of the febrile energy coursing through more modish parts of the capital had nevertheless seeped under the door of number 39. Behind it, rooms were crowded with miscellaneous ornaments and ill-assorted furniture. Combined, the effect was of tawdry opulence teetering on the brink of outright chaos. The décor was a manifestation of the flamboyant personality of Cora Crippen, a blowsy but attractive figure who had once yearned for stardom. Her life to date had been an itinerant one. Of German and Polish-Russian immigrant stock, she had been married at the age of seventeen in Jersey City in 1894. She and her husband had then wandered rootlessly through the United States and Canada as his job blew him from city to city. Around the turn of the century, they had headed to England where, since 1905, they had rented the property on Hilldrop Crescent for £52 10s per annum.

For an aspiring performer, London was the place to be. In 1879, a dozen theatrical companies had toured the British Isles. By 1900, that number had swelled to at least a hundred and forty. Every sizeable town possessed one theatre, and sometimes several. Ranging in price from fourpence to half a guinea, tickets were within reach of all but the poorest.

Enthusiastic audiences took their cue from the King, whose passion for the stage was as legendary as his appetite. Besides attending as many as sixty plays and operas a year, he regularly commanded private performances at Windsor and Sandringham. Knighthoods were bestowed on the actor John Hare in 1907, and the actor-manager Herbert Beerbohm Tree and playwright Arthur Pinero in 1909. Even Willie Clarkson, the man who dressed the *Dreadnought* hoaxers, was honoured with an appointment as 'Royal Perruquier and Costumier'.[15] Frank Verity, the architect who remodelled the ballroom at Buckingham Palace, was known for his lavish theatre interiors, including that of the Imperial for Edward's former mistress, Lillie Langtry. His Majesty's Theatre on Haymarket was so grand its ushers wore powdered wigs as if they were footmen in a ducal residence. Cora Crippen could not have landed in a more receptive city at a more propitious moment in its history.

There was one snag. She had no talent. In her youth, she had dreamed of being an opera diva, like the world-famous Nellie Melba. Then, lowering her sights, she had aimed for the music halls, where she performed as 'Belle Elmore'. Even there, she overreached her modest abilities. Forced to acknowledge that she would never receive top billing, Cora called it a day. Thankfully, she retained her ample nature and considerable charm, and made friends easily. Her connection with the theatre was retained through her involvement with a charitable body, the Music Hall Ladies' Guild, for which she served as honorary treasurer.

Compact and slight, with a walrus moustache, thinning hair and wide-set eyes peering through spectacles, Cora's spouse was as pallid as she was colourful. Everything about him was nebulous and ill-defined. Born in Coldwater, Michigan, in 1862, he was at least ten years older than his wife, and had already been widowed by the time they wed. Christened Hawley Harvey Crippen, he preferred to answer, for some unknown reason, to 'Peter'. Understood to be a doctor, his credentials were obscure. It was as a moderately successful representative of Munyon's Remedies that he had moved to London in the first place. He had then set himself up as a tooth specialist, trading out of premises on New Oxford Street. Summed up by his business partner as a 'humble, unassuming little man', his appeal to the voluptuous Cora was a mystery. In spite of their all too obvious differences, the childless couple seemed content with their lot.

On the evening of 31 January 1910, Paul and Clara Martinetti visited Hilldrop Crescent for supper. Mr Martinetti was a retired music-hall artiste; Clara had met Cora around eighteen months earlier through their activities with the Ladies' Guild. The Crippens didn't employ a cook, so the meal was necessarily a simple one of soup and beef salad. The atmosphere was informal but convivial. A pack of cards was produced, and the couples played whist until well past midnight. At 1.30 a.m., the guests took their leave. In high spirits, Cora came out onto the front steps to bid them farewell. There was not the slightest indication anything was amiss.

The following morning, Dr Crippen paid a courtesy call on the Martinettis to enquire after the health of Paul who had suddenly come down with a cold. Clara asked after Cora (whom she knew as Belle) and was assured her friend was quite 'all right'.[16] Then, after another week had elapsed, came a surprise. Crippen announced that Cora had sailed for America, where she would make for California immediately upon landing. To Clara and her associates at the Guild, this seemed strange. Transatlantic crossings were not lightly undertaken. Under normal circumstances, a traveller would have received a decent send-off, then have kept in touch with postcards throughout their journey. Clara had received not a word. As yet indistinct, her suspicions began to crystallise at a benefit ball held at the Criterion in Piccadilly on 20 February. It was not lost on Clara or any of Cora's other acquaintances that Crippen attended with another woman: his pretty, if somewhat insipid, twenty-seven-year-old secretary, Ethel Le Neve. Nor did it escape Clara's beady eye that Ethel appeared to be wearing one of Cora's brooches. Within a month, Crippen was putting it about that his wife, by then supposedly in Los Angeles, was dangerously ill with double pleuro-pneumonia. On 24 March, he telegraphed the Martinettis to tell them she had passed away.

It was shocking news. Cora had last been seen in London at the end of January, when she had been in perfect health. Her precipitate departure to the United States, and the letter subsequently passed to the Guild by Le Neve, ostensibly from Cora but not in her handwriting, in which she resigned her post as treasurer, didn't add up. Crippen himself seemed at a loss to know exactly when and where she had died. Still, he observed all the conventions of middle-class mourning. His own letters were written on paper with black borders, and he took to wearing a black hat and armband. When two more of Cora's theatrical friends, the manager John Nash and his wife Lillian, known by her stage name 'Lil Hawthorne', visited the widower to tender their condolences, they found him tearful. Crippen was, Nash believed, 'much cut up'.[17] They had no way of knowing he harboured a secret that would, when uncovered, rivet the attention of the entire Western world.

The apparent sleepiness of Hilldrop Crescent could be attributed to the fact that, by 1910, more and more Londoners were opting out of inner-city life to set up home in the suburbs. Even as the West End burgeoned in size and splendour, as many as seven hundred thousand people made the move out of the cramped and smoky metropolis in search of wider streets, fresher air and more modern conveniences. The outer ripples of this shift in population spread as far afield as the south coast of England. During the closing decades of the nineteenth century, William Bowerman, whose start in life had been distinctly unpromising, had amassed a handsome fortune through canny investment in property in the flourishing towns of Hastings and St Leonards. A staunch Methodist, his ironclad values and strong work ethic were shared by his wife, Edith Barber, whom he married around 1888. In spite of a thirty-year age difference, their union was surprisingly successful. Bowerman may have been frugal and abstemious, but he was no martinet. One of the earliest memories of his only daughter Elsie, who was born in late 1889, was of belting out Sankey and Moody hymns with her elderly father at their upright piano.

William's wealth ensured Edith's comfort during his lifetime. After his death, when Elsie was just five, it guaranteed her independence. Having little interest in social aggrandisement, with the endless tea-drinking, call-paying and card-leaving it would have entailed, she set her sights on the wider world. The moment her mourning could be laid aside, she began to travel. One year, there was a trip to Paris, the next a holiday in Rome. Then, in a spirit of adventure, she sailed from Marseille on a cargo steamer. Having taken in Naples, Sicily and Alexandria, she arrived in Cairo, where she and Elsie sat on the balcony of Shepheard's Hotel for hours on end, watching the exotic street life with fascination. Growing up in rural Suffolk, Edith had been acquainted with hardship and, worse, limitation. She now resolved her daughter should enjoy all the opportunities she had been denied. When they rode on camels to the foot of the Pyramids, they did so in the knowledge their horizons had expanded far beyond East Sussex.

At home, Edith worked hard to encourage curiosity and resourcefulness in Elsie, employing hands-on methods that had little to do with the stereotype of the distant and uninvolved Victorian mama. There were word games, nature rambles, sewing classes and kitchen tutorials. A puppy inculcated a sense of responsibility, while riding lessons fostered physical courage. Elsie scarcely knew a moment of inactivity or boredom. When the question of school arose, Edith consulted her most progressive friends. On their advice, she settled on an establishment that was to change Elsie's life.

Situated on the outskirts of High Wycombe in Buckinghamshire, Wycombe Abbey had been founded as recently as 1896 by Frances Dove, a clergyman's daughter who had been in the vanguard of the strides in education made since the 1840s. One of the first students at Girton College, Cambridge, she had formulated a dream of a school 'at which lonely country girls could gain the same advantages of intellectual stimulus and the inspiration of noble ideals of life as their brothers did at their schools'.[18] This emphasis on equality was to become the guiding principle of Wycombe Abbey. The teaching, much of which was done by mistresses who had themselves attended Girton, was of an extremely high calibre. Pupils were trusted to regulate their own conduct without the usual plethora of rules and restrictions. There was little snobbery, and neither was it assumed that marriage and motherhood were the only avenues open to ambitious young women upon leaving. Dove's model equipped her girls to avail themselves of all the exciting possibilities of the twentieth century.

Ahead of her departure, Elsie was avid with a curiosity not even the tedious rigmarole of the sewing on of endless nametapes could diminish. If, at the age of twelve, she felt apprehensive about her despatch into what she termed a 'strange new world', she didn't show it. Despite being two years younger than the other entrants, she was so cheerful when she disappeared through the school gates that her mother, in spite of herself, was crestfallen.[19]

Elsie loved every minute of her time at Wycombe Abbey. She relished its communal routines and rituals and threw herself with gusto into the packed programme of lessons and games. Her classmates became her surrogate family. Inspired by Dove's ethos of 'corporate values', she grew into a confident, motivated and boundlessly energetic young woman who retained an open-minded innocence that led her not only to embrace but actively seek out fresh challenges. At Girton, to which she almost inevitably progressed in 1908, she read Medieval and Modern Languages while immersing herself in college sports, amateur dramatics and missionary work. Coming hard on the heels of her transformative school experience, Elsie's sojourn in Cambridge was happy and fulfilled.

With her grown-up daughter so joyfully spreading her wings, Edith, feeling the need for companionship, made a decision she lived to regret. After William's death, she had withstood the advances of the suitors who swarmed like flies around her and her money. In 1907, she wed a local farmer, Alfred Chibnall, who, like her first husband, was considerably older. By the standards of the day, Bowerman had been a free-thinker. Chibnall proved to be anything but. Within two years, they separated. Her shadowy stepfather features nowhere in Elsie's photograph albums. When at last he died, he left his entire estate to male friends. His wife was not remembered at all.

The failure of her second marriage may have had something to do with Edith's involvement in a cause many men, and not a few women, looked at askance. Closely engaged with current affairs, she was instinctively drawn to the suffragette movement then gaining traction. In the campaign for the vote, she could work towards the attainment of a goal that seemed not only inarguable in its justice but urgent in its necessity.

The advances in education that had precipitated the founding of Girton College and Wycombe Abbey reflected a changing Britain. Of the 230,000 teachers listed in the 1901 Census, three-quarters were female. Although well over a million women remained in service as cooks, maids and nannies, the proliferation of factories and offices provided a wealth of new opportunities for machinists, telephonists, typists and administrators. The first female doctor had qualified in 1865, and the first female dentist in 1895. In 1908, the physician Elizabeth Garrett Anderson was elected Britain's first female mayor. Yet even though these financially independent women had moved far beyond the domestic sphere to which they had previously been confined, they remained without a stake in national government. It was an unacceptable – indeed, untenable – state of affairs that the Women's Social and Political Union, founded by Emmeline Pankhurst in 1903, challenged head-on.

The widow of a Radical barrister from Manchester, Mrs Pankhurst exhorted women to take positive action to bring about meaningful change. Her fight to overcome sex discrimination was framed as a crusade that required its adherents to 'rise up'[20] from the ranks of male-dominated society. Brooking no opposition and tolerating no dissent, she was an autocrat who exacted absolute loyalty from her followers. In return, she promised to 'sacrifice life itself'[21] if by doing so she could further their cause.

A messianic figure who kindled rebellion with her firebrand conviction, Mrs Pankhurst was profoundly troubling to the Edwardian patriarchy. Early attempts to dismiss her crumpled in the face of her 'great revolt',[22] which appropriated the language and trappings of an army. The very word 'suffragette', coined in a spirit of derision by the *Daily Mail* in 1906, had martial overtones. Rejecting polite activism, the WSPU honed its methods and expanded its outreach at an astonishing rate. Targeting the broadest possible range of women, from peeresses to factory hands, it had its own newspaper, *Votes for Women*, which printed its first issue in 1907, and its own colour scheme of purple, white and green, devised in 1908. Joan of Arc was adopted as its patron saint. Highly visible and extremely vocal, Mrs Pankhurst and her equally committed daughters, Christabel, Sylvia and Adela, were in constant movement around the country. Flying squads of suffragettes could be deployed at short notice to bolster the activities of those working in the provinces. Within a remarkably short period, the question of the suffrage became the most pressing, as well as the most divisive, in the public arena.

The King had no truck with any of it. For all his love of women, he expected them to exercise their influence softly and discreetly. There was no place in his conception of boudoir politics for suffragettes causing trouble in a sphere so clearly not their own. 'God put you in the world to be different to us,' he growled to Lady Warwick, 'but you don't seem to see it.'[23] To the Prime Minister, Sir Henry Campbell-Bannerman, he wrote vituperatively of the 'outrageous' conduct of the 'so-called "Suffragettes"', which he held to be detrimental to a cause 'for which I have no sympathy'.[24] Over lunch at Windsor, Margot Asquith was amused to discover that the suffragettes were 'the *pièce de résistance* for Court abuse'.[25] In January 1910, the Countess of Fingall, who had earlier been teased by her fellow guests for her feminist sympathies, found herself seated beside Edward at dinner. 'What do you want with votes?' he asked her. 'You women have quite enough power already! You can get all you want without the Vote.'

Lady Fingall was unapologetic. 'Some of us, Sir,' she countered bravely.[26]

His enmity had been incurred by the disturbances that had, since 1905, come to define the movement. In early 1908, women had chained themselves to railings in Downing Street. Two even slipped into Number 10, from where they had to be bodily evicted. A few weeks later, in the so-called 'Trojan Horse' stunt, a party of suffragettes hid in delivery vans and tried to infiltrate the Palace of Westminster. Discovered before they could gain entry, they were subjected to rough handling by the police. At the end of the year, the Chancellor of the Exchequer, David Lloyd George, was heckled at a mass meeting in the Royal Albert Hall. One of the women turned a dog whip on the men who tried to remove her, but not before they had pummelled her breasts and burned her with a cigar.

Far from being deterred, Christabel Pankhurst urged the suffragettes to devise new and ever more disruptive methods to force the Government to capitulate. 'I say to you that any woman who is content to appeal for votes for women instead of demanding and fighting for it is dishonouring herself,' she declared.[27] Cabinet ministers, and particularly the Prime Minister, Herbert Henry Asquith, were subjected to continual harassment. Pasting a caricature of a snarling harpy into her diary, Margot Asquith scrawled a jeremiad against the 'disgusting women' who were making her family so miserable. They had, she wrote, smashed the windows of Number 10, incited the 'scum of the streets' to storm the House of Commons, and made themselves so objectionable in the Ladies' Gallery that the Speaker had been forced to close it. Worse, Margot herself was the recipient of numerous poison-pen letters, one of which had actually threatened the lives of her husband and children. 'When women get excited,' she concluded furiously, 'they become violent, cruel and senseless.'[28]

In 1909, suffragettes who had been sentenced to gaol for acts of civil disobedience went on hunger strike. In response, the authorities resorted to a policy of force-feeding. It was a brutal remedy, and caused widespread revulsion, even among those who deplored militancy. One prisoner to undergo the harrowing ordeal was force-fed by nasal tube and stomach tube simultaneously. In a graphic account, she described it as:

> most painful – the drums of the ears seem to be bursting, a horrible pain in the throat and the breast. The tube is pushed down twenty inches. I have to lie on the bed pinned down by wardresses, one doctor

stands up on a chair holding the funnel at arm's length, so as to have the funnel end above the level and then the other doctor who is behind forces the other end up the nostrils.[29]

The WSPU bestowed silver medals on women who had been force-fed. On purple, white and green ribbons, their bars were engraved 'FOR VALOUR'. Separate bars were awarded for each hunger strike, with some suffragettes collecting several. Edward professed himself in favour of whatever 'strong measures' the Government chose to employ against the prisoners. If they had to be force-fed, that was preferable to releasing them early just because they wouldn't eat. Such martyrdom, he maintained, would only serve to attract more trouble-makers to the cause. 'Thank heaven those dreadful women have not yet been enfranchised,' he wrote to his son, George.[30]

In spite of the escalation of violence, and the increasingly draconian measures taken against it, the beginning of 1910 found the suffragettes in rude health. Over the previous twelve months, the weekly circulation of *Votes for Women* had surged from 30,000 to 40,000. At Selfridges, supporters could buy everything from blouses and gloves to ribbons and stationery in the suffragette colours. Membership fees and donations paid the salaries of almost a hundred organisers and administrators who worked alongside an army of volunteers. In Sussex, Edith Chibnall was a paid-up member of the Hastings chapter of the WSPU: just one of twenty-three regional branches that spanned the country from Torquay to Dundee, with a further twenty branches in London alone. In the general election that January, the issue of women's suffrage was mentioned in the speeches of two hundred candidates. To Christabel Pankhurst, it was proof that they were on the right track. 'Militancy,' she claimed, 'had floated the Cause. All that remained was to get it into port.'[31]

For there was reason to expect a breakthrough. In the new year, an all-male, cross-party Conciliation Committee was formed under the auspices of the Radical journalist Henry Brailsford and the 2nd Earl of Lytton, respectively the husband and brother of militant suffragettes. They proposed a Bill that would, if passed, enfranchise up to a million women based on property holdings and marital status. More limited in scope than any of the campaigners would have liked, it would at least be better than nothing. At a meeting in the Queen's

Hall on 31 January, Mrs Pankhurst announced a suspension of militant activity – in effect, a ceasefire – which would see the WSPU throw in its lot with the non-militant National Union of Women's Suffrage Societies and the Women's Freedom League while the Bill was being considered. It was a brittle truce, and one that could be preserved in the face of cynicism and mistrust only by Pankhurst's 'extraordinary powers of gentle persuasion'.[32] Still, for most of 1910, relative calm prevailed. Hoping for the best, the suffragettes held their breath.

6: 'The Camel and the Needle's Eye'

The opulence of the Edwardian rich threw the plight of the Edwardian poor into stark relief. The rarefied worlds of Escoffier and Mewès and Davis, of Selfridges and the Savoy, were far removed from the deprivation that abounded in London, and in every other town and city in the British Isles. In 1906 – the same year the Ritz opened its doors – as many as twelve million men, women and children were estimated to be malnourished and on the verge of chronic hunger.

In the final weeks of 1909, a blistering assault on such flagrant inequality was launched from an unlikely quarter. Arthur Ponsonby, whose book *The Camel and the Needle's Eye* was published that December, was firmly embedded in the class he set out to excoriate. For twenty-five years his father, Sir Henry Ponsonby, had served Queen Victoria as her Private Secretary. When, in 1895, Sir Henry had a stroke, his second son Frederick, known as 'Fritz', was promoted from equerry to Assistant Private Secretary, a post he retained under Edward VII. Arthur himself had been inducted into life at Court at a tender age. In 1882, when he was just eleven, he had accompanied the Queen to the wedding of her youngest son, the Duke of Albany, to Princess Helen of Waldeck-Pyrmont. The pair had posed for the camera of the fashionable photographer Alexander Bassano: Victoria diminutive but dignified in Honiton lace and diamonds, Arthur, in his uniform as page of honour, almost swamped by the voluminous train it was his responsibility to manage.

After Eton and Oxford, followed by diplomatic postings in Constantinople and Copenhagen, Ponsonby entered Parliament in the spring of 1908. Almost immediately he landed in hot water when he was among the MPs to protest the King's upcoming voyage to Reval to meet the Tsar. Edward was so angry he gave orders that three of those who had signalled dissent should be scratched from the guest list of a garden party due to take place at Windsor Castle on 20 June. Of the offending trio, the socialists Keir Hardie and Victor Grayson, who loathed the Russian autocracy on principle, were particularly vocal. Nevertheless, once the party had been and gone, Edward let it be known that he considered their sins expiated. He was less inclined to forgive the third, Ponsonby, who in his view had been both disloyal and discourteous. No more invitations would be sent his way until he tendered an explanation and apology. Extremely embarrassed, Fritz managed, with some difficulty, to extract a letter of contrition, which saw his errant brother reinstated in time to attend a Court ball in July. Still, Arthur had made his point. When it came to matters of conscience, he was not, and never would be, constrained by his proximity to the throne.

Even as the debacle rumbled on, Ponsonby was evolving the outline of a book that would examine, as he put it, 'some of the most important bearings of the question of the expenditure of riches'. While admitting that he was no expert, he was at pains to stress his 'deep conviction' in the truth of arguments to be laid out by one who, far from being a passive spectator, was in fact 'infected with the malady he is studying'.[1] Taking his title from a New Testament proverb – 'It is easier for a camel to go through the eye of a needle than for a rich man to enter into the Kingdom of God' – he intended to hold up a mirror to the hedonism of the leisure class by demonstrating that dire poverty was the inevitable by-product of its 'purely selfish satisfaction of animal appetites and material pleasures'.[2]

Ponsonby began by suggesting his readers stroll the Thames from Westminster to Waterloo Bridge. Not far from the bright theatres and luxurious hotels of the West End, a different sort of show was playing:

> It is a long run, every night and all night, and has gone on ever since the Embankment was constructed. As they pass along, they can see the seats packed closely with men and women leaning against each other in an exhausted or half-drunken slumber. They can see the ragged and filthy bundles of humanity lying round the parapet at the foot of Cleopatra's Needle, or the rows of wretched caricatures of men and women lined along the wall under the shelter of the bridges. If they go late enough, there is a strange silence which at first gives the impression that the place is deserted. But it only means that these waifs and strays, these wretched outcasts, are enjoying the few hours' reprieve given even to them by the blessed oblivion of sleep. The moon shines on them from over the river, but no melodrama can reproduce that scene.[3]

In Edwardian London, such sights were inescapable. Lady Cynthia Asquith experienced them viscerally, like a poison that tainted the air she breathed. Walking from her parents' house in Cadogan Square, she passed 'haunting beggars – some distressingly crippled, others with faces pitted with smallpox, and sealed eyes. Bloodless supplicating lips quivered into tremulous thanks when with a "tonk" my halfpenny fell into a tin mug.'[4] Violet Asquith was deeply disturbed by 'the crossing-sweepers who held out their tattered caps for pennies, the children in rags, fluttering like feathers when the wind blew through them, the down-and-outs sleeping under the arches or on the benches in the parks with an old newspaper for cover'.[5] Researching his book, Ponsonby drew upon the account of a journalist who had recently visited the metropolis from Canada. What had struck him in the seat of imperial government were not Britain's 'statesmen or pro-consuls or heroes or scholars'. Rather, 'the thing that impressed me most, the thing that stands out as the background of every reminiscence, was the bloodless, mirthless, hopeless face of the common crowd'. Put simply, wrote the Canadian, 'the social problem everywhere is appalling, almost to the point of despair. Wherever we went, it forced itself upon us.'[6]

Charity had a discomfiting way of illuminating the gulf between wealth and poverty. Newly installed as the chatelaine of Blenheim Palace, Consuelo Marlborough noticed that the butler left a basket of tins on the sideboard in the dining room. These, she learnt, were intended for leftovers from the ducal table. The scraps would be packed into the tins, then taken, in feudal fashion, to the poorest residents in the surrounding villages. At no stage had it ever been thought necessary to separate savoury dishes from sweet: all were jumbled together. Revolted, Consuelo made a point of sorting through the viands before they were despatched. Although her in-laws found her departure from tradition to be 'impertinent', the recipients were, she noted, surprised and delighted that somebody had bothered to take the trouble.[7]

Social reform had not been high on the agenda of the Conservative Government Edward had inherited from his mother. Magnificently patrician, Robert Gascoyne-Cecil, 3rd Marquess of Salisbury, had been Prime Minister since 1895. Filling his Cabinet with men much like himself – some titled, most blue-blooded, all rich – he was the last British premier (with the exception of Alec Douglas-Home, who in 1963 renounced his earldom to take office) to hail from the House of Lords. Mistrustful of democracy, he believed it was the privilege – moreover, the right – of the aristocracy to rule. In time, even the members of his own party came to see him as a brake on progress. To Lord Curzon, he was 'that strange, powerful, inscrutable, brilliant, obstructive deadweight at the top'.[8]

Upon his retirement in the summer of 1902, Salisbury was succeeded by his nephew, Arthur Balfour. Erudite and aloof, he was far too cerebral to appeal to the resolutely unbookish King. Nevertheless, he presided over a government that broke with the policy of 'Splendid Isolation', allowing Edward to work towards the attainment of the Entente Cordiale with France. In December 1905, Balfour, much exercised by divisions within the Conservative ranks, resigned. Edward sent for the Liberal leader, Sir Henry Campbell-Bannerman, who pledged to form a minority government of his own. Somewhat against the odds, for the Liberals were themselves deeply divided on various issues, he managed to do so. Parliament was dissolved in January 1906, paving the way for a general election. The result was a landslide in which the Liberals secured almost four hundred seats. The Conservatives were left with barely a hundred and fifty. The House of Commons seemed to have been completely reborn. Margot Asquith was startled by the profile of a chamber that suddenly seemed alien: 'sadly unfamiliar to me, fearfully over-crowded and full of strangers'.[9] Balfour, who lost his own seat, wrote that 'The election of 1906 inaugurates a new era.'[10] Francis Knollys, the King's Private Secretary, agreed. To his mind, the change was not for the better. 'The old idea that the House of Commons was an assemblage of "gentlemen" has quite passed away,' he grumbled.[11]

If Knollys and Mrs Asquith were nonplussed by the abrupt revolu-tion in their party's fortunes, the Conservatives were downright apprehensive. In opposition, the Liberals had discovered a new purpose. They would be a party of reform, dedicated to the better-ment of the majority of the population. The initiative was long over-due. During the nineteenth century, the male electorate had greatly expanded. The landed elite gravitating, as it always had done, to the Tories, it was left to the Liberals to represent the interests of the middle and, latterly, the working classes. The emergence of the Labour Party, which returned nearly thirty members in 1906, threat-ened that dynamic. Mindful of the lure of socialism, the Liberals planned to head it off with a legislative programme designed to allevi-ate the worst of the evils that so bedevilled the lives of the poor, the elderly, the incapacitated and the unemployed.

Personally, Campbell-Bannerman was more to Edward's taste than Balfour. Superficially, the two men had much in common. Blessed with a good sense of humour – or at least one that saw him laugh convincingly at the royal jokes – the Prime Minister was notably cosmopolitan. A heavy eater and pronounced Francophile, he spoke several languages fluently and holidayed in Marienbad, Edward's spa of choice. Indeed, it was owing to the fact they shared a physician there that Edward gleaned, quite early on, that Campbell-Bannerman's health was so precarious his long-term prospects as Prime Minister were in doubt. Setting those affinities aside, the King could not regard with equanimity a government committed to reforms that would inevitably lead to friction, and conceivably open warfare, between the classes.

As President of the Board of Trade, Campbell-Bannerman selected David Lloyd George, a forty-two-year-old firebrand who had entered Parliament as the Member for Caernarvon Boroughs in 1890. Speaking Welsh as his first language, he was a product of his lower-middle class, Nonconformist upbringing. For him, wrote Violet Asquith, 'Poverty was not a political concept but a stark fact which had entered into his being, bringing with it an instinctive hatred of the rich. Squires, landowners and even parsons were his hereditary enemies.'[12] Intensely charismatic, as well as an orator of pyrotechnical if not incendiary brilliance, Lloyd George swiftly alienated the King by taking his name in vain during one of his 'violent tirades' against the House of Lords. Via Knollys, Edward requested Campbell-Bannerman 'to take the necessary steps to prevent a repetition of this violation of constitutional propriety and good taste.'[13]

The appointment of Herbert Henry Asquith as Chancellor of the Exchequer was even more consequential. Born into a prosperous family in Yorkshire in 1852, he had climbed the social ladder thanks to a combination of aptitude and luck. A brilliant student, he passed from the City of London School to Balliol College, Oxford, where he read Classics. Called to the Bar in 1876, he married Helen Melland, the daughter of a doctor from Manchester, and settled with her in Hampstead, where they had five children before her death from typhoid in 1891. Entering Parliament in 1886, Asquith's clear head, strong work ethic and talent for public speaking saw him become Home Secretary under William Gladstone in 1892. In 1894, a year before the Liberals went into opposition, he married Margot Tennant, the daughter of the Scottish industrialist Sir Charles Tennant, whose factory chimneys dominated the Glasgow skyline. The union was to revolutionise his way of life.

Vibrant, witty and chic, Margot pulled her husband into a far grander milieu than the one to which he had been accustomed. Herself a study in upward mobility, she had first caught the approving eye of Edward as Prince of Wales at Ascot in 1883. Basking in the royal favour, her prospects had improved in a heartbeat. 'I felt my spirits rise,' she recalled of that transformative encounter, 'as walking slowly across the crowded lawn in grilling sunshine, I observed everyone making way for us with lifted hats and low curtsies.'[14] Bankrolled by their father's immense fortune, Margot and her sisters diffused through the ranks of late Victorian Society. Founder members of 'The Souls', the coterie of aesthetically inclined aristocrats who defined their high-minded pleasures against the grosser ones of the Marlborough House Set, they were plugged into a network of influence that proved extremely useful to the ambitious Asquith.

During its first two years, the Liberal Government pursued a modernising and moderately progressive agenda. Under Campbell-Bannerman, the underground railway network was expanded, wireless telegraphy became more widespread, the electrification of London was completed and the programme of naval shipbuilding inaugurated by the *Dreadnought* advanced. It also legislated to improve conditions for the lower classes. By 1908, the Trades Dispute Act, the Workmen's Compensation Act, the Probation of Offenders Act and the Coal Mines Regulation Act had all seen the light of day. Alone, those successes might have implied an acquiescent House of Lords. Nothing could have been further from the truth. In 1906, having already rejected a Plural Voting Bill, the Lords mauled an Education Bill that proposed that religion in public elementary schools should be taught on non-denominational lines. That interference prompted Lloyd George to demand to know 'whether this country is to be governed by the King and his peers, or by the King and his people'.[15] Scenting trouble, Edward exerted himself to bring about some sort of compromise. His efforts were to no avail. The Education Bill having been modified out of all recognition in the Lords, the Government felt compelled to withdraw it. Frustrated and indignant, Liberal minds began to focus. At the end of the year, Campbell-Bannerman fired a warning shot across the Lords' bow. 'A way must be found, and a way will be found,' he declared to an enthusiastically applauding Commons, 'by which the will of the people, expressed through their elected representatives in this House, will be made to prevail.'[16]

For all his championing of new money, Edward never lost his faith in the function of the aristocracy. When, in 1868, Queen Victoria had remonstrated with him over his headlong plunge into high society, he had returned a spirited, if repetitive, response. 'In every Country a great proportion of the Aristocracy will be idle and fond of amusement, and have always been so,' he wrote, 'but I think that in no Country more than ours do the Higher Classes occupy themselves, which is certainly not the case in other Countries. We have always been an Aristocratic Country, and I hope we shall always remain so, as they are the mainstay of this Country.'[17]

Some might argue that the King had done more than any man to dilute what had once been an exclusive caste personified by the likes of Lord Salisbury and his Cabinet. As Prince of Wales, he had facilitated a process of assimilation, drawing parvenus into the patrician fold. By the turn of the century, only mid-Victorian relics like Lady Dorothy Nevill could lament the 'mob of plebeian wealth which surged into the drawing rooms, the portals of which had up till then been so jealously guarded'. For the most part, the distinctions between old blood and new money had long since melted away. In any case, Lady Dorothy noted, 'Not a few of that mob have themselves obtained titles, and now quite honestly believe they are the old aristocracy of England.'[18]

Whether ancient or modern, a peerage conferred privilege. In his youth, Thomas Lister, 4th Baron Ribblesdale, was encouraged by an elderly relation to take advantage of his seat in the House of Lords:

'You will find it,' he said, 'a pleasant lounge.' So it is. Many people are of my relative's opinion, especially after Easter, when the daily attendance gets quite respectable. The pleasant walk across the lawns of St James's Park, the comfortable crimson benches inviting repose of mind and body alike, the certainty of getting home in good time to dress for dinner, and of a season of immunity from the door-bell and her ladyship's notes and telegrams, become matters of agreeable habit with an average of say from fifty to seventy peers from May to July. The routine business gets through quickly; questions are asked and answered, attention called to this or that without interruption, whether of approval or dissent. Ninety-nine nights out of every hundred the House of Lords is a machine with neither pulse nor temperature.[19]

The soporific atmosphere belied the fact that the Lords wielded serious political power. Ramified by generations of intermarriage, its members belonged by hereditary right. Exercising that right, they could veto almost any piece of legislation sent up to them by the Commons. Having no need to concern themselves with votes, it was their duty to mitigate the risk of elected government deploying what Lord Salisbury described as 'an accidental, temporary and unreal advantage . . . for the purpose of permanently modifying the constitution.'[20] In the process, they could force a dissolution of Parliament and a general election, thereby batting contentious issues back to the nation to decide at the ballot box. What came to be known as the 'referendal theory' worked very well – for the Lords.

It was less palatable to the Liberals of 1906. The power of the aristocracy was vested in its ownership of land; and land at the turn of the century was no longer the asset it had been. In the forty years before 1910, its stake in the economy dwindled from one-quarter to one-twelfth. An acre worth £54 in 1875 was worth £19 by 1897.

Simultaneously, the electorate had expanded. Since 1832, successive Reform Acts had enfranchised the middle and working classes. With the passing of the Third Reform Act in 1884, the claim that the House of Lords represented 'the people' had become more tenuous than ever – not least because the allegiance of its members so clearly remained with the Conservatives. Even after his defeat in the Commons, Arthur Balfour could confidently declare that his party would continue to control the fate of the Empire 'whether in office or out of office' thanks to its overwhelming majority in the second chamber.[21] In the eyes of the Liberals, the 'referendal theory' was outdated fiction. In practice, the only interests the Lords felt obliged to represent were its own.

The prognosis of Dr Ott, the fashionable physician consulted by the King and the Prime Minister in Marienbad, had been correct.

In rapidly deteriorating health, Campbell-Bannerman resigned on 3 April 1908. Nineteen days later, he was dead.

Edward had grown to like Campbell-Bannerman, whom he considered a 'great gentleman'.[22] He was less enamoured of his successor, Asquith, who now assumed the party leadership. In the Cabinet reshuffle, Lloyd George became Chancellor of the Exchequer. The post of President of the Board of Trade fell to the up-and-coming Winston Churchill, who had defected from the Conservatives in 1904 in protest against their drift towards protectionism. Campbell-Bannerman's seat, Stirling Burghs, was won in a by-election in May by his Private Secretary, Arthur Ponsonby, who immediately incurred the wrath of the King by opposing his voyage to Reval to meet with the Tsar.

As Prime Minister, Asquith introduced the 1908 Budget he had prepared as Chancellor. In it, he made provision for a long-cherished Liberal dream, an old-age pension. Passed by the Commons, the relevant Bill stumbled in the uncooperative Lords. Even though it would allow just five shillings a week to those with an annual income of £21 and under, it was decried by Lord Lansdowne as a step that would 'weaken the moral fibre and diminish the self-respect of the people'. Lord Rosebery held that 'a scheme so prodigal of expenditure' would deal 'a blow at the Empire which might be almost mortal'.[23] Still, the Lords, which by convention did not exercise the power of veto over what it judged to be 'Money Bills', grudgingly signalled assent on 30 July.

If the Government derived any satisfaction from its pension victory, it was mingled with growing frustration that the Liberal agenda had progressed as far as it could without being hobbled in the second chamber. On 11 December, Asquith made an appeal to his party:

> The question I want to put to you and to my fellow Liberals outside is this: 'Is this state of things to continue?' We say that it must be brought to an end, and I invite the Liberal Party tonight to treat the veto of the House of Lords as the dominating issue in politics – the dominating issue because in the long run it overshadows and absorbs every other.[24]

The following spring, matters came to a head. On 29 April 1909, Lloyd George presented what came to be known as his 'People's Budget' – or, as he put it, 'a war Budget':

> It is for raising money to wage implacable warfare against poverty and squalidness. I cannot help hoping and believing that before this generation has passed away, we shall have advanced a great step towards that good time when poverty and wretchedness, and the human degradation which always follows in its camp, will be as remote to the people of this country as the wolves which once infested its forests.[25]

For all his fanciful rhetoric, the Chancellor's talent for public speaking for once failed him. Extraordinarily convoluted, his address to the Commons lasted nearly five hours. Even the Prime Minister's daughter Violet, who had been 'agog' to hear it, admitted she was unable to sit through the whole thing. She wondered if Lloyd George himself understood half of his circumlocutions.

Once the full implications of the Government's proposals had sunk in, there was consternation and fury in the Lords. To finance the ongoing programme of reform, as well as to cover the cost of the eight new dreadnoughts demanded by the public to counter the perceived threat of German aggression, income tax was to be raised and death duties increased. Besides the introduction of a so-called 'supertax', there were to be taxes on tobacco, spirits, petrol and motor licences. Most controversial of all would be a parcel of land taxes. A levy of 20 per cent would be introduced on the increase of value of land whenever it changed hands; a duty on the capital of undeveloped land was to be imposed; and all the land in the country was to be surveyed and valued. In other words, it wasn't just the rich the Liberals intended to squeeze. It was the aristocracy.

The Government claimed it hadn't set out to goad the Lords to the point it might, in defiance of convention, reject the Budget, thereby sparking an all-out war between the Houses. Even so, the impact of the Bill might have been foreseen. Contemplating provisions that Balfour, the leader of the Opposition, deplored as 'vindictive, inequitable [and] based on no principle'[26], the Lords embarked upon a counter-offensive. First into the fray were the dukes, the most senior-ranking peers, whose prestige was inextricably bound up with their great estates. To the Duke of Rutland, the Liberals were nothing but 'a crew of piratical tatterdemalions'. The Duke of Beaufort expressed his desire to see Lloyd George set upon by 'twenty couple of dog-hounds'. In anticipation of the state of poverty into which the Budget would throw him, the Duke of Buccleuch stopped his guinea subscription to the Dumfriesshire Football Club. The Duke of Somerset withdrew *all* his charitable subscriptions and sacked a number of his workers. Really, remarked an incredulous Margot Asquith, 'the speeches of our Dukes have given us a very unfair advantage'.[27]

If the ducal gestures were petty, the ducal invective smacked of Gilbert and Sullivan. Both played straight into the hands of the anti-aristocratic Lloyd George. Even before the Budget had cleared the Commons, he flung himself at the Lords with relish. He was joined by the almost equally pugnacious Churchill who, as President of the Budget League, travelled the country delivering rabble-rousing speeches to whip up popular support. Dubbed 'the Terrible Twins' by their Conservative opponents, they made a formidable, headline-grabbing double-act.

Throughout the summer and autumn of 1909, the critical issue was ostensibly the Budget. Trusting in precedent, Lloyd George had incorporated schemes for social reform on the understanding the Lords wouldn't dare reject a Money Bill. Still, he and Churchill now had the second chamber firmly in their sights. 'Is it not an extraordinary thing that upon the Budget we should be discussing at all the action of the House of Lords?' enquired Churchill on a platform in July. It was, he maintained, 'an institution absolutely foreign to the spirit of the age and to the whole movement of society'. Likening the Lords to Punch and Judy shows and other picturesque anachronisms, he claimed it had been roused from its pleasant slumber under Salisbury and Balfour to obstruct the work of democratically elected government. He clearly articulated the outcome if the peers, in a reckless act of class warfare, chose to exercise their veto now. By plunging the nation into fiscal chaos, in the process creating 'a Constitutional deadlock of novel and unmeasured gravity', they would hand the Liberals a golden opportunity, 'clear, brilliant and decisive', to deal with them once and for all.[28]

Lloyd George was no more conciliatory. That same month, the Chancellor poured scorn on the cynical machinations of idle land-owners who enjoyed great wealth they had done nothing to create. The dukes of Northumberland, Norfolk and Westminster were singled out for scorn and ridicule. 'No country, however rich,' he said, 'can permanently afford to have quartered upon its revenue a class which declines to do the duty which it was called upon to perform.'[29]

The King was incensed by these gratuitous thrusts. To Lord Crewe, the Liberal leader of the House of Lords, Francis Knollys conveyed Edward's extreme displeasure. The Chancellor had, he wrote, packed his oration full of 'false statements, of Socialism in its most insidious form and of virulent abuse against one particular class, which can only have the effect of setting "class" against "class", and of stirring up the worst passions of its audience'. He had displayed 'gross vulgarity', been 'in the highest degree improper' and come close to offering 'an insult to the Sovereign'.[30]

Although personally against the Budget, Edward let it be known that, officially, he had 'no opinion' on its provisions. He did, however, deplore the rancour between the Houses, and did what he could to persuade the Lords to pass the Bill. After a meeting with Balfour and Lord Lansdowne, the leader of the Opposition peers, at Buckingham Palace in October, he was forced to confess he was no nearer to determining what their course of action would be. In his darker moments, dismayed by his apparent inability to halt the constitutional crisis heaving into view, he expressed doubts about the survival of the monarchy, an institution that, like the Lords, was grounded in the hereditary principle. When, at a party, he discovered that the Prince of Wales was unacquainted with Richard Haldane, the Secretary of State for War, he led his son over and presented him as 'the last King of England'.[31]

Passed by the Commons with a healthy majority in early November, the Budget made its way to the Lords. Jolted out of its club-like torpor, the atmosphere in the second chamber was explosive. Above, the galleries were packed with duchesses and countesses determined not to miss a moment of the action. Below, their husbands, sons and brothers lined the red leather benches in serried ranks. Seasoned statesmen found themselves far outnumbered by the so-called 'back-woodsmen': peers so parochial they had had to ask for directions to Westminster, but who had been prised from their far-flung estates to register their horror at the proposed new taxes.

For several days, the debate raged back and forth. The most eloquent speeches were delivered by those who, like Lord Rosebery, Lord Cromer and the Archbishop of York, despised the Budget but realised that a far graver question would arise if the Lords exercised the veto now. Lord Balfour of Burleigh (not to be confused with Arthur Balfour) set out the risks in no uncertain terms. 'My Lords,' he pleaded, 'if you win, the victory can be at most a temporary one. If you lose, you have altered and prejudiced the position, the power, the prestige, the usefulness of the House.'[32]

The peers remained obdurate. On 30 November, the Budget was overwhelmingly rejected by 350 votes to 75. Among those who ranged themselves in opposition were no fewer than seventeen dukes. Faced with what he called a 'breach of the Constitution and a usurpation of the rights of the Commons',[33] Asquith sought an immediate dissolution of Parliament, to be followed in the early weeks of 1910 by a general election. It would be fought not just over the Budget but over the prerogatives of the House of Lords.

Up at Sandringham, the King was immersed in the festivities to mark Queen Alexandra's sixty-fifth birthday. A thousand schoolchildren sat down to a series of celebratory teas. For the Norfolk gentry, there was a command performance of *The Little Damozel* starring Charles Hawtrey. And, for the amusement of the inner circle, the Russian Balalaika Court Orchestra was imported from London, where it had been playing to packed houses at the Coliseum. Each day, in fine but windy weather, there was shooting in the royal coverts. On 2 December, the Prince of Wales, Lord Derby, Lord Ripon and Arthur Sassoon blasted 1,427 pheasants, 517 rabbits, 35 ducks and 27 hares. Under normal circumstances, Edward would have been in his element.

But circumstances were anything but normal. The day before the birthday, the peers in the party made their excuses and returned to town to cast their votes. When the result came through, the King was unable to accompany the guns as he was obliged to preside over a council to prorogue Parliament. If that were not bad enough, he had such chronic toothache that a dentist had to be summoned for an emergency extraction. Staring into a new year that portended nothing but strife, Edward was convinced the political atmosphere was more acrimonious than at any stage in living memory. He had never, he admitted to his guests, been more miserable.

7: 'We shall have some very bad luck this year'

The turmoil in Parliament was ill-timed. Edward's health invariably took a turn for the worse during the winter months. In early 1905, Queen Alexandra had harboured doubts about leaving her husband in damp and sooty London while she undertook an official visit to Lisbon, followed by a cruise in the Mediterranean. He had had bronchitis and was, as she put it, 'very pulled down'. 'These fogs are very bad for Papa who nearly chokes, it frightens me *dreadfully*,' she wrote to one of their children.[1]

She was not the only one to notice that Edward was often – too often – racked with uncontrollable coughing fits. In January 1908, Sybil Cust, the wife of the Surveyor of the King's Pictures, was at a dinner at Windsor Castle when her host was convulsed with 'an awful choke' so violent she feared he might break in two. She and the other ladies at table averted their eyes until he had had a chance to recover.[2]

He was his own worst enemy. Prince Albert had granted his son permission to take up smoking when he turned nineteen. He hadn't stopped since. Each day, he puffed his way through a dozen Havana cigars, and at least twenty Egyptian cigarettes. Mingled with the citrusy aroma of eau de Portugal, his signature scent, clouds of expensive tobacco enveloped him wherever he went.

Complaining of lethargy, breathlessness, sleeplessness and ever more frequent bouts of depression, Edward was regularly seen by his doctors. Biddable when ill, he slipped back into bad habits the moment his condition, however fleetingly, improved. In 1907, the royal physicians sent a confidential memo to Francis Knollys in which they summarised the King's recurrent attacks of bronchial catarrh. They concluded on a warning note:

> It is obvious that His Majesty's health, even when it appears excellent to the world at large, unfortunately always is in a somewhat precarious state, and that, whilst it must be devoutly hoped that his extraordinary vitality and the comparatively very slow progress of all the processes we have mentioned may presage many more useful years of this most precious life, it cannot be gainsaid that either a more rapid progress of any of the degenerative changes now at work or an acute complication of any kind may bring about, apparently suddenly, very serious results.[3]

Bowed by the accumulated stress of domestic and European affairs, Edward began to age perceptibly. As active as ever, he looked much older than his sixty-eight years.

Since the mid-1860s, Edward and Alexandra had spent most of their Christmases at Sandringham. Fully planted and much improved, the estate was no longer the barren wilderness bemoaned by Lady Macclesfield at the time of its acquisition. The house, however, remained irredeemable in its rambling, pseudo-Jacobean ugliness. Visiting in 1956, the historian and biographer James Pope-Hennessy compared it to a provincial hotel in the depths of rural Scotland: 'tremendously vulgar and emphatically, almost defiantly, hideous and gloomy'.[4] Inside, it was cluttered with reproduction furniture, family photographs and taxidermy. In the hall, a stuffed baboon clutched a tray on which callers could leave their cards. From sentimental knick-knacks to exquisite bibelots by Fabergé, ornaments littered every surface. Homely at best and oppressive at worst, the atmosphere was curiously at odds with the personality of the sophisticated and luxury-loving sovereign.

Still, Edward liked it. When in residence, he played the part of country squire to the hilt. Guests were escorted on tours of the stables, kennels and model farm of which he was inordinately proud. So excellent was the shooting that clocks and watches were set thirty minutes ahead of time to allow the guns to make the most of the winter daylight. Alexandra loved the Norfolk landscape, which reminded her of her native Denmark. In 1892, Sandringham had witnessed tragedy when their elder son Albert Victor, known as 'Eddy', had died of pneumonia at the age of twenty-eight. Some mothers might have shied away from such an unhappy association. Not Alexandra. She kept Eddy's tiny bedroom as a shrine to his memory, strewing the counterpane with flowers and gazing at his uniforms, which were mounted in a glass cabinet on the wall.

In the run-up to Christmas 1909, the weather across much of Britain was severe, with deep snow and heavy frosts. Then there was a thaw that left rivers swollen and fields too waterlogged for hunting. At Sandringham, the wind was bracing but the sun was bright. Edward arrived from Buckingham Palace on 23 December to join his wife and their unmarried daughter, Princess Victoria. At nearby York Cottage, the Prince and Princess of Wales, George and May, were ensconced with their children, who were constantly in and out of the 'Big House' during the holiday period. 'Dickens in a Cartier setting'[5] was how the future Duke of Windsor remembered Christmas with his grandparents: a neat summary of the blend of Victorian cosiness and Edwardian glamour that characterised the royal festivities. On Christmas Eve, gardeners decked the halls with holly, ivy and mistletoe. Slabs of beef from a specially reared cow were distributed to workers on the estate: a pound for every adult, half a pound for every child. There were concerts and dances for the domestic staff and members of the Household, and gifts were handed out from an enormous tree.

Shortly before midnight on 31 December, Sandringham was emptied of its inhabitants so that Edward and Alexandra could be the first to step across its threshold into 1910. Slipping away from the family group, one of the children entered through the back and opened the door ahead of them. It seemed an ill omen. 'We shall have some very bad luck this year,' remarked the King, perturbed.[6]

On 3 January, having ploughed manfully through an avalanche of New Year greetings, Edward, unaccompanied by his wife, motored to Elveden, the estate of Lord Iveagh near Thetford. Few houses, and few hosts for that matter, were more calibrated to his taste. Edward Guinness was the most prominent member of the so-called 'Beerage', the coterie of ennobled brewers who, during the late nineteenth century, had accrued considerable financial and political influence. The chairman of the board of his hugely profitable family business, Guinness had risen from a baronetcy in 1885 to a barony in 1891, and then to a viscountcy in 1905.* His private fortune was so immense that even the grandest members of the old aristocracy didn't scruple to beg for favours. 'Do you know Lord Iveagh?' enquired the 4th Duke of Sutherland of a friend. 'If so, would you ask him if he would take Dunrobin and Stafford House for a year?'[7]

But Iveagh had no need to rent a country seat. He possessed a splendid one of his own. Acquired from its previous owner, the Maharaja Duleep Singh, Elveden had doubled in size between 1899 and 1904. A florid example of High Edwardian Baroque, its domed and pedimented mass was more akin to a town hall than a grand hotel. Inside, it was, in the words of the writer Augustus Hare, 'almost appallingly luxurious',[8] with banks of orchids and Cassano's band to serenade guests as they made their way in to dinner. At the heart of the house was a stupendous space in the Indo-Islamic style. Clad in intricately carved marble, it was said to be the coldest room in Britain.

The sport was as opulent as the décor. Dozens of gamekeepers tended more than a hundred thousand birds. Each beat was connected to its neighbours by telephone. At Holkham, the estate of the Earl of Leicester, even royal guns made do with beer, bread, cheese and Spanish onions. At Elveden, multi-course shooting lunches were served by liveried footmen at tables groaning with glittering plate and exotic blooms. 'The general magnificence would be overpowering,'

---

* Lord Iveagh would finally be raised to an earldom in 1919.

wrote the *Tatler*, 'if Lord and Lady Iveagh were not the kindest and pleasantest of hosts.'[9] It said much about the calibre of their hospitality that Elveden was one of two great houses in which Edward liked to begin each year. The other was Chatsworth.

In January 1910, thick fog blanketed the country for miles around. The Iveaghs' guests spent much of their time indoors, eating, gossiping and playing bridge into the small hours. To avoid agitating the King, politics were studiously avoided. The Countess of Fingall, whose bedroom adjoined Edward's, realised that he was much frailer than he looked. Through the closed door, she could hear his doctor administering oxygen to assist him with his breathing. As a result, he was querulous and morose. A cheerful Irishwoman, Lady Fingall was an amusing but sympathetic dinner companion. As they left the table one evening, Edward asked to speak with her alone. In a corner of the drawing room, looking very solemn, he announced, 'Your friend Mrs Jameson has hurt me deeply.'[10] Lady Fingall was taken aback. The sister of the distinguished army officer Douglas Haig, Mrs Jameson was an acknowledged eccentric. She was convinced her dead brother George sent her messages from beyond the grave, which she would transcribe and relay to their sceptical recipients. Lady Fingall enquired about the nature of her offence.

> He said, 'She knows how much I loved my sister Alice, and she has written to me, giving a message, which she says is from her, sent through her brother, George.'
> 'What was the message, Sir?' I asked.

He hesitated a moment. Then he said: 'It was "The time is short. You must prepare."'[11]

Lady Fingall was shocked. Princess Alice had been the second daughter of Queen Victoria. Married to the Grand Duke of Hesse, she had had several children, one of whom, Alexandra, was now the wife of the Tsar. Intelligent and altruistic, she had been Edward's favourite sister, and he had been grief-stricken on her death from diphtheria in 1878. At a loss for words, Lady Fingall asked if Mrs Jameson had provided any evidence to substantiate her distressing claim.

'Yes,' he said, huskily. 'She said that I was to remember a day when we were on Ben Nevis together and found white heather and divided it.'

I said, 'But, Sir, how could Mrs Jameson or her brother have known that?'

He only repeated that he had been very much hurt and that I must write to Mrs Jameson and tell her so.[12]

It was just one of several small but inauspicious signs to trouble Edward during the first few days of the new year. When the party at Elveden broke up on 8 January, he returned to London by train. Disembarking at King's Cross, he was greeted by the usual crowd of well-wishers. As he walked to the royal motor, a newsboy wormed his way to the front of the throng. By chance, the placard he carried bore the headline, 'The Monarchy in Danger!'[13] Coming hard upon the heels of Mrs Jameson's prophecy, the sight might have unnerved even a less sensitive man.

Anticipation of a rare phenomenon had sparked atavistic fears in other breasts too. Halley's Comet was due to make its first appearance since 1835. Throughout the winter, scientists wrote articles and delivered lectures for the benefit of the curious, and sometimes apprehensive, public. The comet was represented at the children's fancy-dress party given at the Mansion House on 5 January (where other topical costumes included 'The People's Budget', 'The House of Lords' and 'United South Africa') and Lloyd George managed to work it into one of his tub-thumping speeches on unemployment. To allay anxieties of interstellar collision, Robert Ball of the Observatory in Cambridge reassured readers of *The Times* that they should worry about it no more than a charging rhinoceros should fret about a cobweb. From his home in Cavendish Square, a Mr Crawford pointed out that, in earlier generations, a comet was believed to portend some terrible event. The residents of all 'civilised countries' knew better, but might it not be a good idea, he suggested, to publish a simple explanation in the local vernacular for the benefit of those 'peoples and nations whose education has not advanced as rapidly as with us', lest ancient superstitions 'make opportunity for the agitator'?[14] Amateur astronomers were put on notice that the comet would be clearly visible in the skies above

Britain in about five months' time. Experts predicted that it would be at its most brilliant in mid-May.

Gusting in from the North Sea, the winter winds hardened the constitution of Elsie Bowerman as she cycled the three miles of exposed road that separated Girton College from Cambridge town centre. After each round trip, she huddled with hot cocoa beside the fire in her sitting room, discussing team sports, amateur theatricals and, most vital of all, Votes for Women with her many friends.

Even in Bloomsbury, where ideas were preferred to activism, the question had become too difficult to ignore. In the final days of 1909, Virginia Stephen had had a conversation with her private tutor, Janet Case, who had impressed upon her 'the wrongness of the present state of affairs'.[15] On 1 January, Virginia made a resolution. Writing to Case from Fitzroy Square, she requested some pamphlets, or perhaps the address of her local suffrage society where she could volunteer her services. 'I could neither do sums nor argue or speak,' she warned, 'but I could do the humbler work if that is any good.'[16] Low-level administrative tasks would, she suggested, suit her very well.

Case was pleased to make the proper introductions. Within weeks, Virginia was spending hours every Tuesday writing improbable names on envelopes. She was not convinced it made much difference to the cause. 'People say that Adult Suffrage is a bad thing,' she admitted to her confidante Violet Dickinson, 'but they will never get it owing to my efforts.' Nor did she have much in common with her fellow helpers: 'ardent but educated young women and brotherly clerks'[17] who might have strayed from the pages of a novel by H. G. Wells. It was very worthy but terribly dull.

That same month, an encounter took place that was to have far-reaching consequences. Returning home from a trip to Cambridge with her husband Clive, Vanessa Bell spotted a familiar figure on the station platform. At the age of forty-three, Roger Fry would have been unmistakable anywhere. Unusually tall, his chiselled features and unruly shock of greyish hair were offset by enormous spectacles. His air of physical distinction was belied by his unorthodox dress sense. The effect of his well-tailored suits was marred by his predilection for dubious accessories: gaudy ties, strange hats, and brown sandals when black lace-ups would have been more appropriate. Commanding but quizzical, he resembled, in Clive's opinion, nothing so much as 'a highly sagacious rocking horse'.[18]

Although Fry had studied science at university, his first love was art. An aspiring painter, he was to win greater acclaim as a critic and connoisseur. Over the previous decade, he had extended himself in many different directions. He wrote for the *Athenaeum*, was instrumental in the founding of the *Burlington Magazine*, and was active in both the National Art Collections Fund and the New English Arts Club. A scholar of the Renaissance, he placed his expertise at the disposal of American millionaires as they developed their collections. Under the auspices of the financier J. Pierpont Morgan, he was appointed curator of European Paintings at the Metropolitan Museum of Art in New York in 1906. That plum post turned out to be a poisoned chalice. Even as he continued to assist Morgan in a private capacity, Fry was making acquisitions for the museum of which Morgan was president. Within a year, he traded his curatorship for a less restrictive brief as an adviser. Even then, the conflict of interest was insoluble. After a spat with Morgan over a Fra Angelico – Fry wanted it for the museum, Morgan wanted it for himself – he was served with six months' notice at the close of 1909. The timing could not have been worse. His wife Helen had long suffered from mental illness, and she was about to be institutionalised. With two children to support, Fry cast around for alternative employment. The Slade professorship at Oxford was his preference, and he lobbied vigorously to obtain it. If it was not forthcoming – and, in the event, it was not – he would have to join a newspaper or launch himself on the lecture circuit.

Preoccupied by his accumulated woes, Fry was oblivious to the presence of the Bells until Vanessa went over and introduced herself. It was not their first meeting. They had encountered one another some years earlier at a dinner party in London. Then in her mid-twenties, Vanessa had been nervous of an already celebrated critic who 'seemed somehow to have the secret of the art universe'[19] within his grasp. Plucking up her courage, she had ventured a tentative remark, and was surprised to find it was listened to and understood. The conversation had flowed from there, animatedly, and then heatedly.

Between 1901 and 1904, Vanessa had attended classes at the Royal Academy Schools, where she had studied under John Singer Sargent, the most sought-after portrait painter of the day. Initially, she had dismissed him as nothing but a slick propagandist for the rich and fashionable. Then she had been forced to recant. 'I had for long doubted, denied his merits, thought him vulgar,' she wrote, 'but had at last gone over with vehemence, overcome by what seemed such superb painting.'[20] That night in Chelsea, Fry had begged to differ. Sargent couldn't draw at all, he insisted – a singular assessment of one of the most superlative draughtsmen of his, or any, age. Vanessa countered with the famous portrait of *Madame X*. 'Yes,' Fry had conceded, 'you've hit upon the one thing – perhaps the arm in that *is* drawn, I agree.'[21]

The spirited opening had not been followed by much of a sequel until the pair met by chance that January morning in Cambridge. When their train puffed in, they climbed into the same compartment. Fry had a manuscript with him and obviously intended to write. As soon as he and the Bells began to talk, his papers were set aside. By the time they reached King's Cross, they were well on the way to becoming friends. For both Bells, it was a *coup de foudre*. Less loquacious than her husband, Vanessa contemplated Fry with her painter's eye. 'As he sate [*sic*] opposite me in the corner,' she remembered, 'I looked at his face bent a little down towards his MS, but not reading, considering, listening, waiting to reply, intensely alive but quiet. "What astonishing beauty," I thought, looking at the austere modelling in the flat bright side lights from the train windows.'[22]

For Clive, the thrill was intellectual. As his dismissal of Sargent had demonstrated, Fry was unafraid to defy consensus. Notwithstanding his credentials as a historian, he was increasingly drawn to modern painters who were barely known in a Britain belatedly coming to terms with Impressionism. Clive, who had been converted to the *avant garde* during his time in Paris in 1904, was a well-informed and receptive interlocutor, and he relished the opportunity to discuss his ideas with a kindred spirit. Some years later, his sister-in-law recalled his exhilaration:

It must have been in 1910 I suppose that Clive one evening rushed upstairs in a state of the highest excitement. He had just had one of the most interesting conversations of his life. It was with Roger Fry. They were discussing the theory of art for hours. He thought Roger Fry the most interesting person he had met since Cambridge days.[23]

The euphoria was contagious. Virginia soon discovered for herself that Fry possessed 'more knowledge and experience than the rest of us put together'. Under his guiding hand, 'the old skeleton arguments of primitive Bloomsbury about art and beauty put on flesh and blood'.[24]

According to Clive, it was during that first meeting – in fact, while they were still on the train – that Fry mentioned his intention to stage an exhibition in London of works by 'the newest French painters'.[25] Clive immediately pledged his support. In early 1910, the world seemed alive with possibilities. Anything, even a miracle, might happen. Still, the British public was notoriously conservative. Was it ready for exposure to the bold, and potentially shocking, canvases of Matisse, Cézanne and Gauguin? Clive had his doubts. Fry's scheme didn't strike him as premature so much as downright fantastic.

The *Tatler* hailed February as the 'month of promise'[26] when the first forecasts could be made of the forthcoming Season. Even at that early stage, there were indications the spring and summer of 1910 would be unusually brilliant. In May, the eagerly anticipated Japan-British Exhibition would open at White City. To celebrate the spirit of friendship engendered by the brokering of an alliance that predated even the Entente Cordiale, the organisers planned an extravaganza to educate and enthral. Wandering through the lavishly decorated halls, visitors would be able to admire displays of rare antiquities and demonstrations of wrestling and traditional handicrafts as the Great Imperial Japanese Band ('Never before out of Nippon') played around the clock. The King agreed to loan paintings, tapestries and swords, as well as the bullet that had felled Lord Nelson. The Queen would lend fans from her personal collection.

In the meantime, gossip columnists surveyed a particularly note-worthy crop of debutantes. Leading the pack was Edward's grand-daughter, Princess Maud, who was something of an unknown quantity, given that her parents, the Princess Royal and the Duke of

Fife, preferred to seclude themselves on their Scottish estate. Lady Moira Osborne, the daughter of the 10th Duke of Leeds, would likely be overshadowed by Lady Diana Manners, the daughter of the 8th Duke of Rutland, whose reputation as a dazzling beauty was already established. Worldlier than the majority of her contemporaries, the Honourable Victoria 'Vita' Sackville-West was dreading her first Season. She was besotted with Knole, her family's ancestral seat in Kent, and unable to reconcile herself to the fact that, as a woman, she wouldn't one day inherit it. Some years earlier, she had met Violet Keppel, the elder daughter of the King's mistress. Over time, their relationship would become progressively closer and more intense.

Seventeen-year-old Lady Victoria Stanley was just one of several earls' daughters projected to make her debut. Her father, the 17th Earl of Derby, could trace his lineage back to 1125. His estates in and around the port city of Liverpool yielded as much as £300,000 in rent each year. Robust and no-nonsense, with a happy knack of getting along with men of all stripes and conditions, he had married Lady Alice Montagu, a daughter of the 7th Duke of Manchester, in 1889. Their wedding was attended by the then Prince and Princess of Wales and all five of their children, who had grown up with the bride and knew her affectionately as 'Starling'. In due course, Alice would be appointed a Woman of the Bedchamber to Queen Alexandra.

As yet only skirting the fringes of the social scene, Victoria could look forward to two coming-out dances. One would be given by her maternal grandmother, the so-called 'Double Duchess', who had married the 8th Duke of Devonshire after the death of her first husband. The other would be hosted by her parents at Stratford House, which had been acquired by Lord Derby as recently as 1908. The already impressive mansion on the north side of Oxford Street had since been extensively remodelled. That spring, the finishing touches were being put to a magnificent new ballroom, which was to be inaugurated in the presence of the King and Queen in June. Victoria's debut would be 'big business', the *Tatler* predicted, 'and her future outlook is cheery in the extreme'.[27]

Lady Derby's plans for her only daughter's first Season likely included a series of visits to Lucile Ltd at 23 Hanover Square.

Founded in the mid-1890s, it was the most celebrated dressmaking establishment in London. Its proprietress, Lady Duff Gordon, was a brilliantly talented designer, whose vision and drive had enabled her to rise to the uppermost tier of a notoriously fickle and cut-throat industry. Drawing inspiration from the eighteenth-century portraits of Boucher, Fragonard and Vigée Le Brun, the Lucile look was a significant departure from the whaleboned richness of the late Victorian era. Ethereal colours, delicate lace, lavish applications of sequins and hand-stitched flowers conspired to create an impression of swooning femininity in elegant salons carpeted in soothing grey and garlanded with innumerable pink silk roses.

From the outset, Lady Duff Gordon, who had been born Lucy Christiana Sutherland in 1863, was informed by a flair for the dramatic. In a theatre-loving age, she assiduously courted playwrights and impresarios, creating costumes for top actresses in plays sure to be seen by the well-connected and fashion-conscious. When she dressed the female cast members of Henry Arthur Jones's *The Liars* in 1897, she made great use of figure-hugging chiffons naughtily reminiscent of sexy lingerie. It was an audacious decision, and one that helped to crystallise her signature style. With imagination and ingenuity, she bridged the gap between propriety and decadence, nudging but never quite transgressing the boundary of respectability. To the members of the luxurious, lascivious social set that surrounded Edward as Prince of Wales and King, it was irresistible.

In 1900, Lucy married Sir Cosmo Duff Gordon, a handsome baronet who would serve on the organising committee of the London Olympic Games in 1908. Her title generated press coverage her competitors could only envy. It stood her in particularly good stead in New York where, in a bold but inspired move, she established a branch of Lucile Ltd at the tail-end of 1909. At the same time, she engaged the services of a professional publicity man who was soon shouting her name from the rooftops. 'The newspapers came out with columns about the first English lady of title who was to open a shop to dress the Four Hundred,' she recalled, referring to the number of individuals held to constitute the elite of Manhattan. 'There were stories of myself and of my husband's family, even the Duff Gordon ghost had half a column to itself, and the coat of arms was reproduced in a dozen illustrations.'[28] At first embarrassed by a marketing blitz so relentless it caused her to be lampooned as 'Lady Muff Boredom', Lucy came to appreciate that what seemed vulgar to the self-effacing English was indispensable in modern America. It wasn't long before she was sharing her thoughts on style with the readers of the Hearst-affiliated newspapers to which she contributed lively, if necessarily self-promoting, articles.

Having seeded the ground in New York, Lady Duff Gordon dashed back across the Atlantic in the early weeks of 1910 to unveil her latest collection in London. One of her most talked-about innovations had been the introduction of lyrical names to convey the unique 'character' of each of her diaphanous creations. On the afternoon of 22 February, an aristocratic audience that included the Duchess of Rutland, the Countess of Dudley and Margot Asquith assembled in Hanover Square to gaze enraptured at trailing gowns of pink taffeta ('The Eternal Feminine'), green tussore ('Sea Lady') and pale sapphire and silver chiffon ('After the Darkness Cometh Light'). Amid the shimmering hues, one dress in particular stood out. Of deepest black velvet, it struck a sombre note: 'Incarnate Woe'.[29]

Lucile Ltd was the most prestigious member of the elite band of 'Court dressmakers' versed in the complicated etiquette that underpinned the sumptuous ensembles worn by women upon presentation to the sovereign. It was fortunate for Lady Duff Gordon that, under Edward VII, life at Court was a great deal more glamorous than it had been under Queen Victoria. In an attempt to recreate something of the theatrical splendour of the Tuileries which had so impressed him as a boy, Edward pushed the timing of the presentation ceremonies way back, from mid-afternoon to 10 p.m. and beyond. Beneath the blaze of the newly electrified chandeliers, debutantes made their way along crimson carpets into the white and gold ballroom banked with palms and hothouse flowers. Tasked with providing an ambient background, Sir Walter Parratt, the high-brow Master of the King's Musick, was so appalled by Edward's preference for easy-listening that, eventually, the band over which he presided was dissolved to make way for one that specialised in sparkling Offenbach, rousing Sousa and merry Lehár. Usually held on Fridays, at least one Court a year was scheduled for another night of the week to permit the attendance of practicing Jews.

Taking place on Friday, 4 March, the second Court of 1910 was a typically dazzling affair. Wearing the uniform of Colonel-in-Chief of the Grenadier Guards, Edward was observed to be looking 'wonderfully well'.[30] Still in mourning for her sister-in-law, Princess Valdemar of Denmark, who had died four months earlier, Queen Alexandra had scattered her sequined black gown with the spectacular Cullinan diamonds. The ladies making their curtsies were hardly less splendid. Lady Magdalen Williams Bulkeley wore silver satin with a train of lime-blossom green velvet edged with cloth-of-silver. Lady Nina Balfour wore Egyptian blue satin and chiffon with crushed pearl embroidery and a platinum-embroidered train. Mrs Harry Graham wore anemone pink embroidered with silver and trimmed with tulle. Surveying the panoply of colours, fabrics and jewels, few would have disputed what the *Tatler* held to be true: that 'the English Court is among the most brilliant in Europe, and the London Season is after Paris the gayest of any capital in the world'.[31]

The following evening, the King hosted a large, men-only dinner party. To Lord Redesdale, he seemed in excellent spirits as he chatted cheerfully about his imminent departure for Biarritz. Members of the inner circle were aware that Edward's health was precarious, yet Redesdale could detect no trace of illness in his old friend. The King, he thought, resembled a happy schoolboy about to break up for the holidays. Relieved, he remarked upon this to one of the royal physicians. The reply brought him up short. 'Only we,' whispered the doctor, 'know how serious his condition is. If he had been a private individual, we should have had him away long ago.'[32]

8: 'That horrid Biarritz'

Edward's high spirits stemmed, at least in part, from the prospect of escape from an unusually fraught political atmosphere. Ever since the Lords' rejection of the Budget in late November, there had been discussions about the ways in which the deadlock between the Houses might be broken. As early as 2 December, Edward's Private Secretary, Francis Knollys, had learnt that the Cabinet was mulling two courses of action. The first was to advise the King to make a permanent transfer of his power to create peers to the Prime Minister of the day.

The second was to devise a Bill that would abolish the veto of the Lords, and would be accompanied by a pledge from the King that he would, if necessary, create a sufficient number of peers to see it through a House that would otherwise reject it. Knollys was horrified by both suggestions. The former, in particular, was to his mind so 'outrageous' that he believed Edward should abdicate altogether rather than consent to such an infringement on his prerogatives.[1]

In the event, it was the second proposal that gained traction. Scarcely more palatable to the King than the discarded alternative, it would, he maintained, be tantamount to the destruction of the House of Lords. Furthermore, it would place him in an invidious position by ranging the Crown against the interests of the Conservatives by forcing it to intercede in favour of the Liberals. From the moment Asquith opened his election campaign on 10 December, he stressed that he and his party were seeking the complete control of the House of Commons over finance bills, as well as a curtailment of the power of the House of Lords – objectives they meant to pursue in spite of the assurance of Lord Lansdowne, the leader of the Opposition peers, that the second chamber would pass the Budget without delay if the Liberals emerged victorious.

In a confidential exchange between Knollys and the Prime Minister's Private Secretary, Vaughan Nash, it was explained that Edward could not possibly countenance the creation of an extraordinary number of peers without a *second* election. The King favoured a practical demonstration of the referendal theory, in which the electorate would have its say before the Government could legislate to amend the Constitution. In the meantime, the contested Budget would still have to be passed.

The early weeks of 1910 were anxious ones for Edward. Most worrying of all was his fear that the obdurate 'backwoodsmen' might again reject the Budget. Then there was Asquith's allusion to the 'safeguards' he had publicly declared would be a condition of the Liberals taking office. From that, many in both parties assumed that the King had already guaranteed a creation of peers. He had done no such thing but was uncertain he would be able to resist the call if the Prime Minister, as seemed likely, was returned.

When they came in February, the results of the election were inconclusive. The massive majority the Liberals had achieved in 1906 was catastrophically reduced to the point that Asquith was compelled to parley with Labour and the Irish Nationalists to face down the Conservatives. The number of seats held by Labour had increased to forty, but it was the Irish, with nearly double, who had the whip hand. Committed to Home Rule for Ireland – for decades, one of the most insoluble issues in British politics – they threatened to vote with the Conservatives unless a Bill was introduced that would limit the power of the Lords and, in the process, abet their own agenda. It was not an appealing prospect for Asquith who wished to focus, first and foremost, on the Budget.

For the King, the loss of the Liberals' majority was good news, for it meant that the Prime Minister, lacking a clear mandate, would not be able to browbeat him over the creation of peers. Then again, the machinations of the Irish sparked fears that the Cabinet would be forced to resign. As he attempted to manoeuvre between the competing factions – including those within his own party, where Lloyd George hoped to smash the veto right away, while Churchill, who had been promoted to Home Secretary, was mooting the total abolition of the Lords – Asquith delayed the reintroduction of the Budget. In perplexity, he wrote to his daughter Violet of 'all the worries and anxieties of the political situation'. To his knowledge, there had never 'been anything quite like it; one party is as badly off as another, and it looks as though we might find ourselves in an impasse from which there is no visible outlet'.[2]

In spite of the prevailing uncertainty, Edward opened Parliament in his customary state on 21 February. The speech he read – badly, in the opinion of Margot Asquith – was thankfully short, as he was once again suffering from bronchitis. Its content, though, was electrifying:

Recent experience has disclosed serious difficulties, due to recurring differences of strong opinion between the two branches of the Legislature.

Proposals will be laid before you, with all convenient speed, to define the relations between the Houses of Parliament, so as to secure the undivided authority of the House of Commons over Finance and its predominance in Legislation. These measures, in the opinion of my advisers, should provide that this House should be so constituted and

empowered as to exercise impartially, in response of proposed legislation, the functions of initiation, revision, and, subject to proper safeguards, of delay.[3]

With the 'daring challenge', as the *Daily Telegraph* put it, thus thrown
down – a challenge 'so complete that compromise seemed once more
to be remote and impossible'[4] – Asquith, back in the Commons,
delivered an extraordinary speech of his own. The result of the recent
election, he insisted, had indeed furnished the Liberals with a mandate
to deal with the Budget, and then with the Lords. What astounded
his listeners was his admission that, contrary to widespread belief, he
had neither sought nor received guarantees about the creation of
peers before he had taken office. To have requested them would have
revealed him to be an unconstitutional statesman, and the King, in
granting them, to be an unconstitutional monarch. It was his duty as
a loyal subject to keep the sovereign and his prerogatives outside the
domain of party politics.

Aware of just how badly his apparent volte-face would go down with
Labour, the Irish and a large number of Liberals – in fact, with practically everybody but the gleeful Conservatives – Asquith read from his
notes with less than his usual confidence. His denial did, however, afford
the King some breathing space. Assured by the Prime Minister that he
foresaw no immediate crisis that would require his presence in London,
Edward confirmed arrangements for his annual trip to Biarritz.

At 9 p.m. on Sunday, 6 March, a closed carriage clattered out of
the gate of Buckingham Palace. Inside were the King, his Physician-
in-Ordinary, Sir James Reid, his Assistant Private Secretary, Colonel
Sir Arthur Davidson, and his equerry, Lieutenant Colonel George
Holford. Having travelled the short distance to Victoria station, the
royal party took its leave of the Prince of Wales and a delegation of
railway officials, then crossed a crimson carpet to a private saloon
coupled to a train to Dover. As the engine pulled away, the crowd of
well-wishers gathered at a respectful distance broke into enthusiastic
cheers. By midnight, Edward was asleep aboard the royal yacht
Alexandra, ready to sail for Calais on the morning tide.

Biarritz had been a late addition to the King's yearly itinerary. In
early 1906, his doctor prescribed a restorative sojourn in the

pine-scented resort on the Côte Basque where he would be able to expel the winter smog from his sorely tried lungs and replace it with invigorating Atlantic ozone. As a palliative, it had surpassed all expectations. Edward was enchanted. 'Though this place is quieter than the Riviera,' he reported to the Marchioness of Londonderry, 'it is more bracing, and I am sure healthier.'[5] The following year, he urged the town's charms on the ailing Sir Henry Campbell-Bannerman; and, again to Lady Londonderry, he lauded its sea air and sunshine, which 'always agree wonderfully well with me'.[6] In 1908, there was a furore when he summoned Campbell-Bannerman's successor, Herbert Henry Asquith, all the way to Biarritz, where the new Prime Minister kissed the royal hand in a hotel room, rather than at Buckingham Palace as was customary. Asquith hadn't really minded. The indignant press, feeling he had been unfairly put upon, had minded very much indeed.

Salubriousness aside, the appeal of Biarritz wasn't hard to fathom. For a start, there was its association with Napoleon III and Empress Eugénie. Oppressed by the grandeur of the Tuileries, the Empress had enjoyed relative freedom in what had once been a fishing village nestled between the Pyrenees and the Bay of Biscay. Delighting in the rugged coastline and mild, if sometimes unpredictable, weather, she took up residence in the palace her husband had constructed for her high above the sand dunes.

Gutted by fire at the turn of the century, the Villa Eugénie, as it had been called during her tenure, was rebuilt as the elegant Hôtel du Palais. It was there, in the same ground-floor suite, that Edward stayed for several weeks every March and April. As rarefied as it was self-selecting, the company invariably included what the King described as 'a great many English'.[7] In his first year alone, he discovered that the Devonshires, the Roxburghes, the Dudleys, the Poltimores, the Dowager Duchess of Manchester and Lady Yarborough were all settled nearby. Together, they kept him company as he recruited his strength ahead of the London Season.

'There is so much virtue in the air of Biarritz that there is none left for the inhabitants,' quipped one of its habitués.[8] Thanks to Edward's patronage, the resort became as fashionable as Nice, Cannes and Monte Carlo. There was golf, pigeon-shooting and gambling for high stakes at the casino. A new hotel, the Carlton, was inaugurated in 1910 to cater to the demands of a glittering international clientele. In spite of its up-to-date amenities, it couldn't compete with the supremacy of the Palais, which, frequented as it was by sundry Rothschilds and Ephrussis, was snidely dubbed 'the House of Israel' by those who couldn't afford its exorbitant rates.[9]

Rising early each morning, Edward breakfasted heartily, then tackled the voluminous correspondence couriered out to him in sealed canvas bags. A leisurely stroll along the promenade preceded a lazy lunch, which would be followed by a motor drive to one of the local beauty spots. Occasionally, he would cross the border into Spain, where his niece, Victoria Eugenie, or 'Ena', was the wife of young King Alfonso XIII. Back at the hotel, he would go over his papers again, then dine in-house, or at the villa of one of his friends. Retiring to bed around midnight, he was soothed to sleep by the susurration of the rolling waves, which he described as 'not unpleasant'.[10]

Edward's trips to Biarritz, like his visits to Marienbad, were undertaken in a private capacity. It was only in Biarritz, however, that he considered himself to be on holiday. It helped that he travelled incognito as the 'Duke of Lancaster'. At no point was he mistaken for anybody other than himself. The flimsy alias was merely a signal to foreign dignitaries that he expected to be greeted with the minimum of fuss: no fanfares, no presentations and no receptions. Untrammelled by etiquette, Edward was, for the duration of his stay, as anonymous as he could ever be.

It was thanks to this cloak of semi-secrecy that he was able to enjoy the almost constant companionship of a woman whose presence was rarely if ever reported by the eagle-eyed press. Accounts vary as to how Alice Keppel had entered his life. Some said they had been introduced by Lady Howe, a daughter of the 7th Duke of Marlborough, others by Mrs Henri Bischoffsheim, the wife of a prominent Jewish banker. A third scenario places their first meeting at the races at Sandown Park. Regardless of the circumstances, Mrs Keppel was, by the beginning of 1898, firmly established. Over the next twelve years, she assiduously, if gracefully, consolidated her privileged position until she became indispensable to Edward's happiness and well-being.

Prior to her advent, he had had two 'official' mistresses. The first, in the late 1870s, was Emilie 'Lillie' Langtry, the daughter of the Dean of Jersey, who had risen from provincial obscurity to take Society by storm as an artists' muse and 'Professional Beauty'. In 1881, she had launched herself as an actress. Edward endorsed the venture, and his support set Lillie on the road to transatlantic stardom. Their friendship endured. Their liaison did not.

By 1889, the royal affections had been transferred to the Countess of Warwick. Edward so adored her that he took to addressing her as 'my little Daisywife'. Sweetly pretty, she was also woefully indiscreet. Her inability to keep the kinds of secrets that might imperil the reputation of the Prince of Wales earned her the nickname 'Babbling Brooke' in a pun on her husband's courtesy title. By the end of the 1890s, that affair, too, was over – no doubt to the relief of Edward's advisers who, with Queen Victoria in her dotage, saw the throne slowly but inexorably approaching.

By contrast, Mrs Keppel was as low-key as Mrs Langtry was celebrated and as guarded as Lady Warwick was loose-lipped. When they met, she was twenty-nine to Edward's fifty-six. Her antecedents were impeccably patrician. Her mother was the daughter of the governor of the Ionian Islands, while her father, Admiral Sir William Edmonstone, was a Scottish baronet and Conservative MP. The youngest of many girls, she was brought up at Duntreath Castle near Glasgow.

In 1891, Alice married the Honourable George Keppel, the third son of the 7th Earl of Albemarle. Over six feet tall – in the bonnet of his regiment, the Gordon Highlanders, closer to eight – he was black-haired, blue-eyed and immaculately turned out. His bristling moustache was kept in curl with tiny silver tongs. Holding his country, family and inherited traditions to be sacrosanct, he was everything an English gentleman should be. Everything, that is, except rich. His lack of funds obliged his wife to leverage her own assets to ensure they would remain in the social swim.

Statuesque but alluring, Mrs Keppel exhaled a miasma of sensuality all the more potent for being combined with a practical outlook and extreme good nature. Her younger daughter, Sonia, retained an indelible impression of her 'as she lay back among her lace pillows, her beautiful chestnut hair, unbound around her shoulders, her alabaster skin, her turquoise-coloured eyes. She had all the qualities and none of the defects of an Alma-Tadema beauty.'[11] Her bedroom was aromatic with the scent of fresh flowers 'and a certain elusive smell, like fresh green sap, that came from herself'.[12] Older, more dispassionate, observers were equally impressed. Jean, Lady Hamilton, the wife of a senior-ranking army officer who dipped in and out of the King's milieu, was transfixed by Alice's eroticism:

> Mrs George Keppel, to my surprise, fascinates me – sometimes she looks beautiful – she is absolute woman, fully developed, strong and capable. In her soft, long, chiffon tea-gown she looked beautiful at tea, but at dinner, in a very low blue satin, with purple and green grapes wreathed in her hair, I did not admire her. She has beautiful shoulders, and her dress is cut very low at the back to show a brown mole in the centre of it, I could not help wondering how many men had kissed that mole?[13]

The men in question – Ernest William Beckett, later Lord Grimthorpe, Humphrey Sturt, later Lord Alington, and Lord Stavordale, heir to the 5th Earl of Ilchester – were chosen for their wealth and connections. Edward's financial adviser, Sir Ernest Cassel, did not, so far as is known, number among Mrs Keppel's lovers, but his backing, from the early days of her affair with the King, was to prove even more remunerative. His sagacious advice, which saw her stock portfolio bulge with share certificates in American railroads and South African mining companies, took the Keppels, in the space of a decade, from the brink of penury to great riches. 'Throughout her life, Mamma was irresistibly attractive to bank managers,' wrote Sonia, who recognised that money and power were the corollaries of beauty and charm.[14]

Yet Mrs Keppel was neither grasping nor mercenary. In the back-biting world of Edwardian Society, few had a bad word to say about her. Among her many qualities, one above all equipped her for her role as a latter-day Madame de Pompadour. Charles Hardinge put his finger squarely upon it:

> I would like here to pay a tribute to her wonderful discretion, and to the excellent influence which she always exercised upon the King.

She never utilised her knowledge to her own advantage, or to that of her friends; and I never heard her repeat an unkind word of anybody. There were one or two occasions when the King was in disagreement with the Foreign Office, and I was able, through her, to advise the King with a view to the policy of the Government being accepted. She was very loyal to the King, and patriotic at the same time.[15]

Wise in the ways of the world, Mrs Keppel nurtured some improbable but useful friendships. Sensing that he was a rising star in the political firmament, she cultivated Lloyd George and did her best to smooth his troubled relations with the King. The Kaiser, whom she wooed over dinner in late 1907, was so captivated by her that he took receipt, with copious thanks, of a photograph of her seductive portrait by the French artist François Flameng.

In his mistress's presence, Edward was observed by Lord Esher to be 'perfectly happy'. His admiration of her was 'almost pathetic. He watches her all day and is never happy when she's talking to someone else.'[16] Her hold over him was so complete he seldom made an important decision without discussing it with her first. Late one evening in a country house, the Honourable Muriel Beckett was chatting on Mrs Keppel's bed when Edward unexpectedly materialised in his dressing gown 'just as any husband would':

> Muriel was also in her dressing gown and didn't know whether to get up and drop him a sweeping courtesy, or sit tight – the King signed to her not to move and after consulting Alice about some State papers he carried in his hand, he departed like an ordinary husband by the door wherein he came.[17]

It said much about Mrs Keppel's management of the men in her life that she remained on excellent terms with her actual husband. If anything, he was proud to share his wife's favours with the King. According to Sonia, their marriage was 'a comradeship of love and laughter'.[18] As a couple, they knew the cardinal rule that there should be no scandal, and each played the game with skill.

Queen Alexandra preferred to avoid what she called 'that horrid Biarritz',[19] and so did George Keppel. The absence of their respective spouses enabled Edward and his mistress to place their relationship on an almost conjugal footing. In the interests of propriety, Alice was chaperoned, unusually but effectively, by her daughters. In early March, elaborate preparations began ahead of their departure for the Côte Basque. At Woollands in Knightsbridge, Sonia and her elder sister Violet were fitted for stylish new toilettes. They each possessed a large trunk in which their clothes were packed, but their luggage was dwarfed by that of their mother: 'studded wardrobe-trunks, standing up on end, and high enough to stand in; hat-boxes; shoe-boxes; rugs; travelling cushions; her travelling jewel-case', all of which caused her lady's maid, Miss Draper, considerable anxiety as she struggled to keep track of the innumerable pieces en route.[20]

The journey itself was a matter of quasi-state, with private railway carriages and a special cabin on the ferry from Dover to Calais. At every step along the way, Mrs Keppel was 'treated like royalty' by fawning customs officials, couriers and attendants.[21] In Biarritz, the family stayed, not at the Hôtel de Palais, but at the nearby Villa Eugénie, which was rented by the ever-obliging Sir Ernest Cassel. With its glass doors and marble floors, it was glamorous but intimidating. To Sonia, it resembled a conservatory more than a house, 'always prepared for an invisible party . . . with its inmates potted about in it like plants'.[22] Cassel was often there for the duration, as were his elegant invalid of a daughter, Maud Ashley, whose early patronage of Lady Duff Gordon had helped cement the prestige of Lucile Ltd, and his granddaughters, Edwina and Mary. Her host caused Sonia no small mystification as she was never able to tell him apart from the King. As alike as Tweedledee and Tweedledum, they were both stout and bearded, and both chomped on enormous cigars. Over time, Sonia came to realise that Edward was more fun than Cassel, laughing more easily and joining in with her games. Maud detested Biarritz, where she could never fully relax in case the King needed to be kept company. 'We are his servants quite as much as the housemaid or the butler,' she complained.[23] Carefully supervised, the children had a less onerous time, playing on the beach and drinking spiced hot chocolate on their excursions to picturesque towns on the Spanish border.

On Easter Sunday, tiny jewelled and enamelled eggs were exchanged before the royal party set out in a cavalcade of motors for a picnic lunch. A brace of footmen staggered under the weight of tables, chairs, linen, silver, crystal and hot and cold food packed into special containers. In spite of the elaborate arrangements, Edward took perverse delight in eating by the side of the dusty road. It was an idiosyncrasy that soon became known to the resort's more indefatigable social-climbers, whose own cars, trailing at a discreet distance, had a habit of breaking down close to the chosen spot.

As ubiquitous in Biarritz as he was everywhere else was the wire-haired fox terrier Caesar. Bred by the Duchess of Newcastle and presented to the King in 1903, he was adored by his master. Noisy and ill-disciplined, he ruthlessly exploited Edward's affection, safe in the knowledge he would never be punished for his many misdemeanours. At most, the King would ineffectually shake his stick and admonish him with the words, 'You naughty dog, you naughty, naughty dog.'[24] Dismissed by Lady Fingall as a 'horrid little snob',[25] he was one of the most pampered animals in Europe. In 1907, Fritz Ponsonby had had to dissuade Edward from rushing a vet from London to Marienbad at the cost of £200 a day to attend to Caesar, who had been taken ill there. Restored to health, he was modelled by Fabergé in white chalcedony with cabochon rubies for eyes and a gold collar embossed, as in life, with the legend 'I Belong to the King'. On their picnic excursions, Caesar liked to settle himself in Violet Keppel's lap; for her, a dubious honour, as she claimed he smelt. His attentions were more warmly received by Sonia. The terrier had, she remembered, 'a fine disregard for the villa's curtains and chair-legs, but a close personal regard for me'.[26]

In the spring of 1910, nothing – not the best-laid plans, or the reassuring presence of his mistress and dog – could arrest a sudden deterioration in Edward's health. The previous year, Wilfrid Scawen Blunt had noted in his diary that he had heard there was 'something seriously the matter' with his throat.[27] In fact, the situation was more precarious than the gossips of London Society realised. Arriving in Paris on 7 March, Edward attended a performance of Edmond Rostand's new play, *Chantecler*. His high hopes were swiftly dashed. The production was, he wrote, nothing but a 'stupid and childish' pantomime.[28] Worse, the auditorium was overheated, and a sense of acute physical discomfort exacerbated his excruciating boredom. The result was an attack of chronic indigestion, accompanied, more worryingly, by what was subsequently described as 'considerable cardiac distress'.[29] Somehow, Edward rallied. The city was basking in early spring sunshine, and he made the most of his short stay to pay his respects to President Fallières at the Élysée Palace, dine with the British ambassador, lunch with his fashionable friends and make a second trip to the theatre. Departing from the Gare d'Orsay on the morning of 9 March, he trundled leisurely south-westward, arriving in Biarritz that evening. Edward told the town's mayor, who had turned out to greet him, that he was delighted to be back in his beloved France, and particularly in a resort that never failed to put him back on his feet.

Alas, the good weather that accompanied him from Paris didn't hold. Beneath lowering skies, the Atlantic was sullen and grey. An enervating breeze 'with a disagreeable suggestion of the "sirocco" in it' blew ceaselessly, rendering the atmosphere muggy and oppressive.[30] Feeling less than his best, Edward struggled gamely on. On his first full day, he took a walk on the beach, then called upon a fellow holiday-maker, Queen Amélie of Portugal, who had been sensationally widowed two years earlier in a double assassination that had not only felled her husband, King Carlos I, but also her eldest son, Luís Filipe. When the wind dropped, so did the thermometer. A wet and wintry chill set in. The royal physician, Sir James Reid, advised the King, who by now had a high temperature and hacking cough, to keep to his rooms. On Monday, 14 March, Mrs Keppel dashed off a note to the Marquis de Soveral, who was also in Biarritz, with an urgent request:

> The King's cold is so bad that he can't dine out but he wants us all to dine with him at 8.15 at the Palais, SO BE THERE.
>   I am quite worried *entre nous* and have sent for the nurse . . .[31]

'Much alarmed'[32] by her lover's condition, Mrs Keppel derived comfort from the ministrations of Reid, who seldom left Edward's side. Aged sixty, he had chalked up three decades of service to the Crown. A brisk and no-nonsense Scot, he had been engaged in 1881 to look after the health of the Household at Balmoral. Over time,

Queen Victoria had come to depend so completely upon his judgement that her invariable reply whenever she was approached for advice was 'Ask Sir James.' Reid, who had delivered several royal babies, was equally familiar with royal deathbeds. He was in close attendance on Victoria during her final illness and helped to execute the detailed instructions for her burial.

In the autumn of 1907, Francis Knollys had summoned Reid to a private meeting at Buckingham Palace, where he informed him that the King had lost confidence in his Physician-in-Ordinary, Sir Francis Laking. He proposed that, from now on, responsibility for the King's health should be shared. Laking would continue to deal with his more trifling ailments, while Reid would supervise his long-term conditions. The scheme worked well. Unlike many members of the aristocracy, Edward was not snobbish about the medical profession, treating his doctor as a personal friend as much as an employee. It was Reid who accompanied the King on his holidays to Biarritz, where they were often photographed strolling together along the promenade. The privilege of intimacy was some recompense for a meagre retainer of five pounds a day.

That March, every penny was earned. Edward's cold turned, yet again, into bronchitis, accompanied by an accelerated pulse, rapid breathing and 'physical signs in the chest'[33] that caused Reid considerable anxiety. Fearful of a sudden emergency, he took to sitting up all night in case he was needed. Soveral and Mrs Keppel were constantly in and out of the royal suite, but otherwise the crisis was kept firmly under wraps. The British public was given no reason to suppose the King suffered from anything worse than a passing indisposition. It was assured his temperature was normal, his appetite was good and 'everyone about him is quite contented with the excellent progress he continues to make'.[34]

In fact, behind the scenes, the Palace and the press had entered into a gentlemen's agreement. Fritz Ponsonby recalled that the editor of the *Daily Mail* had decided that it would 'not be right'[35] to frighten his readers with the full details of the King's illness until such a time when suppression became unfeasible. The other papers followed his lead. Ponsonby continued to feed what he believed to be unvarnished updates to the *Mail*, but when he arrived in Biarritz in early April to relieve Sir Arthur Davidson, he was astonished to discover just how grave the situation on the ground had been. The conspiracy of silence had been so scrupulously maintained that even the staff and guests at the Hôtel du Palais had been none the wiser.

It was testament to Edward's stamina that, on 21 March, he emerged, apparently much improved, and immediately threw himself into the social whirl. In a letter to Cassel, who that year had carried the sickly Maud Ashley off to Egypt, he wrote:

> Unfortunately, not long after my arrival here, I developed a cold and bronchial attack and Sir J. Reid would not let me go out of my rooms for a week. It has greatly pulled me down, but I am now getting daily stronger and better.[36]

Whether Edward believed that is debatable. Certainly, he seemed eager to make up for lost time. For a whole month, he was rarely still, delighting his fellow holidaymakers with his willingness to amuse and be amused. In spite of inclement weather, which 'has recalled nothing so much as the Scottish climate in its grumpiest mood',[37] he played croquet, joined a meet of the Biarritz Foxhounds and presented prizes at the local golf club. There were motor excursions to Bayonne, to Lourdes, and to a Bernardine convent where the rule was absolute silence. On 29 March, he attended the opening day of Aviation Week, watching the flying demonstrations with interest and congratulating Louis Blériot on his skill. On 10 April, he lunched with his niece, Grand Duchess Xenia Alexandrovna, the younger sister of the Tsar. There were nightly dinners for his English friends and endless games of bridge. 'His Majesty, God bless him, looks strong and well, and so he should,' observed the *Tatler*, complacently.[38]

On the evening of Monday, 25 April, Biarritz staged a lavish farewell ceremony for its most illustrious visitor. The courtyard of the Hôtel du Palais was animated with a military tattoo. There was a march past by the soldiers of the local garrison, who carried flags, flaming torches and Chinese lanterns. The King graciously returned the officers' salute, which was accompanied by the British and French national anthems. Afterwards, there was a spectacular fireworks display over the seafront. The following morning, Edward, having arranged the distribution of medals and other souvenirs to the officials who had rendered him particular service, as well as a gift of eighty pounds to the town's poorest inhabitants, stood in his suite as his trunks were removed one by one. Stepping out onto the balcony, he gazed at the view he had come to know so well. 'I shall be sorry to leave Biarritz,' he said quietly, 'perhaps for good.'[39]

9: 'In case I don't see you again, goodbye'

More than medical complications had arisen from Edward's illness. Had she known of its true extent, there was little doubt Queen Alexandra would have rushed to Biarritz to nurse him in person. Sensitive to the predicament of Mrs Keppel, Sir James Reid was keen to spare all parties unnecessary embarrassment. He opted to downplay the gravity of a situation that had caused him such alarm.

On Alexandra's part, there was perhaps a willingness to be deceived. For almost half a century, she had been required to display unusual forbearance in the face of Edward's serial infidelities. Frequently dismissed as a featherbrain, she was sufficiently astute to realise the surest way to alienate his affection would be to cause a scene. 'Jealousy,' she had once written, 'is the bottom of all mischief and misfortune in this world.'[1] Well-practised in the art of turning a blind eye, she was alternately cordial and cool to her husband's mistresses, tolerating liaisons she had every reason to resent.

With his instinctive understanding of image and performance, Edward appreciated that Alexandra's preternatural glamour was an important factor in his own popularity. Lionel Cust was struck by the 'special deference' paid by the King to the Queen as a token of his gratitude for her part 'in the hearty welcome which he had received from the nation on his accession to the throne'.[2] Like an indulgent parent pricked by an uneasy conscience, Edward permitted Alexandra the freedom to do exactly as she pleased. Over time, she became spoiled, self-centred and chronically unpunctual. 'It is queer,' puzzled Lord Esher, 'her determination to have her way. As Princess of Wales she was never, so she says, allowed to do as she chose. "Now, I do as I like" is the sort of attitude.'[3] Her son George was more trenchant. 'Mama, as I have always said, is one of the most selfish people I know,' he wrote.[4]

Alexandra's worst fault was a failure of imagination. Unwilling or unable to comprehend the effects of her often infuriating behaviour, she exacted complete devotion from servants, courtiers and family members. Nobody suffered more under her velvet-gloved rule than her three daughters. Early on, Edward had observed that 'A child is always best looked after under its mother's eye',[5] a maxim that freed him from the obligation to supervise his offspring too closely. In complete agreement, Alexandra was doting but possessive. Born in rapid succession, Princess Louise, Princess Victoria and Princess Maud were high-spirited, and even boisterous, in the nursery. With maturity, they shrank inward. As shy and self-effacing young women, they were dressed alike, to the extent they became virtually indistinguishable to strangers. Lumped together as 'the Whispering Waleses' – more unkindly still as 'the Hags' – the sisters remained single long after they should have found husbands. When a concerned Queen Victoria began asking questions, she was assured by Edward that 'Alix found them such companions that she would not encourage them marrying, and they themselves had no inclination for it'.[6]

In reality, Alexandra's selfishness, as well as her ingrained detestation of Germany, that hotbed of royal suitors, blighted their prospects. In 1889, she consented to lose plain and silent Louise to Lord Fife, who was immediately raised to a dukedom. Thereafter, the couple retreated to Scotland, and were seldom seen in Society. In 1896, pretty Maud married her cousin, the handsome but penniless Prince Charles of Denmark. Much to her father's delight, they were elected King and Queen of Norway nine years later. That left attractive and intelligent Victoria as the reluctant stay-at-home. Forever at her mother's beck and call, she was, in the words of Grand Duchess Olga Alexandrovna, reduced to the status of 'a glorified maid'.[7]

Blithely unaware of the seriousness of Edward's illness, Alexandra was not on hand to welcome him home. Accompanied by Victoria and a coterie of favourite retainers, she had departed for Genoa and a Mediterranean cruise on 14 April. In view of the circumstances, it seemed an eccentric, and even cavalier, decision. 'Dear Mama, fancy going all the way to Corfu for a fortnight, and what a fatigue just before the Season,' wrote the Princess of Wales in disapproving wonder.[8]

When his train pulled into Victoria station on the afternoon of Wednesday, 27 April, Edward was irked to find the Prime Minister and the Home Secretary waiting for him on the platform. By that stage, he considered himself so ill-used by both men that the very sight of them was distasteful to him.

Even as he had immersed himself in the pleasures of Biarritz, he had followed events in Westminster closely. The outlook was grimmer than ever. The Cabinet had declined to strike terms with the Irish Nationalists over the increased duty on whisky included in the Budget. In consequence, the Irish had threatened to ally themselves with the Conservatives. If they did so, there was a danger the Budget would be rejected in the Commons and the Government would be forced to resign. That raised the dreadful prospect of 'a crisis of an unexampled and most embarrassing kind',[9] Asquith admitted, whereby a second general election would have to take place three months after the first.

To bring the Irish onside, he resorted to the course of action he had publicly repudiated on 21 February. A Parliament Bill had just been introduced, which would see the Lords lose their power of veto: a development that would greatly assist the cause of Home Rule. Since the Lords would never legislate against their own interests, the Prime Minister had little choice but to allude to the possibility of a guarantee from the King that he would create a sufficient number of peers to swamp the second chamber. Were he to extract such a promise, a scandalised Francis Knollys believed, he would perpetrate 'the greatest outrage on the King which has ever been committed since England became a Constitutional Monarchy'.[10] Usually more temperate than his Private Secretary, Edward was, on this occasion, no less indignant. Asquith had gone back on his word in a manner that was 'simply disgusting'.[11] He wished his government to understand 'that I look upon them with the greatest displeasure and can no more be on friendly terms with them. They are not only ruining the Country but maltreat me personally, and I can neither forgive nor forget it.'[12]

The long-delayed Budget, which had been reintroduced on 20 April, was finally passed by the Lords the following week. Attention now turned to the looming showdown between the Houses. Whatever benefits Edward had derived from his holiday were visibly effaced the moment he set foot in the toxic atmosphere of London. That night, Wilfrid Scawen Blunt found himself in a railway carriage with two strangers who had seen the King drive away from the station. He had, they reported, 'looked very white and flabby'.[13]

The prevailing uncertainty played havoc with the fledgling Season. 'Never in the annals of London entertaining have social fixtures been so few and far between as now,' lamented the *Tatler*.[14] With a general election a distinct possibility before the end of the summer, it was difficult to schedule dinners and dances. It fell to Mrs John Jacob Astor, Mrs Frank Mackay, Mrs Miller Graham and other expatriate American hostesses to save Mayfair from 'total stagnation'. Immune to the hurly-burly in Parliament, they pledged to do their bit to 'make things hum' until, one way or another, the crisis was resolved.[15]

Sensing his subjects craved reassurance, Edward was back in the public eye within hours of his return. In spite of his fatigue, he was at Covent Garden that very evening for a performance of *Rigoletto*. The next day, Thursday, 28 April, he had a half-hour audience with the Prime Minister. Both men dreaded the meeting, but professional courtesy saw them through. Their first encounter in weeks was to be their last for a further fortnight. Asquith was about to sail from Portsmouth on the Admiralty yacht *Enchantress* for an inspection of the naval establishments at Gibraltar. The King commissioned him to call at Lisbon to pay his respects to Queen Amélie and her son, King Manuel II. Asquith, who told his wife he had found Edward 'most reasonable'[16], may have been chastened by an open letter in the following morning's *Times*. In a crisp but pointed missive to a concerned correspondent, Francis Knollys reiterated that 'The King is at all times anxious that his name should be kept out of all controversies of a political nature.'[17]

After the Prime Minister had taken his leave, Edward had a longer audience with Lord Kitchener, the former Commander-in-Chief, India, on whom he bestowed a field marshal's baton; lunched with his eldest daughter, Louise, who was paying a rare visit to London with her husband, the Duke of Fife; then drove to the Royal Academy for a private viewing of the Summer Exhibition, which traditionally inaugurated the most intensive phase of the Season.

The artistic standard was deemed to be decent, if unexceptional. Since the mid-1880s, the field of portraiture had been dominated by the American painter, John Singer Sargent. Regarded as the successor to Van Dyck, Reynolds and Lawrence, he had furnished the aristocracy with superlative images of itself. Conferring grandeur on the very rich and glamour on the very grand, he was celebrated for his fearless brushwork and bravura handling of colour and chiaroscuro. Even Roger Fry conceded that he was 'a brilliant ambassador between [his sitters] and posterity'.[18]

Yet even at the height of his stellar career, Sargent had been unwilling to sublimate self-expression to prestige. In 1902, he had refused a commission to paint the Coronation. Neither had there ever been a one-to-one sitting with the King. It was a strange lacuna, for Edward made no secret of his admiration. At the beginning of 1907, he had nominated Sargent for a knighthood, declaring him 'simply the most distinguished portrait painter in England'.[19] The honour was courteously but firmly declined. Sargent had no right to aspire to a title, he explained, 'as I am not one of His Majesty's Subjects but an American citizen'.[20] Later that same year, weary and disaffected, he had slammed his studio door on his blue-blooded clientele. From now on, he intended to focus only on projects that interested and inspired him. To that end, he had submitted four landscapes to the Summer Exhibition of 1910. Lauded by the critics, they were no substitute for the brilliant portraits with which he had made his name. Fans of the genre had to make do with an enormous canvas by the President of the Royal Academy, Sir Edward Poynter, in which Edward was depicted in the full regalia of the Order of the Garter. Stately, pompous and utterly pedestrian, it was dutifully but unenthusiastically commended by *The Times* for its 'highly decorative qualities'.[21]

In the evening, the King was back at the Opera House for a single act of *Siegfried*. By chance, Lord Redesdale was in the audience. He kept an eye on the sovereign seated in solitary splendour in his box. He looked, Redesdale thought, 'very tired and worn'. When the curtain fell, Edward rose to his feet with an audible sigh. Making as if to leave, he turned abruptly on the threshold, surveying the glittering auditorium 'with a very sad expression in his face – so unlike himself . . . as if to bid it farewell'.[22]

The elegiac account of his last sighting of his old friend is belied by that of Fritz Ponsonby, who was in attendance upon the King when he, with a party of male courtiers, travelled to Sandringham to inspect some alterations in the gardens. Edward was on his usual form, regaling his suite with 'amusing incidents of former years'.[23] He worked on his papers, played bridge and went to church. In the absence of Queen Alexandra, orders had been given that the drawing rooms were to be kept closed. The King settled himself in Francis Knollys's office, where there wasn't even a fire to keep the Norfolk chill at bay.

On Monday, 2 May, driving rain set in. On the train to London, Edward was uncharacteristically subdued. At Buckingham Palace, he changed his clothes, then went straight back out again. His destination was 17 Grosvenor Crescent, where he was to dine quietly with his friend, Agnes Keyser. The unmarried daughter of a wealthy stockbroker, she dextrously straddled the worlds of healthcare and high society. When the Boer War had broken out in 1899, she had offered her townhouse in Belgravia as a private hospital for wounded officers, capably tending many of the patients herself. Close to the then Prince of Wales, she had obtained generous donations from the likes of Lord Iveagh and Sir Ernest Cassel. The enterprise was so successful that, even after peace returned, the hospital continued to thrive, patronised by, and eventually called after, the supportive King.

Brisk and matronly – not for nothing was she known to her staff as 'Sister' – Miss Keyser was the best person with whom Edward could have spent that particular evening. He was so obviously unwell that she scribbled a note in pencil and despatched it to Sir James Reid. The King had 'a cold and a little cough'. Would Reid be kind enough to attend him at 11.15 p.m.?[24] A summons so late at night, and from one well-equipped to recognise a medical emergency, alerted the doctor to the seriousness of the situation. Arriving at Buckingham Palace, he found his patient in his dressing gown. He was feverish, with a high temperature and accelerated pulse. Between bouts of coughing, his breathing was rapid. Reid mixed two poultices of linseed and mustard and applied them to Edward's back and chest to aid respiration. After administering chlorodyne and morphine to help him sleep, he wrote a full report for Sir Francis Laking, with a request that they should convene at nine the following morning. He gave no hint of how worried he felt. When he got home at 1 a.m., he was greeted by his wife, who had waited up for news. Reid pulled no punches. 'The King may recover, as he did at Biarritz,' he told her, 'but if not, he will be dead in three days.'[25]

Over breakfast on Tuesday, 3 May, Edward assured his doctors that he felt better after an uncomfortable night. His pulse had slowed and his temperature had dropped. Reid arranged to check up on him at intervals as he worked his way through a packed programme of appointments. Grand Duke Michael Mikhailovich of Russia came to lunch. The Bishop of Norwich did homage. There was an audience with Field Marshal Lord Roberts, and another with the American ambassador, Whitelaw Reid, whom Edward liked enormously. Furiously social, the ambassador spent a great deal of his time attending the weddings of Dollar Princesses to British aristocrats. The marriage of his own daughter, Jean, to a younger son of the Earl of Dudley had been one of the highlights of the 1908 Season. As a token of his esteem, the King had permitted the ceremony to take place in the Chapel Royal at St James's Palace.

That day, the pair discussed arrangements for the reception of former President Theodore Roosevelt, whose arrival in London was imminent. In spite of Edward's best efforts to mask his discomfort, Reid was not deceived. In a letter to President William Howard Taft, he wrote that 'The general public think him in perfect health; but I am impressed with the notion that in the inner circles there is more anxiety about him lately than I have ever observed at any time before.'[26]

When his doctor called in the evening, the King, who was seated at his desk, complained of 'malaise'. Reid applied the same poultices as on the previous night.[27] Fritz Ponsonby, who had been informed by Laking that there had been a recurrence of bronchitis, was appalled to see Edward smoke an enormous cigar after a dinner he had barely been able to touch. In the Japanese Room, the King played bridge with Mrs Keppel and Mrs Arthur James, the wife of a wealthy racehorse owner who never failed to divert him with her witty chatter. Cards would, he explained, remove the obligation to talk. Even then, Ponsonby couldn't bring himself to believe that he was seriously ill.

Yet more meetings with statesmen and military personnel took place on Wednesday, 4 May. For the first time, the King admitted the possibility he might be dying. When it was suggested that he should go to bed, he rejected the idea out of hand. 'No,' he protested, 'I shall not give in – I shall work to the end. Of what use is it to be alive if one cannot work?'[28]

The Prince of Wales had been a frequent visitor since Edward's return from Biarritz. Now Reid took the opportunity to prepare him for the worst. George, who until then had believed his father to be suffering from a cold, immediately crafted a tactful but pressing letter to be delivered to his mother at Calais. For the past fortnight, Queen Alexandra and Princess Victoria had been dawdling in the Mediterranean. At Corfu, they spent several days with the family of Alexandra's brother, the King of Greece. Turning for home, they called at Venice, then drifted inland to Lake Como. George urged them not to waste another hour, but to make for London with all possible speed.

In the meantime, Edward battled on. His nights were restless, and Reid judged his condition to be deteriorating. Oxygen and amyl nitrate provided only temporary relief. The doctors resorted to injections of strychnine to stimulate his heart, which they feared might fail

King Edward VII painted by Sir Luke Fildes shortly after his accession in 1901. Copies of this portrait were distributed to British embassies and legations around the globe.

The preternaturally youthful and perennially glamorous Queen Alexandra painted in satin, tulle and diamonds by François Flameng in 1908.

A model of tact, graciousness and discretion, Edward's mistress Alice Keppel was indispensable to his happiness and well-being during his final years.

Kaiser Wilhelm II of Germany in all his glory. Edward was sorely tested by his insecure, overbearing and unpredictable nephew.

Three generations of British kings photographed during the visit of Tsar Nicholas II of Russia to the Isle of Wight in the summer of 1909. Edward is seated beside his nephew in the centre. The future Edward VIII stands on the far left. His father, the future George V, is on the far right. Princess Victoria is in the middle of the back row.

Virginia Stephen (later Woolf, far left) and her fellow conspirators in blackface as Abyssinian royalty prior to their tour of HMS *Dreadnought* in February 1910. The audacious hoax was front-page news.

Student and suffragette Elsie Bowerman in uncharacteristically demure mood around 1910.

The pioneering couturière Lady Duff Gordon – 'Lucile' – whose designs epitomised Edwardian elegance.

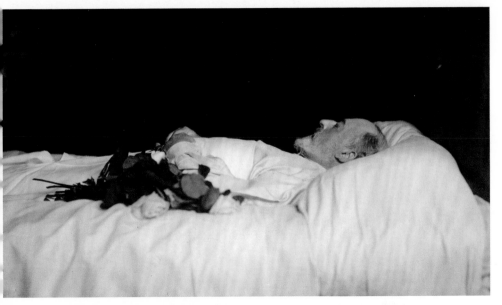

This photograph of Edward's corpse was authorised for reproduction in newspapers and magazines, as well as on innumerable picture postcards.

Hundreds of thousands of Londoners of every age and background queued for hours to pay their respects to the late King as his body lay in state in Westminster Hall prior to his funeral.

Edward's relationship with Prime Minister Herbert Henry Asquith was strained by the long-running battle between the Commons and the Lords.

Devoted to his duty and his wife, Queen Mary, Edward's successor George V was an unglamorous but dependable king during an era of unprecedented upheaval.

One emperor and eight kings – of Britain, Germany, Belgium, Denmark, Norway, Spain, Portugal, Greece and Bulgaria – gathered at Windsor Castle for Edward's funeral on 20 May 1910.

The Countess of Derby and her daughter Lady Victoria Stanley conversing with the Marquess of Londonderry at 'Black Ascot' in June 1910. Lady Victoria was one of the debutantes whose first Season was derailed by the King's death.

'They looked like nothing so much as an immense flight of crows that had just landed!' In memory of a king who had adored racing, head-to-toe black was mandatory in the Royal Enclosure at Ascot in 1910.

BEFORE THE HALF-MOURNING PERIOD: *The Blackness of Society up to the 17th of June.*

THE UNRELIEVED BLACKNESS OF SOCIETY AS SHOWN AT ASCOT LAST WEEK

Owing possibly to the official reminder that was issued to the effect that the period of full mourning would not expire until the 17th, Ascot opened with an unmitigated blackness of aspect not hitherto witnessed by this generation. Individually the cut of the gowns was very smart, but in the mass the effect was astonishingly sombre

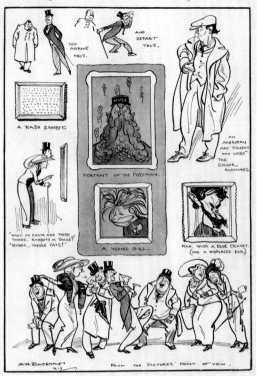

Organised by Roger Fry and his friends in Bloomsbury, 'Manet and the Post-Impressionists' exposed the wider British public to a kind of art hitherto familiar to a select few. Hilarity and outrage soon gave way to avid attention.

With numerous instances of verbal, physical and even sexual assault, the violence that erupted on the threshold of Parliament on so-called 'Black Friday' in November 1910 reignited the suffragettes' militant campaign for the vote.

at any moment. There was still no cessation in official business. At noon on Thursday, Lord Islington, who had recently been appointed Governor of New Zealand, arrived for an audience. Edward was up and dressed, but looked, Islington thought, 'ghastly'. Like the American ambassador before him, he left with no illusions. 'I don't know what other people think,' he told his wife, 'but I think I have been seeing a dying man.'[29] When Asquith, from the *Enchantress*, reported on his reception in Portugal, he received a polite acknowledgement: 'Very glad that you liked your stay at Lisbon and that the King was so pleasant. Edward R.'[30] It was the last communication between the Prime Minister and the sovereign he had so sorely vexed.

Mrs Keppel was at Buckingham Palace that day but left before the Queen's return in the late afternoon. Even her son's letter, which she had received before her storm-tossed crossing from France, had not prepared Alexandra for the gravity of her husband's condition. Realisation dawned at Victoria station, where she was greeted not by the King, as was customary, but by the Prince and Princess of Wales. At the Palace, she was aghast to discover an ashen-faced Edward struggling for breath and unable to sit upright. Profoundly shaken, Princess Victoria dashed off a postcard to her childhood friend Lady Derby, who had sent her a note of concern. 'Dearest Starling,' she scrawled, 'so like you writing. It has indeed been an *awful shock* coming home not knowing anything & finding him *so* ill. God grant his precious life . . .'[31]

That evening, the King sent for Fritz Ponsonby, who found him huddled at his desk, a rug tucked around his knees. Edward read the Foreign Office telegrams and signed some papers. Determined he should be spared exertion, Ponsonby withheld everything he believed might require discussion. As his secretary prepared to take his leave, Edward said, in a gasping voice, 'You managed so well at Biarritz. I hope everyone was thanked.' After a painful pause, he added, 'Especially the Press.' Feigning a cheerfulness he was far from feeling, Ponsonby wished him a rapid recovery. 'I feel wretchedly ill,' Edward admitted. 'I can't eat, I can't sleep. They really must do something for me.' Then, recollecting that Ponsonby was to go out of waiting the following day, the King shook his hand. 'In case I don't see you again, goodbye,' he wheezed.[32]

At 6 p.m., the first bulletin was issued. It announced that Edward was suffering from 'a severe bronchial attack' and had been confined to his room for the last two days. Around 8 p.m., a second bulletin, signed by Laking and Reid, as well as a third Physician-in-Ordinary, Sir Richard Douglas Powell, concluded with the ominous statement that 'His Majesty's condition causes some anxiety.' The press, which until then had continued to observe its self-imposed moratorium, had no choice but to come clean. Over the next twenty-four hours, the headlines became ever more portentous as a stunned nation scrambled for updates.

'The news of the illness,' wrote Keble Howard in the *Sketch*, 'came down on London, rumours notwithstanding, with the force of an unexpected and shrewdly planted blow. In the streets, in the trains, in clubs, in shops, in theatres, one found the depressing effect of it all day long.'[33] In an era before radio, television and the internet, those who craved the latest information had little choice but to go and obtain it themselves. On the sunny morning of Friday, 6 May, a river of pedestrians and cyclists, carriages and motor-cars flowed towards Buckingham Palace. Among the anonymous hordes were numerous notables: the Duke of Devonshire and the Marquess of Salisbury; Lord Rosebery and Lord Rothschild; Sir Luke Fildes and Sir Lawrence Alma-Tadema; the Belgian and Chinese ministers. Only members of the Royal Family were admitted into the King's presence, but the Archbishop of Canterbury, Randall Davidson, was received by the Queen, and then by the Prince of Wales. A visitors' book was made available in which callers could inscribe their names. Demand for it was so great that a second volume was opened at the Ambassador's Gate. Lest the incessant din of hoofs and wheels penetrate the sickroom, peat was laid between the stone arches leading from the forecourt to the quadrangle.

Activity was the only thing that kept Margot Asquith from breaking down. Having signed the book, she returned to Downing Street to find Charles Hardinge looking quite miserable. Francis Knollys was in tears, he told her. He recommended that she cable her husband aboard the *Enchantress* without delay. Feeling 'shattered & deeply moved', Margot received her lunch guests in near-silence. Throughout a cheerless meal, bulletins arrived at intervals. Lady Frances Balfour infuriated her hostess by pointing out that 'the Tory Party would blame us if he died & that I must be prepared to see cold faces.'

Asquith's Private Secretary, Roderick Meiklejohn, was hardly more consoling. 'Nothing,' he said, 'except any disaster happening to the Prime Minister cd have been more awful for the Liberal Party.' It was, Margot thought, 'like a dream and all London is standing still with anxiety'.[34]

At the Palace, Sir James Reid and his colleagues kept vigil. The King was settled in an easy chair, Queen Alexandra and Princess Victoria at his sides. Oxygen was administered ever more frequently. Close friends were summoned to say farewell. Sir Ernest Cassel had not been certain his own audience would go ahead. At 11 a.m., Arthur Davidson had telephoned to cancel it, only for Francis Knollys to call again half an hour later with an urgent request to come at once. Having been briefed on the latest by Laking, Cassel saw the Queen first. She begged him to stay awhile. Then he was taken to the King. Edward, who had insisted on dressing, rose to greet his visitor with the words, 'I knew that you would not fail me.'[35] His voice was indistinct, and Cassel believed him to be in great pain. Describing himself as 'very seedy', Edward enquired after the health of Maud Ashley, who had just returned from Egypt.[36] Implored by Laking not to keep the King talking, Cassel took his leave as soon as he could. Before he did so, he handed the monarch an envelope containing ten thousand pounds in banknotes.

Edward's final meeting with his mistress was as harrowing as that with his banker was dignified. Even before the news was broken to the nation, the atmosphere surrounding Mrs Keppel was fraught. From her nursery window, nine-year-old Sonia could see knots of people clustered on the pavements, and strangers buttonholing each other for the latest. Inside, the servants were distracted and grim. Fifteen-year-old Violet was clearly in on the secret but refused to divulge any details.

That afternoon, Mrs Keppel presented a letter to the Queen, which Edward had written to her almost a decade earlier. In the event he was ever taken seriously ill, he asked her to come and see him 'so that I may say farewell and thank you for all your kindness and friendship since it has been my good fortune to know you'. He concluded with a thinly veiled order to his wife and children: 'I feel convinced that all those who have any affection for me will carry out the wishes which I expressed in these lines.'[37]

Always magnanimous to her husband's lovers, Alexandra invited Mrs Keppel to the Palace at 5 p.m. By then, the King was being kept alive with strychnine. At 1 p.m., he had had a heart attack and was believed to be dead. Coming round, he had drifted in and out of consciousness for several hours. At 4.30 p.m., the Prince of Wales informed him that his horse, Witch of the Air, had just won by half a length at Kempton Park. 'I am very glad,' Edward murmured.[38]

When Mrs Keppel arrived, he barely recognised her. According to Lord Esher, who heard a full account from Francis Knollys, the Queen shook hands and told her, 'I am sure you have always had a good influence over him.' She then withdrew to the window. Flanked by nurses, the incoherent King fell forward in his chair. The sight was too much for Mrs Keppel, who lost her nerve completely. 'Almost shrieking,' she was bundled out of the room by Princess Victoria. In the corridor, she became hysterical, repeating over and over again, 'I never did any harm, there was nothing wrong between us,' and 'What is to become of me?' To Esher's mind, the most egregious thing about this uncharacteristic lapse in decorum was that it occurred in full view of the pages and footmen. The princess attempted to calm her father's mistress, who was in a 'wild fit'. Eventually, she was carried into Fritz Ponsonby's room, where she remained for several hours. 'Altogether,' observed the acid Esher, who was one of the few people to dislike Mrs Keppel, 'it was a painful and rather theatrical exhibition, and ought never to have happened.'[39]

As the sun-dappled afternoon gave way to a showery dusk, the tension across London thickened. In St James's, club lobbies were thronged with members monitoring the ticker tapes. In Mayfair and Belgravia, maids took mourning apparel out of mothballs. Anticipating a rush, some women went to the department stores early. Margot Asquith ordered a black dress at Woollands, where her son Anthony disrupted a spring fashion show with his toy aeroplane. One of the assistants callously remarked, 'This is bad news, madam. The King's death will spoil the Season.' Dashed, Margot 'felt the smallness of human outlook'.[40]

Swelled by successive waves, the crowds milling around the base of the still unfinished Victoria Memorial were larger than ever. First had come the bowler-hatted office-workers, then the young suburbanites who had bicycled into the city from their homes in Clapham, Brixton and Ealing. They were followed by the rich, who, in spite of sudden downpours, lingered in their evening finery to inspect the now sodden and dog-eared bulletins fastened to the gilded gates. Occasionally, there was a slight commotion. At one point, an open-topped taxi cruised up and down The Mall. In the rear, a cinematographer cranked the handle of a motion-picture camera, recording the scenes for posterity. With darkness descending and lights snapping on all over the soot-encrusted Palace façade, a ragged Irishman pushed his way through the throng. Whether drunk or distraught, he was clearly much affected. Tears coursing down his grimy cheeks, he saluted as he fixed his eyes on one illuminated window. 'God bless you, Ted!' he sobbed.[41]

But Edward was moving beyond help. At 6.15 p.m., the gravest bulletin yet announced his condition to be critical. Those of his relatives who were not already present, as well as the Archbishop of Canterbury and the Home Secretary, arrived one by one. Many members of the public turned to prayer. At the Shakespeare Festival in Stratford-upon-Avon, Ellen Terry gave a performance to a packed house. At its close, the National Anthem was played, and the audience bowed their heads in silence. In the nursery at Number 10, Margot Asquith knelt on the floor with seven-year-old Anthony and his thirteen-year-old sister Elizabeth to beseech God to save the King. Margot, who had pulled out of Consuelo Marlborough's farewell dinner for the Islingtons, called on Charles Hardinge's wife, Bina. There she encountered the Foreign Secretary, Sir Edward Grey, 'looking ill with sorrow'. Later, they hailed a cab in the pouring rain. 'This is a very big thing,' Grey observed. 'These things have to come, but it came as a terrible shock in its suddenness.'[42]

Exhausted and cold, Margot was approached in her bedroom by Downing Street's head messenger, Mr Lindsay, who begged her for an update. Hovering behind him in the corridor was his wife in her nightgown. When Margot told them it was 'practically all over', Lindsay assured her that he would wait up for further news. Not many more minutes elapsed before he knocked gently at the door. Entering, he stood at the foot of Margot's bed. 'His Majesty passed away at eleven forty-five,' he told her.[43]

Margot burst into tears. In the darkness outside the streaming window, the bell of Westminster Abbey began to toll.

A thousand miles away in the Mediterranean, the *Enchantress* was racing for home. At Gibraltar, a wireless message from Francis Knollys had alerted the Prime Minister to the emergency in London. Asquith replied that he would return immediately.

At 3 a.m., he was roused from an uneasy slumber and handed a scrap of paper. It read:

I am deeply grieved to inform you that my beloved father the King passed away peacefully at a quarter to twelve tonight (the 6th). George.

Stunned, Asquith stumbled up on deck. Already, thoughts of the as yet unresolved crisis in Parliament churned. 'At a most anxious moment in the fortunes of the State,' he wrote later, 'we had lost, without warning or preparation, the Sovereign whose ripe experience, trained sagacity, equitable judgement, and unvarying consideration, counted for so much.'[44]

As the Prime Minister brooded, he turned his eyes towards the heavens. For the first and only time during the voyage, he saw Halley's Comet streaking across the sky.

10: 'The meaning of everything seems gone for the moment'

Like his mother nine years earlier, Edward was surrounded by a bevy of relations – wife, children, siblings, in-laws – during his final hours. Among those who knelt on the floor of his bedroom as he slipped away was his son George, who invited the Archbishop of Canterbury to lead them all in prayer. It was a throwback to an era of Christian piety Queen Victoria would surely have approved.

At the time of his accession, Edward had remarked that the Crown had come to him two decades too late. George, who was just shy of his forty-fifth birthday, believed his own elevation to be premature. He had been devoted to, if somewhat frightened of, his ebullient father. Unusual in the annals of royal history, their bond was remarkable given the diversity of their characters and outlooks. Edward was charismatic and cosmopolitan. George was dependable and dull. Since his marriage to Princess May of Teck in 1893, he had displayed not the slightest interest in other women. Temperamentally averse to the very idea of 'Abroad', his grasp of European languages was limited. Slim and abstemious where his father was stout and self-indulgent, his favourite hobbies were shooting and stamp-collecting. Edward could enter into the former easily enough. The latter was incomprehensible to him.

Against those considerable odds, they had co-existed in surprising harmony. A waspish cousin might declare that the King's affection for the Prince of Wales stemmed from the latter's willingness to be his 'complete slave',[1] but that was to do both men an injustice. George never challenged his father politically, and he had neither the aptitude nor the inclination to rival him socially. On the other hand, his commitment to his duty was total. It was an admirable trait, and one Edward rewarded with love and affection.

Lord Esher kissed the hands of the new King and Queen at Buckingham Palace at 12.15 a.m. Usually undemonstrative, May sobbed uncontrollably. 'This is going to be a terrible time for us, full of difficulties,' she said. 'I hope you will help us.'[2] The couple resembled, Esher thought, 'two poor storm-battered children'. Outwardly stoic, George was fearful of the future. 'I am quite stunned by this awful blow,' he confided to his diary.[3]

Still, private grief could not be permitted to interfere with good manners. Before he departed for his home at Marlborough House, the King remembered to thank Sir James Reid for all he had done.

Early on the morning of Saturday, 7 May, Jean, Lady Hamilton, who had often glimpsed Edward on the Society circuit, gazed out of her window in Mayfair. The sun was shining, and she could see people riding and talking beneath the fresh green foliage of the early summer trees. She was struck by the incongruity of the scene. Life went on as usual, yet London felt different in some indefinable but fundamental way. 'The King is dead,' she wrote. 'The meaning of everything seems gone for the moment.'[4]

Her sense of dislocation was shared by countless others. The antithesis of all that was remote and inscrutable, Edward had been vibrant, familiar and intensely alive. His sudden demise, after an illness that had lasted, as far as the majority of his subjects were concerned, barely twenty-four hours, tore a gaping hole in the fabric of the nation. To Lionel Cust, the Surveyor of the King's Pictures, it was not, like the passing of Queen Victoria, 'the removal of one who to many was more like a permanent institution'. It was the loss of both 'a personal friend' and 'a great personality who radiated something special and indescribable from his throne'.[5]

Over the next few days, men and women from every walk of life attempted to articulate what Edward had meant to them. *The Times*, which had been so tepid upon his accession, now believed it held the key to his phenomenal popularity. In its first full-length report on his death, it identified the King's *joie de vivre* as 'the real secret of the spell which he undoubtedly exercised, not only over those with whom he came into contact, but over the masses of his peoples'.[6] The Foreign Secretary Sir Edward Grey concurred. He was convinced that 'The humblest devotees of horse racing in a Derby Day crowd knew that the King was there to enjoy the national festival in precisely the same spirit as themselves; that he wished them to enjoy it too; that their enjoyment was part of his own.'[7]

After the high-minded but censorious Victorian era, Edward's scintillating reign had sluiced away the last dregs of Puritanism. The King had hardly been a model of virtue, but neither was he a bigot or hypocrite. Lord Granville had summarised it best when he drew a comparison between father and son. Whereas the worthy Prince Albert had been unloved 'because he possessed all the virtues which are sometimes lacking in the Englishman', Edward was loved 'because he has all the faults of which the Englishman is accused'.[8]

Obituarists kept circling his all-conquering charm. It was, Lord Esher considered, 'invincible. The individual man succumbed to it, and the multitude went down before it. When the King walked into a room everyone felt the glow of a personal greeting. When he smiled upon a vast assemblage everyone replied unconsciously.'[9] Edward may have lived his life at the apex of an intensely hierarchical society, but he had possessed what Lord Fisher (the former First Sea Lord who had been raised to the peerage at the close of 1909) called an 'astounding aptitude of appealing to the hearts of both High and Low'.[10] To every domestic servant, he had expressed his appreciation. To every beggar, he had tipped his hat. G. K. Chesterton described the King 'as a kind of universal uncle. His popularity in poor families was so frank as to be undignified; he was really spoken of by tinkers and tailors as if he were some gay and prosperous member of their own family. There was a picture of him upon the popular retina infinitely brighter and brisker than there is either of Mr Asquith or Mr Balfour.'[11]

To those who had reached adulthood since the turn of the century, Edward had embodied the hedonistic spirit of the age. Violet Asquith, who was staying with the Viceroy in Dublin, was brought the news of his death in the middle of the night. 'The King dead – *dead*,' she wrote in her diary. 'I can't realise it.' He had been 'a splendidly characteristic figurehead – full of personality'.[12] The brilliant young scholar Patrick Shaw-Stewart mourned Edward as 'my favourite institution. There will be no more fun now of any sort.'[13] From Balliol College in Oxford, the Honourable Billy Grenfell reflected on the tragic turn of events. 'I am sad about King Edward, aren't you?' he asked his parents, Lord and Lady Desborough. 'It seems as if the glory has departed; and there will be lots of war and mother will have to worry considerably.'[14]

A startling transformation was soon under way in every city, town and village in the country. Blinds in embassies, banks and offices were pulled down as flags dipped to half-mast. The black borders that framed the pages of the newspapers were mirrored in the stark black lettering on the placards that loomed at railway stations and on street corners. The Stock Exchange ground to a virtual halt. At an emergency meeting of the managers of the West End theatres, it was agreed that no performances should take place until after the funeral. The fledgling Season threatened to implode as hostesses cancelled balls and dinner parties by the hundred. The 'national calamity' saw thirty-eight functions called off at the Ritz alone.[15] Concerts, lectures and general meetings were postponed, and so was the opening of the Japan–British Exhibition, which had been due to take place on 12 May. The Royal Academy closed its doors. Restaurants remained open but were empty of diners. The WSPU let it be known that gatherings of suffragettes would be restricted to those in private

houses. For good measure, Annie Kenney, one of the most prominent militants, sent a telegram to Queen Alexandra in which she
conveyed the 'loving sympathy' of the members of the Bristol
chapter.[16]

In the heart of St James's, Rosa Lewis, the proprietor of the
Cavendish Hotel, convened her staff and guests. Good-looking, feisty
and determined, she had transcended her working-class origins to
establish a reputation as the pre-eminent female chef in England.
Even the mighty Escoffier hailed her as the 'Queen of Cooks'. Much
in demand in London Society, she had brought her uncompromising
vision of hospitality to bear at the Cavendish, which she had transformed into a home-away-from-home for male members of the aristocracy. The King himself had looked in upon occasion. On 7 May,
champagne was poured, and a toast was drunk to Edward's memory.
Then Rosa descended to the wine cellar, where the racks were lined
with the precious vintages she had reserved for the royal table. There
were Veuve Clicquot 1904, Château Pontet-Canet 1895 and Schloss
Johannisberg Cabinet 1893, besides all manner of ports, brandies and
rare liqueurs. With a last, sad look, Rosa locked the door and pock-
eted the key. It would not, she declared, be opened again in her
lifetime.[17]

In spite of unsettled weather, which saw shafts of bright sunshine
alternate with squalls of rain, hail and even snow, the crowds outside
Buckingham Palace had not abated. If anything, they had grown.
Hushed and respectful, they watched the carriages and motor-cars
come and go, bowing their heads to any that contained members of
the Royal Family. Hawkers did a brisk trade in hastily printed memorial cards and knots of white and purple ribbon. Save for the occa-
sional footman who wore a band of black crêpe over the left arm of
his scarlet livery, the massive forecourt was deserted.

Only clothes shops were lively. Margot Asquith's instinct to procure
her mourning early had been wise. Almost immediately, the Lord
Chamberlain's Office published instructions for ladies and gentlemen
intending to go to Court: full mourning of unrelieved black until 7
November, reduced to half-mourning of black with touches of white,
grey, lavender and mauve for six months thereafter. But it wasn't just
the elite who wished to display their sorrow sartorially. Men and
women of all ages and backgrounds rushed to purchase the trappings

of grief. Department stores stripped their windows of coloured goods and substituted black ones instead. Retail establishments and whole-sale houses alike were, in the words of the *Illustrated London News*, 'at once thrown into a state of the utmost activity'. Harrods, Selfridges and Debenham & Freebody were 'literally besieged' from morning to night.[18] Maison Lewis, Madame Louise and the other fashionable milliners of Regent Street extended their opening hours until 7 p.m. to cope with demand. It was as well that Lady Duff Gordon had included a black dress in her latest collection at Lucile Ltd. She and her fellow couturiers had to scramble to adapt their polychromatic designs to the dictates of mass mourning.

The iconoclastic playwright George Bernard Shaw judged the whole business to be gratuitous, if not downright reprehensible. Making a plea on behalf of lower-middle-class parents who found themselves obliged to kit out their offspring with new outfits they could ill afford, he demanded to know 'why our schools should be deliberately made hideous with black because an honourable public career has come to its natural close'. He suggested that little boys and girls should sport violet ribbons as a gesture 'correct, inexpensive and pretty'.[19]

For the most part, his words fell upon deaf ears. Even the poorest were determined to do what they could to project an appropriate sense of loss. On her way to pay her condolences to Edward's sister, Princess Louise, Mrs Arthur Thesiger passed an elderly tramp on the pavement outside Kensington Palace. His coat and trousers were in rags, but he wore a clean new mourning tie around his neck. When she heard about it, the princess burst into tears. 'It was so touching,' she told Queen Alexandra.[20]

At Belvoir Castle, Lady Marjorie, Lady Violet and Lady Diana Manners were caught short. From childhood, they had been encour-aged in their flamboyant dress sense by their mother, the Duchess of Rutland, whose unconventionality had so perturbed Edward that he had once called upon her to remonstrate. As everyone around them donned mourning, the sisters discovered that their wardrobes were unequal to such a sombre occasion. Forced to improvise, they swathed themselves in yards of black chiffon, which they hoped would obscure their embarrassingly bright colours. They looked, Diana admitted, 'the fulfilment of make-shift'. Their mood was not improved by the atmosphere that prevailed right across the county. The flags at Belvoir were lowered while church bells tolled all day long. The family butler, Nixon, only depressed them further with his grim prognostications. 'I tell you what *I* think, milady,' he kept repeating. '*I* think it's very serious, not so much for the royal circle, but for the country!' Diana, whose official debut was now deferred until 1911, bit her tongue. 'I longed to say it was a hundred times worse for Mrs Keppel than all put together,' she wrote to a friend.[21]

Edward's mistress was having a difficult time. On Saturday afternoon, Sir Ernest Cassel visited Margot Asquith at 10 Downing Street. Visibly shattered – 'he really loved the King,' Margot realised – he told her he had heard that Queen Alexandra had refused admittance to Mrs Keppel, adding, 'It would not have been unnatural,' if that had been the case. Margot couldn't bring herself to believe anything so heartless.[22] Jean Hamilton was outraged when an ill-disposed acquaintance, 'so spiteful and nasty, in her black clothes', called it 'disgraceful' that the royal favourite had been allowed anywhere near the dying man in his final hours.[23] For his part, Lord Esher was keen to have it understood that Mrs Keppel's version of events, disseminated at the Ritz by Mrs Arthur James, was a tissue of lies, and that the Queen, far from kissing her upon her arrival and assuring her that the Royal Family would 'look after her', had been polite but glacial throughout.[24]

To escape the wagging tongues – and, it was whispered, their creditors – the Keppels fled Portman Square to seek sanctuary with Mrs James on Grafton Street. Violet and Sonia followed. Increasingly distressed by a mysterious development nobody troubled to explain, Sonia was thrown completely off balance. Lined with yellow marble and staffed by menservants of 'untouchable dignity', the house was opulent but unwelcoming. Black hats, black frocks and black stockings appeared overnight. Even the girls' frilled petticoats were threaded with black ribbon. When they attempted to see their mother, who was prostrate in bed, they were denied entry. When at last they were told they could go in, they found she could only look at them blankly 'and rather resentfully, as though we were unwelcome intruders'. Sonia ended the day by sobbing out her confusion on her father's starched shirt-front. 'Why does it matter so much, Kingy dying?' she demanded to know.

George did his best to console her. 'Poor little girl!' he said. 'It must have been frightening for you. And for all of us, for that matter. Nothing will ever be quite the same again. Because Kingy was such a wonderful man.'[25]

Mrs Keppel soon discovered that her days of influence were at an end. At Marlborough House, she was informed that King George had given orders that she should not be allowed to sign the visitors' book. Even her financial situation seemed suddenly uncertain. The envelope stuffed with banknotes Sir Ernest Cassel had left with Edward during their final meeting was returned to him by Francis Knollys. Cassel sent it straight back. He explained that the cash (the equivalent of more than a million pounds today) represented interest on business he had transacted on the King's behalf. His biographer, and Mrs Keppel's, have speculated that it had been meant for her. If so, there is no evidence it ever reached her. The former favourite was almost destroyed by the abrupt downturn in her fortunes. 'Life with all its joys have [sic] come to a full stop, at least for me,' she wrote.[26]

Beyond the narrow confines of London Society, few people had heard of Mrs Keppel. Everybody had heard of Queen Alexandra, who now found herself the focus of the nation's grief. Desolate but dignified, her apparent composure belied her dread of the scrutiny to which she would be subjected during the impending state funeral. To Fritz Ponsonby, she confessed she 'felt as if she had been turned into stone, unable to cry, unable to grasp the meaning of it all, and incapable of doing anything'.[27]

As intricate plans were formulated around her, Alexandra stayed close to Edward, who lay uncoffined in the bed in which he had died. His hands were laid on the unwrinkled counterpane, while his head was inclined to one side 'as if in comfortable sleep'.[28] His face displayed not the slightest sign of suffering or pain. He looked so tranquil that his widow decided that all those who had not already said farewell should do so now. Over the course of the following week, an ever-lengthening list of relatives, friends and courtiers were invited to Buckingham Palace to view the body. They included the dukes of Norfolk and Abercorn; the Lords Roberts, Kitchener and Fisher; the French, German, Russian and Austrian ambassadors; the Marquess and Marchioness of Londonderry; Sir Edward Grey and Lord

Lansdowne; Arthur Balfour and Charles Hardinge; and two delegations of six members each from the upper and lower Houses of
Parliament. Clad in a simple black dress, Alexandra was so sweet,
pathetic and altogether bereft that grown men were moved to tears in
her presence. 'It is the end of my life,' she told one. 'They want to take
him away, but I can't bear to part with him. Once they hide his face
from me everything is gone forever.'[29] Yet at the same time, she struck
Lord Esher as strangely happy, talking with 'only a slight diminution
of her natural gaiety, but with a tenderness which betrayed all the love
in her soul'. At last, she was in 'complete possession of the man who
was the love of her youth, and – as I fervently believe – of all her
life'.[30]

During the nineteenth century, death had come to be marked by
the observance of elaborate obsequies that fused new technology
with age-old traditions. Prevalent in many generations and cultures,
the practice of making a visual record of the deceased had derived
fresh impetus from the invention of photography. The royal families
of Europe were quick on the uptake. Prince Albert was photographed on his deathbed in 1861, and so were his son-in-law,
Emperor Frederick III, in 1888, and his second son, the Duke of
Saxe-Coburg and Gotha, in 1900. Swaddled in tulle and banked
with flowers, the tiny corpse of Queen Victoria was photographed
at Osborne House. On that occasion, the man behind the camera
was probably Hubert von Herkomer, who used the image as the
basis for an ethereal watercolour he presented to the King. Edward
must have endorsed the venture, for he rewarded him with a knighthood in 1907.

In such a context, the decision to invite two of the most prominent
artists of the day to draw Edward as he lay dead was not so outlandish.
Of the pair, Sir Luke Fildes was the more obvious candidate. In 1901,
he had painted a swaggering full-length of the new king in his ermine
and velvet robes. The completed canvas, copies of which were
despatched to British embassies and legations throughout the world,
had been heartily approved by Queen Alexandra. John Singer Sargent,
on the other hand, had twice rebuffed the Palace when it had
attempted to enlist him. Why he accepted a commission now is a
mystery. At least he had experience of the macabre conditions in
which he was to work. Two years earlier, he had drawn the writer and

librettist Henry B. Brewster the day after his death in response to an appeal from the composer Ethel Smyth.

Bidden on 8 May, the artists approached their subject in different but characteristic ways. Infinitely respectful, Fildes sketched the body in profile as a study in noble repose. Sargent opted for a tighter focus on the head settled deep into its pillow. He delineated Edward's brow and Hanoverian nose with the crispness of sculpted marble yet conjured his beard with just a few strokes of charcoal. Presented with the finished drawings, Alexandra seems to have preferred the former. The Sargent was absorbed into the Royal Collection, but it was the Fildes she authorised for reproduction in the *Graphic*.

Private grief notwithstanding, the widowed Queen displayed a remarkable flair for public relations. Sensing the nation craved catharsis, she granted the press privileged access to her private thoughts and feelings, collapsing the barriers that divided her from the people. The result was an effusion of emotion that flowed in both directions. At Alexandra's command, a photograph of the King on his deathbed was released to the *Daily Mail* and the *Sphere*, as well as to various postcard manufacturers. 'Graciously approved' for publication in a special supplement to the *Illustrated London News*, a sentimental drawing by A. Forestier depicted the Queen tucking a single white rose into Edward's hand. It was, the poem printed underneath declared, 'the sad, last token of undying love'.[31]

On 10 May, Lord Esher, at the request of Francis Knollys, applied himself to the task of composing a suitable reply to the messages of condolence that had flooded in from across the Empire. After a struggle of several hours, he had finally hashed out a workable draft that he was reading through with the Private Secretary when Alexandra unexpectedly sent down a draft of her own. She had never been noted for her way with words, yet the four-sided document, which contained not a single erasure or revision, was considered by both men to be so perfect they passed it without hesitation. It came, Esher believed, 'straight from her woman's heart and every word of it rings like a bell'. 'These are things,' he said, 'which women, and especially Queens, do better than any man.'[32]

In five short but extremely personal paragraphs, Alexandra addressed herself directly to her late husband's subjects. 'From the depths of my poor, broken heart', she voiced her sincere appreciation for their sympathy in her 'overwhelming sorrow and unspeakable anguish'. She had, she continued, 'lost everything in Him'. Britain, too, had 'suffered an irreparable loss by their best friend, Father and Sovereign, thus suddenly called away'. Drawing upon her devout Christian faith, the Queen called upon God to 'give us all His Divine help to bear this heaviest of crosses which He has seen fit to lay upon us'. She humbly beseeched the people to 'give me a thought in your prayers which will comfort and sustain me in all I still have to go through'. Last, she confided 'my dear Son into your care'. Supported by his wife, George would, she assured them, 'follow in his dear Father's footsteps'.[33]

Appearing in virtually every local and national paper in the country on 11 May, Alexandra's letter was considered by the more cynical members of London Society to be mawkish. Jean Hamilton gathered as much from Lord Basil Blackwood when he called to see her the next day. She herself maintained the tone had been just right. 'Luckily there are many ways of loving,' she wrote in her diary. 'Love is no less real for being emotional, and every cottage will treasure the Queen's letter.'[34] Her assessment proved to be the more accurate. The text was printed in full on black or purple-edged cards, which were soon in mass circulation.

In her gratitude to the general public, Alexandra did not forget those closer to home. She instructed that a cheque for two hundred guineas should be sent to Sir James Reid so 'that you may know Her Majesty fully appreciated your kind and willing services during King Edward's illness and sad death last week'.[35] Unlike Mrs Keppel, Reid, who had been so close to his patient during his final days, suffered no loss of status with his passing. It was he who composed the official reports for the *British Medical Journal* and the *Lancet*, not neglecting to send a statement to the Kaiser, whom he had known since they had kept vigil beside Queen Victoria's deathbed. In short order, he was appointed Physician-in-Ordinary to George V: the same post he had filled under the previous two monarchs.

Upon the death of her brother-in-law, Tsar Alexander III, in 1894, Alexandra, then Princess of Wales, had journeyed to Russia to console her sister, Marie. The Dowager Empress now returned the favour. Accompanied by a giant Cossack, she descended on London to be greeted by George and May, who conducted her straight to Buckingham Palace. As self-centred as Alexandra, but more strong-willed, she proved to be an unhelpful influence. In Russia, a dead emperor's widow took precedence over a living emperor's wife. With a blithe disregard for British protocol, Marie encouraged Alexandra to adopt a similar point of view. It made things awkward for the new queen, May, whose patience was to be sorely tested over the coming weeks. May had enough to contend with. Her full name, Victoria Mary, had long been regarded as cumbersome by her husband. With his accession, he asked her to choose between the two. 'Victoria' was so closely associated with his illustrious grandmother that 'Mary' was the only alternative. 'It strikes me as curious to be rechristened at the age of 43,' she wrote to her beloved aunt and confidante, the Grand Duchess of Mecklenburg-Strelitz. 'Mary' at least had a regal ring. 'I hope the beautiful old name will come into vogue again,' noted the diarist Lady Knightley of Fawsley with approval on 9 May.[36]

Although Edward's body had eventually been placed in an open coffin, it remained on the bed in which he had died. Alexandra was so reluctant to let her husband go that, day after day, the plans for his removal had to be postponed. Finally, on 14 May, she consented that the coffin, of oak hewn from the forest at Windsor set with the brass insignia of the Crown and the Order of the Garter, should be closed ahead of a private lying-in-state. Followed from the bedroom by Alexandra, George and Mary, as well as by George's three sisters, his uncles, the Duke of Connaught and King Frederick VIII of Denmark, and his aunt, the Dowager Empress, it was carried to the Throne Room in Buckingham Palace, where it rested on a catafalque beneath the gilt-encrusted ceiling. The crimson walls and deep-pile carpet were untouched, but the throne itself had been removed, to be replaced by an altar flanked by towering arrangements of white flowers. The immense crystal chandeliers remained unlit. After nightfall, the only illumination came from tall candles. Draped in the same cream embroidered pall that had been used at the funeral of Queen Victoria, the coffin was covered with the Royal Standard and purple velvet cushions upon which were placed the Orb, Sceptre and St Edward's Crown, and Edward's diamond-studded Garter. On the floor at its foot was spread the Regimental Standard of the Grenadier

Guards. Motionless in their scarlet tunics and towering bearskins, four Grenadiers with reversed arms and bowed heads kept watch at all times.

Over the next three days, there was a series of religious services for the Royal Family and members of the Household: in the private chapel on the morning of Sunday, 15 May, and each evening at 10 p.m. in the Throne Room. Beyond the palace gates, many of Edward's subjects found solace in their faith. In an era when anti-Semitism was endemic at all levels of society, the King's engagement with the Jewish community had been greatly appreciated. To a gathering of several thousand crammed into the Great Assembly Hall in Mile End, Rabbi Schewzik delivered an oration in which he described a three-fold sense of grief. First, there was loyalty to the country in which the Jews had 'found a place of rest' in a hostile world. Second, as a commercial people, Jews required peace for 'enterprise and prosperity', and no man had worked more assiduously to preserve it than Edward. Last, and most significant, the Jews had, with the death of the King, lost 'their best friend, their protector and their father. He had set an example which might well be followed by other European monarchs in associating with Jews and staying at their houses. He had done his best to protect them from persecution, expulsion, torture and torment.' The reason so many Jews had settled in England, the rabbi concluded, was because 'here they were treated as men and as human beings'. With that, *The Times* reported, 'almost the whole of the congregation burst into tears, and for a short time the manifestations of grief were so great as to interrupt the service'.[37]

In spite of the heartfelt tributes of Jews, Roman Catholics, Nonconformists and members of the Orthodox Church, Britain was still, in 1910, predominantly Anglican. As many as thirty million in a population of around forty-five million were born and raised in the Church of England. It was therefore unsurprising that it was from Anglican pulpits that the majority of sermons on Edward's passing were preached. One of the most eloquent was written by the Reverend Henry Scott Holland, Canon of St Paul's Cathedral, and delivered at Evensong on 15 May. A soul-stirring meditation on loss, one part of it in particular has endured. Imagining what the deceased might say to those he or she had left behind, Scott Holland speculated that it might be 'Death is nothing at all. It does not count. I have only slipped away into the next room.' Profoundly moving though the lines were, they vanished into obscurity for decades until their rediscovery in the late twentieth century, when they attained enormous popularity as a stand-alone reading at funerals.

The strong Christian faith Elsie Bowerman had imbibed from her father had been buttressed at Wycombe Abbey, where prayers were said each morning and evening. At Cambridge, she was a regular church-goer, relishing the services that took place in that jewel of the English Gothic, King's College Chapel, where she thrilled to the clear voices of the boy choristers as they soared upward to the fan-vaulted roof. It was to King's that she gravitated after Edward's death, to be rewarded with an experience she never forgot. Upon entry, the early summer day had been flawless. The great doors at the West End were kept open to allow the circulation of air, and through them Elsie could see the velvet lawns stretching down to the peaceful trees and unruffled waters of the Backs. Then, as the Dead March from Handel's *Saul* began, the aspect changed abruptly. From nowhere, a violent storm arose, with flashes of lightning and reverberations of thunder that mingled with the 'grim gloom' of the organ. It was spine-tingling in its drama, and not a little ominous. 'It seemed,' Elsie ruminated in later life, 'to herald the end of an era.'[38]

11: 'They're giving him to us now'

Although Edward's passing had been so sudden, those responsible for arranging his funeral were at least fortunate to have a recent precedent to draw upon. Over sixty-three years had elapsed between the death of William IV in 1837 and that of his niece Queen Victoria in 1901. In the interim, many of the protocols had grown rusty. 'You would think that the English Monarchy had been buried since the time of Alfred,' Lord Esher had scoffed in disbelief.[1]

A decade on, Sir Schomberg McDonnell had his own difficulties to contend with. Familiarly known as 'Pom', the youngest son of the 5th Earl of Antrim had capably served Lord Salisbury as Principal Private Secretary during two of his premierships. Since then, he had clocked up considerable experience in the Office of Works, to which he was appointed Secretary in 1902. Well-versed in the logistics that underpinned state and ceremonial occasions, McDonnell was, at the age of forty-nine, direct, indefatigable and uncompromising. Ramrod-straight, with gimlet eyes that gleamed above a magnificent moustache, he was emotionally as well as professionally invested in his work. Much liked by the Royal Family, he was unafraid to make enemies in his pursuit of perfection.

The most significant difference between the funerals of Victoria and Edward was that the latter was to be preceded by a three-day lying-in-state in Westminster Hall. It was something of an innovation, and one that added an additional layer of complexity to an already intricate exercise. The last monarch to receive such treatment had been George III, whose body had lain-in-state at Windsor for twenty-four hours in 1820. The tradition of lying-in-state at Westminster had been inaugurated with the death of the venerable Prime Minister William Ewart Gladstone in 1898. On that occasion, tens of thousands of members of the public had filed past his coffin prior to his burial in the adjacent Abbey.

Esher, who had preceded McDonnell at the Office of Works, was opposed to the very idea of a lying-in-state for Edward, and at Westminster in particular. He pointed out that the Hall had been the site of the trial of Charles I in 1649, and that the resonance would be unfortunate. His qualms were dismissed by McDonnell as 'foolish'. In any case, he was swiftly overruled by the Archbishop of Canterbury and the new King, both of whom were in favour of the scheme. Perhaps fearing Esher's continued interference, McDonnell welcomed George's decisiveness at such an early stage in his reign. It was, he considered, 'a fortunate omen'.[2]

From the moment the question of the lying-in-state was settled, McDonnell went into overdrive. No detail was too small for his personal attention. On 7 May, he instructed the Controller of Supplies to purchase vast quantities of purple cloth and grey felt. The tolling of Big Ben was arranged; towering candelabra were borrowed from St Paul's Cathedral; electric standard lamps were moved into St Stephen's Porch; and the King's printers, Eyre & Spottiswood, were visited to finalise the Order of Service, which was to be bound in violet leather tooled in gold. There was even a meeting about the pattern of the prie-dieu to be used by Queen Alexandra as she said her prayers. Somehow, he found the time to keep a daily, sometimes hourly, journal, which he wrote by hand on paper headed with the address of the Office of Works in Storey's Gate.

Flitting between Buckingham Palace, St James's Palace, Marlborough House, Westminster and Windsor, where the burial was to take place in St George's Chapel on Friday, 20 May, McDonnell achieved an instant rapport with George V, who, in their first meeting, he found to be 'very much affected but very quiet and business-like'. A consummate courtier as well as a talented logistician, McDonnell tendered his condolences: 'I told him that I could realise what his loss was as I had never seen a more devoted Father and Son than the King and himself.' George's reply was succinct but heartfelt. He had, he said, 'lost the best Father and Friend that any son possessed'.[3] Then, turning to the matter in hand, he signalled his assent to all the proposals McDonnell laid before him.

From the outset, both men harboured doubts about the involvement of the 15th Duke of Norfolk who, as hereditary Earl Marshal, was theoretically in charge of the arrangements. At the age of sixty-two, the duke was a well-meaning but bumbling soul judged by McDonnell to be 'not equal to the occasion'.[4] In that assessment, he was to be proved exasperatingly correct. The organising committee convened from the College of Heralds was 'much too large', and 'great confusion' inevitably ensued. On 16 May, at the rehearsal for the reception and installation of Edward's coffin in Westminster Hall, Norfolk made a verbal statement to all concerned in which he described their various duties, specifically requesting no interruptions should he make a mistake. For McDonnell, it was torture. When, as predicted, he heard the duke veer wildly off course, he was forced to intervene, set him straight and begin the whole speech again. By 18 May, Norfolk, who was by then 'very distraught', was visibly at sea in a meeting to finalise the order of the funeral procession. He looked, McDonnell noted, 'fogged and likely I fear to make a hash of it'.[5]

The following day, the King summoned McDonnell to Buckingham Palace. Their worst fears had been realised. The Earl Marshal had published the entire Ceremonial incorrectly, and a team of five men was now required to rewrite it. George was at his wit's end. 'What is the use of my taking all this trouble and labouring at it as I have done if these stupid men are to upset everything?' he sputtered. 'I love the

Duke: he is a charming, honourable, straight-forward little gentle-man; no better in the world. But as a man of business, he is absolutely impossible. I ask you, Pom,' he concluded piteously, 'is it not hard on me?'[6]

McDonnell could not have agreed more. It was, he replied, 'an outrage which the Sovereign should not be called upon to bear'.[7] The current system, in which an amateur was compelled to grapple with a feat of organisation far beyond his capabilities, was clearly inade-quate. He suggested that he should author a memorandum identify-ing the various defects and proposing appropriate remedies. George wearily concurred.

In spite of the duke's ineptitude, things passed off remarkably smoothly. On Tuesday, 17 May, eleven days after his death, Edward's body was conveyed from Buckingham Palace to Westminster Hall in a procession that marked the first act in his protracted obsequies. The weather was as unsettled as it had been all month. The crowds that began to gather as early as 4 a.m. did so in a light drizzle which soon passed over, but the skies remained overcast and it was unseasonably cool. By 10 a.m., the number of spectators had swelled to the hundreds of thousands. Before the procession, which was due to depart at 11.30 a.m., the Bishop of London, Arthur Winnington-Ingram, conducted a private service for the immediate members of the Royal Family. Twelve men of the Grenadier Guards then lifted the massive coffin onto their shoulders and carried it from the ground-floor Bow Room to which it had been transferred and loaded it onto the same grey gun-carriage used at the funeral of Queen Victoria. Pulled by a team of black horses into the palace forecourt, it was saluted by two guards of honour, one formed of a hundred men of the 3rd Battalion of Grenadier Guards, the other comprising a hundred sailors of the Royal Navy.

Draped with the Royal Standard, the coffin lid was arranged with cushions that bore the Orb, Sceptre and St Edward's Crown, as well as the Ribbon, Star and Order of the Garter. Dressed in the uniform of an Admiral of the Fleet, George walked close behind, followed by his two elder sons, fifteen-year-old David and fourteen-year-old Albert; the Duke of Connaught; King Frederick of Denmark; King Haakon VII of Norway; and a 'gorgeous, scintillating'[8] cavalcade of native and foreign royals, dignitaries and courtiers.

Chilled to the bone in the icy wind gusting down The Mall, Margot Asquith and Mrs Keppel watched the cortège pull out of the palace gate. Margot was crying so bitterly she could barely see, but she was resolved not to miss the cynosure of every eye: Queen Alexandra, who rode in a closed carriage with her sister, the Dowager Empress, and her daughters, the Princess Royal and Princess Victoria. At the sight of her veiled face at the window, the silent spectators instinctively edged closer. Women curtsied and men removed their hats. 'The Queen looked at us,' somebody tearfully exclaimed. 'How good of her!'[9]

Save for the fresh green foliage of the trees, the sea of black that stretched all along the route was virtually unrelieved by any colour. Even where a summer dress or hat supplied what *The Times* called 'a false tone', closer inspection invariably revealed a scrap of black ribbon to demonstrate that the wearer had entered into the nation's grief. Penned in by rows of soldiers, onlookers recognised that Edward was coming among them in death as he had done so often in life. To some, the intimidating grandeur of the ceremony was out of keeping with the character of the deceased. 'When he was alive he never wanted such a sight o' policemen an' sojers to keep the people off,' one man grumbled. 'Not he – he liked to see an' be seen an' be one of the crowd like.' The majority, however, understood that the procession transcended a class system that often seemed immutable. A pale-faced girl in a shabby black frock summed it up best when she was heard to cry, 'They're giving him to us now.'[10]

As salutes thundered in Hyde Park and at the Tower of London – one gun for each year of Edward's life – John Mackenzie-Rogan, the Bandmaster of the Coldstream Guards, was simultaneously exhilarated and terrified. He was determined that the transferral of the King's coffin from Buckingham Palace to Westminster Hall should be marked 'in such a way that it would leave an impression on our countrymen which would never be forgotten'.[11] Central to his vision was the drum: an instrument 'of great potentialities when used not merely as a supplement to the rest of the orchestra, but as a separate and individual thing – an instrument that would, in its primitive and barbaric way, move the human heart even as the organ and violin move it'.[12]

Having received permission to have the drummers and pipers of the Brigade of Guards placed at his disposal, as well as the bands of the four regiments of Foot Guards, Mackenzie-Rogan had drilled them rigorously. After pacing the route in slow time to establish exactly how many bars of music would be necessary, he had submitted a detailed programme to the King. It included funeral marches by Beethoven and Chopin, the Prelude from Handel's *Saul*, and 'Flowers of the Forest' to be played by the pipers alone. George approved his choices on one condition: that the procession, once under way, should neither halt nor 'mark time' until it reached its destination. Too narrow to permit the passage of eight bandsmen marching abreast, the stone arch leading from Horse Guards into Whitehall was an obstacle to be overcome. Mackenzie-Rogan had issued instructions that the gates in the smaller arches on either side should be opened to allow the musicians through.

Now, with the gun-carriage barely thirty yards away, he saw to his horror that the side-gates remained closed. 'I must confess that for a few moments I felt helpless,' he wrote later. 'The bands could not possibly get through the narrow arch without causing a lengthy check to the whole procession.'[13] Dreadful as the embarrassment of that would be, even worse was the thought of the King's ire.

His heart in his mouth, Mackenzie-Rogan passed a lightning order that the two outside men on each flank should fall back on reaching the arch; pass through it in quick time; then fan out and resume in slow time on the other side. It was a gamble, and one he feared would result in an undignified scramble. The next few minutes were, he admitted, the most anxious of his life. Thankfully, his unexpected command was executed so efficiently that only he and the musicians realised anything untoward had occurred. The music continued without cessation.

When conceiving his programme, Mackenzie-Rogan had imagined massed drums opening with a scarcely audible flutter that would swell to a 'tremendous thunder', then die away, 'so that it might seem there had been a visitation . . . from another world'.[14] On the day of the procession, his innovation created an unforgettably eerie effect. The waves of sound, rolling all along the route, silenced the listening mourners:

Whispers and movement ceased; men seemed turned to stone; tremulous women were in tears. The drums carried their awe-inspiring message into the hearts of us all, musicians as well as the rest. Each time the eighty drums played I observed the same effect; they did their work that day, almost terribly.[15]

Wending its way down Whitehall, where every window was filled, and every rooftop crammed, the cortège at last came in sight of the Palace of Westminster. Lionel Cust could barely contain his relief. With its never-ending lines of pale faces on either side, the walk had seemed to him 'almost intolerable and interminable'.[16] As Big Ben tolled monotonously overhead, the gun-carriage clattered into New Palace Yard to be greeted by guards of honour from the Coldstream Guards and the Royal Marines Light Infantry. Simultaneously, the Union Flag on the Victoria Tower was lowered, and the Royal Standard raised to half-mast. The King personally supervised the removal of the Regalia from the coffin, then assisted his mother from her carriage, and his wife and younger children from the one that followed.

Within the Hall, the members of the Lords and the Commons, their differences temporarily suspended, waited in two separate enclosures. The light streaming through the traceried windows was augmented by candles on free-standing candelabra and electroliers suspended from the fourteenth-century hammerbeam roof. The floor was carpeted with felt, which effectively deadened what little sound there was. At the top of the broad stairs at the South End were assembled the choirs of Westminster Abbey and the Chapels Royal under the baton of Sir Frederick Bridge. Two hundred feet away at the North Door stood officers of the Household Brigade, with the Earl Marshal and the Heralds and Pursuivants in their tabards of red, blue and gold.

Resting on the shoulders of a party of Grenadiers, Edward's coffin was carried in at 12.30 p.m. George, Alexandra and the Dowager Empress came immediately after. Alexandra comported herself with dignity, but Marie was convulsed with sobs beneath her veil. Schomberg McDonnell, who had opted out of the procession in order to direct operations, was not so distracted that he failed to observe that it presented 'the most beautiful and impressive sight imaginable'.[17] After the coffin had been installed on the purple-draped catafalque, and the pall, Standard and Regalia arranged on top, he instructed that the tolling of Big Ben should cease and the North Door be closed. There followed a simple service during which the Archbishop of Canterbury delivered a short address, and the choirs sang 'Blest Are The Departed' and 'O God, Our Help In Ages Past'. It was all, McDonnell considered, 'glorious', the only difficulty arising from the acoustics of the wooden roof, which unduly amplified the musical accompaniment. At the end of the service Alexandra, who, in the words of the Lord Great Chamberlain Lord Carrington, 'scarcely looked forty, so slim and upright and trim',[18] knelt for a moment of silent prayer. Then, as the bands gathered outside struck up Beethoven's Funeral March, the Royal Family and foreign dignitaries slowly departed. By 1 p.m., it was over.

The occasion had been a sad one, but George was delighted with how it had unfolded. That evening, he instructed his Private Secretary, Sir Arthur Bigge, to despatch letters of congratulation to the Duke of Norfolk and the Commissioner of Police, Sir Edward Henry. 'His Majesty feels that nothing could have been better than the quiet dignity of the tribute thus paid to the memory of his beloved father,' Bigge wrote.[19]

With a handful of exceptions, 'quiet dignity' was to be the keynote of the next three days. As soon as the royal mourners had dispersed, McDonnell began to prepare for the public part of the lying-in-state. It was fortunate that he was by nature an authoritarian, for colleagues and onlookers had an infuriating habit of interfering with his well-laid schemes. When the Clerk of the Works took it upon himself to erect an iron railing around the catafalque, McDonnell, who deemed it to be both an eyesore and obstruction, had it swept away. A rogue MP who attempted to force his way into the Hall received similarly short shrift. His incursion and subsequent ejection earned the constable on duty a severe reprimand.

Invited by James Lowther, the Speaker of the House of Commons, for a well-earned lunch, McDonnell was back at his post in time to receive a phalanx of fifty accredited photographers who recorded the scene with their cameras. On the whole, he felt that they comported themselves well. After three-quarters of an hour, they were hustled out to make way for the German ambassador, Count Metternich, who laid a wreath on behalf of the Kaiser. Entirely comprised of feathery orchids, it was so large and unwieldy that three men were required to lift it. Once Metternich had said a solitary prayer of remembrance, the doors were opened at 4 p.m.

The crowds that had gathered outside Buckingham Palace during Edward's final illness and in the immediate aftermath of his death had been drawn by a sense of personal connection they had never enjoyed with his mother. His extreme visibility, combined with his appetite for pleasures the majority of his subjects could understand, even if they couldn't share them, had made him seem both accessible and modern: a suitable monarch for a new century that promised much in the way of change. Edward's lying-in-state was conceived as a thoroughly democratic affair that would transcend religion, social status and political affiliations to invite the active participation of a grieving nation. The people responded magnificently. The first to enter the Hall were three women McDonnell judged to be 'of the seamstress class: very poorly dressed and very reverent'.[20] They were followed by a torrent of nameless mourners who came to bid the King farewell.

On the streets of Westminster and all along the Embankment, the lines snaked for miles. Variable weather had little impact on the numbers. In the rain, thousands of black umbrellas were unfurled. In the interludes of oppressive heat, hawkers sold oranges and local householders sent out their maids to circulate with baskets of cups and buckets of water. Clergymen, shop assistants, domestic servants and military veterans took their places alongside dapper clubmen and fashionable ladies. Teachers brought entire schools of children. From grandparents to babes-in-arms, whole families waited their turn. The pace was brisk; uncomfortably so for the elderly and infirm, who struggled to keep up. Members of St John Ambulance attended to those who fainted. Vigilant policemen dealt firmly with would-be queue-jumpers.

When the Hall was attained at last, the mourners entered through St Stephen's Porch. Pouring down the broad stone steps 'like a waterfall', they divided into two streams that flowed on either side of the coffin. At the upper end of the catafalque were posted four members of the King's Body Guard of Gentlemen at Arms in plumed helmets, their long ceremonial battle-axes reversed. In the middle, facing outward, were two pairs of officers of the Grenadiers, their white-gloved hands resting on their swords. At the foot was a single Gurkha. A little further off, four Yeomen of the Guard stood motionless at each corner. The hush was so profound it struck McDonnell like a physical sensation.

During peak periods, as many as ten thousand people an hour streamed through the Hall, pausing for a few seconds to bow or curtsy when they reached the coffin. For observers who attempted to look upon the scene for any length of time, the effect was almost hypnotic. 'The monotonous movement of the crowd . . . worked its way into the brain,' wrote an awe-inspired correspondent from *The Times*.[21] Exiting via the North Door into New Palace Yard, many mourners craned back, as if to impress the scene upon their memories.

If those who came to the Hall during the day were largely anony-mous, it was at night that the native and foreign dignitaries appeared. An unprecedented number of crowned heads had descended upon London for Edward's funeral, and almost all went to Westminster to pay their respects. At 10.30 p.m. on 17 May, King Alfonso of Spain arrived with his mother-in-law, Princess Beatrice. McDonnell, who was by then exhausted, had to delay his departure until they had gone. The following evening, Queen Mary came alone, to be followed by King Manuel of Portugal and the Portuguese ambassador. Soveral, who had been one of Edward's closest friends, was visibly distraught. Clasping the hand of Lord Carrington, he kept repeating, 'This is too awful.'[22]

It was on the third and final day of the lying-in-state, 19 May, that the eagle-eyed McDonnell was tested to his limit. Nobody doubted that the most important royal mourner of all was the Kaiser. The moment he had heard of Edward's death, Wilhelm had shelved his rampant Anglophobia to reinvent himself as a grief-stricken nephew. He had immediately ordered the Court in Berlin into full mourn-ing. The officers of the Army and the Navy were required to wear mourning for eight days, and all German battleships in home waters were instructed to fire mourning salutes and fly their flags at half-mast.

Sailing into Sheerness on the imperial yacht *Hohenzollern*, Wilhelm made his way to the capital, where he was received in great state by his cousin George at Victoria station. He then drove to Buckingham

Palace to pay his condolences to Queen Alexandra. Just after 3 p.m., the King and the Kaiser arrived together at Westminster Hall. Uncharacteristically self-effacing, Wilhelm charmed McDonnell with his pleasantries. He laid an immense wreath of white and purple flowers on the coffin of the uncle he had so loathed, before clasping hands with George in a theatrical gesture of Anglo-German solidarity that pleased spectators greatly.

That evening, McDonnell dined with the brewing heiress Mrs Ronald Greville, fortifying himself against the exertions still to come. When he returned to the Hall, he found the Prime Minister and his daughter Violet watching the tail-end of the crowds. Asquith had arrived back in England on 9 May, to be briefed on the latest developments by his wife, who always kept her ear to the ground. He had since observed the formalities: calling on King George, who had impressed him with his 'modesty and common sense'; viewing Edward's body with Queen Alexandra; and delivering an eloquent oration to the House of Commons in which he paid tribute to Edward's 'personal charm, the warmth and welcome of his humanity, his unfailing considerateness for all who were permitted to work for him'.[23]

Yet he was not oblivious to the upside of the unexpected turn of events. 'All here seem to think the political crisis indefinitely postponed by the King's death, and that Asquith will be able to potter on now till the end of the year,' Wilfrid Scawen Blunt noted in his diary.[24] It may have been relief, or simply the afterglow of a good dinner, but the Prime Minister's demeanour left something to be desired. He lolled against one of the lamp standards in St Stephen's Porch in an attitude McDonnell considered 'rather offensive'.[25] When they had seen enough, he turned to his daughter and cheerfully remarked, 'Now there are no more surprises to be expected. I think we may go home to bed.' It was, McDonnell felt, quite distasteful. Violet, who worshipped her father, ignored his lapses. To her, the Hall presented 'a most extraordinary & impressive sight'.[26]

Most striking of all had been the sudden arrival of Queen Alexandra, who had appeared just after the doors had been closed at 10 p.m. It was then that the foreign deputations were filing past. With her entrance, the ambassadors and envoys fell back on either side, saluting as she made her way slowly up the Hall on the arm of her brother, King

George of Greece. Gracious as ever, Alexandra paused to exchange a few words with those she recognised. Looking 'quite beautiful and very sorrow-worn,'[27] she knelt for a few moments beside the coffin, then tucked little bunches of lily-of-the-valley all around it. McDonnell was deeply touched by her evident reluctance to take her leave.

If the ceremonies in Westminster elicited an extraordinary response from the general public, it would not be true to claim they affected everybody equally. Inevitably, there were dissenting voices. Beatrice Webb was an activist and social reformer closely involved with the left-wing Fabian Society. Stoked as it was by the popular press, she regarded the wave of emotion that had crashed over Britain with unalloyed contempt. 'London and the country generally is enjoying itself hugely at the royal wake, slobbering over the lying-in-state and the formal procession,' she fumed. 'The ludicrous false sentiment which is being lavished over the somewhat common-place virtues of our late King would turn the stomachs of the most loyal of Fabians.'[28]

Bloomsbury, too, remained largely unmoved. The restlessness that had propelled Virginia Stephen towards the suffrage movement in January, then into the *Dreadnought* hoax the following month, had been the prelude to a bout of mental illness that worried the Bells greatly. They had spirited her away to Dorset in the hope that a change of scene, accompanied by a complete cessation of activity, would do her good. Poised on the brink of temporary insanity, Virginia let Edward's death pass without mention.

Her friends elsewhere *did* mention it, but with a mixture of amusement and *ennui*. Duncan Grant looked forward to watching the funeral procession, which he anticipated would be most divert-ing. Lytton Strachey, on the other hand, found the atmosphere in Cambridge, where the university fellows were required to take part in endless services of remembrance and all the colleges were draped in black, so demoralising that he fled to seek sanctuary with the poet Rupert Brooke at Grantchester. John Maynard Keynes stayed put but confessed that he had 'never been so much bored in my life'. The keepers of the city's boarding-houses were equally disgrun-tled. With the cancellation of the May Balls, an important revenue stream had evaporated. Even in Italy, where E. M. Forster had retreated earlier in the year to finish *Howards End*, the knock-on effects of Edward's death were pronounced. In a letter to his friend Syed Ross Masood, he took aim at the English ladies who flocked to the shops of Florence in search of mourning apparel. 'Masood, I am sick of these formalities,' he wailed. 'They are stifling all the heart out of life. Nothing but gossip & millinery, and all real feeling crushed into the background.'[29]

It was unsurprising that socialists and the intelligentsia should hold themselves aloof. What *was* surprising was the questionable conduct of certain figures – aristocrats, ministers – thoroughly embedded in the circles of power. The night before Edward's funeral, Schomberg McDonnell was supervising the team of workmen and -women who were quietly repairing the wear and tear inevitably sustained by the trappings in Westminster Hall during the passage of hundreds of thousands of mourners. It was so stuffy that he ordered the doors to be left open, lest the officers on guard should faint. To his amazement, he saw a party of four hovering outside, apparently wishing to enter. Accompanied by Maurice Baring of the banking family, and the Honourable Evan Charteris, a younger son of the 10th Earl of Wemyss, the Countess of Essex and Lady Desborough fluttered back and forth. The American-born Lady Essex seemed merely curious; but Lady Desborough, a celebrated hostess who was shortly to be appointed a Lady of the Bedchamber to Queen Mary, was determined to push her luck. 'As civilly as disgust would allow,' McDonnell declined to let them in. With a supplicating smile 'which doubtless would have been effective 20 years ago', Lady Desborough pressed their case. McDonnell stood fast. Eventually, Lord Carrington came storming down the Hall. Scandalised by their effrontery, he ordered them off in no uncertain terms: 'He told them openly that he was ashamed of them . . . and the Queen would be hurt and amazed if she heard of their behaviour.' With that, they slunk away.[30]

It had been an unattractive episode, but worse was to come. With the clock close to 11 p.m., Carrington had gone home and McDonnell was just putting on his cloak when the gates of New Palace Yard were flung open and a caravan of motor-cars puttered through. Out of the first scrambled the Home Secretary, Winston Churchill, and his wife, Clementine. The others disgorged Churchill's mother and stepfather; his brother and sister-in-law; and Captain Hugh Warrender and the 9th Duke of Marlborough. Together, they advanced to the door.

Churchill had made himself quite obnoxious in the days after Edward's death. In one of his first meetings with the new King, he had tactlessly picked up where he had left off with his father, insisting that 'a great change was necessary in the Constitution'. George had icily responded that he was 'averse to violent changes'. Now, on the very eve of Edward's funeral, the Home Secretary insisted on his right to a private viewing of the coffin. McDonnell refused point-blank. Churchill attempted to pull rank. Unwavering, McDonnell retorted that if he were not satisfied, he could go and rouse Carrington, who was asleep in a nearby house, and solicit a second opinion. For several minutes, the two men bickered on the threshold until the Home Secretary, thoroughly bested, flounced off with his relations. It was, the incandescent McDonnell wrote, 'an amazing instance of vulgarity and indecency of which I should not have thought that even Churchill was capable'.[31]

As the cars drove away into the sultry night, the constable on duty thanked McDonnell for his firmness in the face of an encounter that had placed him in an awkward position. McDonnell was touched. It was strange, he reflected, that a humble police officer could be far more of a gentleman than the Home Secretary.

12: 'But alas – he has *gone* – and *no* one can help there'

Even as Schomberg McDonnell kept a close and dictatorial eye on the activities in Westminster Hall, he and his colleagues were finalising arrangements for Edward's funeral on Friday, 20 May. The King had been so closely identified with London, and so popular in the country at large, that the Archbishop of Canterbury had initially proposed burial in Westminster Abbey. A less daring suggestion was the royal mausoleum at Frogmore, where Queen Victoria and Prince Albert were interred. Neither venue appealed to George V, who expressed a preference for St George's Chapel at Windsor. There, his father would be laid to rest among his Plantagenet, Tudor, Stuart and Hanoverian forebears.

In the meantime, the capital filled with crowned heads and envoys from every corner of the globe. Many were related to Edward, and most had met him at some point during his uniquely peripatetic life and reign. Some, such as King Frederick of Denmark, King Haakon of Norway and King George of Greece, travelled to Britain in their capacity as in-laws. Others, like King Albert of the Belgians and Tsar Ferdinand of Bulgaria, came to pay their last respects to a great monarch and an even greater European. Franz Joseph, the Emperor of Austria, who was considered by Charles Hardinge to be 'the dearest and most courteous gentleman that lives'[1], had enjoyed an excellent rapport with Edward. However, at the age of seventy-nine, he was too old to participate in person, and despatched his heir, Archduke Franz Ferdinand, instead.

Judged by Lord Esher to be the 'most genuine'[2] of all the foreign mourners, the unpredictable Kaiser was certainly the most conspicuous. Although his Russian counterpart, Tsar Nicholas, did not attend, several other Romanovs did. While the Dowager Empress consoled her sister in private, her younger son, Grand Duke Michael Alexandrovich, was to ride in the funeral procession along with his distant cousin, Grand Duke Michael Mikhailovich, who was resident in England, and who had lunched with Edward just days before his death.

The Tsar's absence in no way implied a lack of regard for his late uncle or his successor. In a personal letter of condolence to the King, he expressed the sorrow of a cousin as well as a fellow head of state. 'Just a few lines to tell you how *deeply* I feel for you the terrible loss you and England have sustained,' he wrote. 'How I would have liked to come now and be near you!'

Constrained by the perennial issue of security, Nicholas reiterated his commitment to the cause of Anglo–Russian relations:

I beg you, dearest Georgie, to continue our old friendship and to show my country the same interest as your dear Father did from the day he came to the throne. No one did so much in trying to bring our two countries closer together than Him. The first steps have brought good results, let us strive and work in the same direction.[3]

The Russian Foreign Minister Count Isvolsky echoed those sentiments. 'Deeply distressed' in the wake of Edward's death, he lamented the demise of one he called 'the mainstay of our foreign policy'.[4]

As the day of the funeral approached, the number of dignitaries pouring into London became so great the resources, as well as the ingenuity, of the Palace were stretched to the limit. Lionel Cust was seconded to look after one of the lesser royals, Crown Prince Danilo of Montenegro, who erupted onto the scene like a character from a comic opera. From the outset, he was a headache. Rather than arriving by special steamer at the appointed time and place, he slunk in on an ordinary ferry upon which he had embarked in an attempt to evade Tsar Ferdinand, whom he detested. Alighting at Charing Cross station hours behind schedule, he incurred the wrath of Edward's nephew, Prince Arthur of Connaught, who headed his welcoming committee, and whose own schedule was now hopelessly derailed. Worse, it transpired that the Crown Prince was accompanied by one of his wife's ladies-in-waiting. Ostensibly on a shopping expedition, her 'great personal attractions', as Cust coyly put it, left nobody in any doubt as to her real function. London was bursting at the seams, and Danilo's minders were at a loss to know where this surprise guest could be accommodated. Frantic applications having been made at every hostelry in town, she was at last shoehorned in at Claridge's.[5]

After a sultry, storm-tossed night, Friday dawned in a burst of radiant sunshine. The route to be followed by the funeral cortège from Westminster Hall to Paddington station would be considerably longer than that of the procession three days earlier, and a far greater swathe of the city centre was now packed with crowds who had turned out to see it pass. By 6.30 a.m., Piccadilly was 'an apparently inextricable jumble of carriages, cabs, motor-cars, all facing towards Westminster, but moving at a crawling pace, so thick were the opposing streams of humanity flowing in different directions'.[6] In spite of a crush on the pavements so dense the six thousand policemen deployed to keep order were in danger of being overwhelmed, it was noted that the public for the most part behaved with courtesy and consideration.

Lest it offend their neighbours, male onlookers refrained from smoking, and women removed their broad-brimmed hats so as not to obstruct the view of those standing behind.

The unexpectedness of the King's death had meant there had been insufficient time to prepare a co-ordinated scheme of mourning for the streets and public buildings. The *Graphic* saw it as a missed opportunity. 'The lack of a master-hand was painfully conspicuous,' it lamented. 'The mourning decoration of London as a whole was unworthy of the greatness of the occasion.'⁷ In the West End, banks, hotels, department stores and clubs had draped their portals and balconies in black and purple cloth, and even the smallest shops displayed portraits of Edward in their windows. For the rest, the only consistent decorative motifs were the tall masts hung with white and purple banners and topped with gilded crowns that lined the processional route at intervals. These turned out to be convenient repositories for the mourning wreaths of laurel and evergreen that had been sent to the capital from organisations and private individuals across Britain. Combined, the result was, as even the *Graphic* conceded, 'surprisingly effective'. Writing for the *Sketch*, Ella Hepworth Dixon took a different line. In her view, the impression created by so much purple and black was far more impressive than the gaudy red, white and blue of the Union Flags that fluttered on happier occasions. In any case, the budding green leaves of the trees in the parks were, she decided, a happy omen for the new reign.⁸

On Downing Street, Margot Asquith had been up since dawn. Insatiably curious, she sallied forth before breakfast to mingle with the crowds in Whitehall. Sir Edward Henry had advised the Prime Minister not to attempt the short journey to Westminster Hall, lest he get caught in traffic and so miss the train from Paddington that was to carry the funeral party to Windsor. Margot was convinced that this was nonsense, and that there would be ample time to watch the coffin start. After a hurried consultation, it was decided the Asquiths would abandon their motor to hitch a lift to the station with the Archbishop of Canterbury. At 8 a.m., they, with their friends Lord and Lady Crewe, set out on foot in front of serried ranks of soldiers beneath cloudless skies. It was already so hot that Margot's mourning headgear – a black tulle toque with a chiffon veil in front and a longer crêpe veil behind – was stuffy and uncomfortable. She consoled herself with the thought that the overall effect, although 'barbarous', was not unbecoming.[9]

Within, Westminster Hall was cool and shady, but the assembled dignitaries were compelled to await the arrival of the cortège on the red carpet laid outside the North Door in New Palace Yard. The Duke of Norfolk was there, and so were Lord Rosebery, Lord Carrington and the Speaker, James Lowther. Margot kept half an ear on the political small-talk as, one by one, the pieces and bit-players assembled. First came the empty grey gun-carriage, then Edward's charger with his top boots reversed in the stirrups. Last and most pathetic of all was Caesar, who was led by a Highland attendant. Margot reached down to pet the little dog, which frisked cheerfully at her feet.

At 9.30 a.m., the royal procession swept into the Yard. A kaleidoscopic patchwork of plumed helmets and glittering breastplates, of scarlet, blue, green and white tunics festooned with medals, orders and gold braid, it was a sight so dazzling that even seasoned reporters struggled to tell the participants apart. At its head was King George in a general's uniform astride a dark charger. He was flanked by the Kaiser on his right and the Duke of Connaught on his left. Both were dressed as field marshals, batons clasped firmly in their hands. Behind rode the Crown Prince of Romania and the Hereditary Prince of the Ottoman Empire, the Grand Duke of Mecklenburg-Strelitz and the Duke of Aosta, Prince Rupprecht of Bavaria and Prince Bovaradej of Siam, and dozens more besides. It was, wrote Lionel Cust, a veritable 'babel of tongues and clashing hoofs'.[10]

Immediately after the horsemen came the state carriages conveying the female members of the Royal Family. In the first was Queen Alexandra, who was accompanied by the Dowager Empress and her two elder daughters. In the second were Queen Mary and her sister-in-law, the Queen of Norway. As they drew to a halt, the excitable Kaiser leaped to the ground, running to first one door and then to the other in order to assist his aunt down the steps. Not content with providing her with a supporting arm, he planted a fervent kiss on her veiled cheek. Alexandra, who loathed Wilhelm even more than Edward had done, bore his unwonted attentions with good grace. She looked, thought Margot as she sank into a curtsy, 'a vision of beauty'.[11]

The only members of the royal party to go into the Hall for a brief service led by the Archbishop of Canterbury were the King, the Kaiser and the Duke of Connaught, along with Alexandra and Princess Victoria. While it was taking place, the Prime Minister's wife scrutinised the foreign guests, who were drawn up in a vast semi-circle. They were not, she decided, a terribly prepossessing bunch. Archduke Franz Ferdinand appeared to be 'not a very good sort', while King Alfonso of Spain 'with his Hapsburg mouth and unworldly chin looked almost as funny as the K. of Portugal'. Silently, Margot gave thanks that, in England, anarchists went unmolested and violence against public figures was a rarity. Her blood ran cold when she imagined the 'terrifying success' of a bomb dropped onto the assemblage from Big Ben.[12]

Preceded by the Archbishop and a chaplain holding a gold cross aloft, Edward's coffin emerged on the shoulders of a party of Grenadiers. George and his mother watched as it was strapped to the gun-carriage and the pall, Standard and Regalia were arranged on top. When Caesar jumped up against her skirts, Alexandra absent-mindedly fondled his ears. All the while, the foreign royals, who had remained in their saddles, saluted. Then, wheeling around, the great procession, with the coffin at its heart, moved slowly out into Parliament Square. The hush was so complete the only sounds were those of tolling bells and rustling leaves.

From Whitehall, the cortège crossed Horse Guards until it reached The Mall. There, it passed Marlborough House, Edward's home of forty years, before cutting through to St James's Street, where the crowds were estimated to be twenty deep. At Piccadilly, it headed west, entering Hyde Park by Apsley Gate, then proceeded northward along the Drive. As many as three hundred thousand mourners were gathered there alone. Barbed wire had been wound around the trunks of the trees to prevent climbing but, far from acting as a deterrent, it had facilitated the ascent of scores of young men who claimed points of vantage high up in the branches. Their antics had been watched with interest by those on the ground, some of whom had shouted advice and encouragement. When the gun-carriage came into view, all movement ceased, save for the bowing of innumerable heads. It was, wrote William Cornwallis-West to his daughter, Princess Daisy of Pless, one of the most remarkable sights it is possible to imagine. I mean a population of millions mourning its King. The number and demeanour of the masses of human beings in the whole three miles of the funeral Pageant was most amazing – all uncovered and silent – one and all felt they had lost a friend as well as a Sovereign. The effect on the popular mind will do wonders for monarchical institutions and this alone will entitle King Edward to everlasting gratitude.[13]

If the procession as a whole was defined by its dignity and sombre magnificence, individual elements within it were unable to suppress their private grievances. Amid the cavalcade of emperors, kings, princes and grand dukes, only two republics were represented. Edward's affinity with France was so well-known, and his role in the brokering of the Entente Cordiale so legendary, that the French Foreign Minister, Stephen Pichon, had been deputised to represent President Fallières. It was an honour that he rode in the procession at all. Almost all of the other non-royal envoys had proceeded straight to Paddington.

The privilege was lost on Pichon. He was assigned to the eighth carriage, which he shared with the representative of the United States. Former President Theodore Roosevelt had never met Edward in person, but the pair had conducted a mutually appreciative correspondence over several years. Following his departure from the White House in 1909, Roosevelt had been on an epic, months-long safari through east and central Africa. Turning for home, he had intended to rendezvous with the King in London. In the event, he was only in time to attend his funeral.

To Pichon, it was an outrage that France and the United States were placed so far back. Even before they set out, he complained to Roosevelt that they were stuck behind 'ces Chinois', who were of far less consequence globally. The American attempted to laugh him out of his pique by pointing out that the Chinese, in their richly embroidered robes, were so gorgeously attired they deserved to take precedence. The Foreign Minister was not mollified. When he discovered that the third occupant of their carriage was to be the representative of Persia – in Roosevelt's estimation, 'a deprecatory, inoffensive-looking Levantine of Parisian education' – Pichon's indignation boiled over. Jumping into the forward-facing seat on the left, he blocked the adjacent seat with his arm so that Roosevelt could claim it first. Torn between amusement and disgust at this flagrant display of bad manners, the former president took his place, to be followed by the discomfited Persian, who looked 'about as unaggressive as a rabbit in a cage with two boa constrictors'.

Along the way, Pichon moaned without cessation about the fact that they were compelled to trail behind '*toutes ces petites royautés*'. Finally, Roosevelt's patience snapped. Nobody could doubt the prestige of either France or America, he exclaimed, and it was terribly gauche to make such a fuss. Pichon pushed back. Precedence was, he huffed, very important, and he invited Roosevelt to join him when he lodged a formal protest. Roosevelt refused. 'I answered that I very earnestly hoped that he would not make a row at a funeral (my French failed me at this point, and I tried alternately '*funéraille*' and '*pompe funèbre*'), that it would be sure to have a bad effect.' With that, he left the disgruntled minister to stew in his own juices for the remainder of the journey.[14]

As the cortège neared Paddington from one direction, Schomberg McDonnell approached from another. Surprisingly, the procession had failed to move him. Indeed, it had made him 'sick at heart – I cannot bear to see the burial of anyone – even a King – made so much of a spectacle'. When he himself was buried, he resolved that it should be 'very quietly' and with the minimum of fuss.[15]

Hopping into a car with Lord Carrington and Lewis 'Loulou' Harcourt, the Commissioner of Works, McDonnell sped along Birdcage Walk and Buckingham Palace Road, and then through Albert Gate into Hyde Park. As they went, the three men aired their frustration with the Duke of Norfolk's continued mismanagement. Carrington confessed that, in spite of his high office as Lord Great Chamberlain, he had never received an invitation to the actual funeral. McDonnell took advantage of the quiet moment to tell his colleagues about his acrimonious exchange with Winston Churchill the previous night, and to canvass their opinion of his handling of that awkward situation. To his relief, they 'entirely agreed that I was right, and W. Churchill was wrong'.[16]

At Paddington, brilliant sunshine poured through the glass roof onto a red carpet laid along a platform temporarily clear of commuters. The unusual calm was shattered with the arrival of the cortège from Westminster. For several minutes, the concourse was animated with colour and movement as royals, ambassadors, ministers, officers and courtiers milled around in their brilliant uniforms. It was, Margot Asquith thought, rather like the Royal Enclosure at Ascot. Edward's coffin was removed from the gun-carriage and reverently placed on a bier in the same coach that had transported the body of Queen Victoria to her burial nine years earlier. Once it had been safely stowed, the dignitaries took their seats in the ten saloons coupled to a gleaming engine named, appropriately, the *King Edward*. The departure for Windsor was timed for 11.57 a.m. precisely.

Not all of the mourners were to continue on. Among those left behind was Caesar, who, upon Alexandra's orders, had trotted in a place of honour behind the King's horse. Of all the memorable sights that morning, none created a greater or more devastating impression. Since Edward's death, the terrier had been at a loss, refusing to eat as he disconsolately roamed the corridors of Buckingham Palace. His appearance in the procession tore the hearts of the sentimental public. 'Everybody cried when they saw the King's little dog following the coffin,' wrote Vita Sackville-West.[17]

When all the guests had boarded the train, there was a brief pause during which the Dead March from *Saul* was played yet again. Then, right on cue, the engine pulled smoothly out. As it did so, a guard of honour presented arms and gave a final salute. Straining at his lead, Caesar stood on his hind legs, whimpering, until the last carriage had rounded a curve in the tracks and passed out of sight.

Begun in 1475 and completed by 1528, St George's Chapel is, in effect, a miniature cathedral of golden stone nestled snugly within the Lower Ward of Windsor Castle. A fairy-tale edifice of pinnacles, buttresses and traceried windows, it looms large in the history of the monarchy. Edward IV is buried there, and so are Henry VIII and Charles I. In 1820, the remains of Edward's great-grandfather, George III, were interred beside those of his wife, Queen Charlotte, who had died two years earlier. In due course, they were joined by their sons, George IV and William IV. Elaborately carved wooden stalls line each side of the Quire, while hoisted high above are serried ranks of heraldic banners that ripple beneath the fan-vaulted roof. St George's is the Chapel of the Order of the Garter, the most venerable order of chivalry in Great Britain, and each Garter Knight is entitled to display his crest and colours there during his lifetime. 'None of our Kings, perhaps,' *The Times* observed, 'was more alive to the dignity and values, even under the changed conditions of modern life, of such associations and their external signs, than King Edward VII; and none set more store than he did by the grandeur and antiquity of this most august brotherhood.'[18]

When the Prince of Wales had married Princess Alexandra of Denmark in St George's in March 1863, the arrangements had been faultless. 'There was no crowding,' Lord Clarendon had written approvingly, 'everybody was in his or her allotted place & not scrambling, as is usual in Engd. [England] on such occasions, for something they ought not to get.'[19] Forty-seven years later, the meticulousness that had defined Edward's wedding was not to define his funeral. The fumbling of the Duke of Norfolk threatened to turn the climactic moment of the obsequies into a fiasco.

Having travelled to Windsor by train with the Crewes and Sir Edward Grey, the Asquiths proceeded straight to the Castle where they lingered in the cloisters, admiring the wreaths that carpeted the pavements and lawns. Then, seeing the other mourners enter the Chapel, they drifted indoors to be greeted by a scene of barely controlled chaos. There was no seating plan, and nobody had any idea where the various dignitaries were to be placed. As Prime Minister, Asquith was fortunate to be allocated one of the best stalls in the Quire. Margot slipped into the same row, where she rubbed shoulders with Queen Alexandra's Mistress of the Robes, the Duchess of Buccleuch, and other senior peeresses. From that vantage, she watched with amazement as the Heralds, who worked under Norfolk, assigned and reassigned the rest of the congregation. The Knights of the Garter, along with Arthur Balfour and the members of the Opposition, were pushed and shoved in the most undignified manner. Immense charts were unfurled and pored over, but they proved to be of little use as verbal instructions were issued and almost immediately countermanded. Dashing backwards and forwards 'in an *Alice in Wonderland* way', the blundering Heralds appeared to be as clueless as those they were attempting to direct. The result was a shambles:

'a mere mosaic of indecision,' as Margot described it in her diary. 'Either the Earl Marshal has no staff or no brain.'[20]

As the music-less wait spilled over into its second hour, the guests sweltered. At first, the ladies kept their faces covered. When at last the heat became intolerable, they threw back their veils for a breath of air. In the 'curiously stupefying' atmosphere, it was difficult to remain awake. Margot rested her elbows on the sides of her stall and nodded off with her head on her clasped hands. She therefore missed the most interesting arrival of all: that of Mrs Keppel, whose discreet entry by a side door had been arranged by Schomberg McDonnell. George V did not look with favour on his father's mistress, but he was not about to bar her from his funeral.

At 12.30 p.m., the bell in the Curfew Tower of the Castle began to toll as a sign that the train carrying Edward's remains was crossing the bridge over the river. Minutes later, its doleful sound was taken up by a second bell in the Round Tower. Removed from the Church of the Twelve Apostles at Sebastopol after the Crimean War, it was only ever rung upon the death of the sovereign. In the Great Park, guns thundered as the final spectators hurried into place along the Long Walk. Those who clustered around the base of the equestrian statue of George III were compelled to use binoculars if they wished to see anything at all.

Necessarily on a smaller scale than that in London, the procession through the streets of Windsor was, in its way, equally memorable. At the funeral of Queen Victoria, the gun-carriage bearing her coffin had been rendered immobile when the horses' harness had snapped. At the suggestion of Prince Louis of Battenberg, ratings from the naval guard of honour had been ordered into the traces. In that moment of improvisation, a royal tradition was born. It was a team of straw-hatted 'bluejackets' who hauled Edward's coffin up the hill to the Castle as the King, the Kaiser and the other crowned heads followed on foot. Then came Queen Alexandra and the Dowager Empress in a closed carriage, and after them the princes, ambassadors and envoys. Bringing up the rear were Queen Mary and the rest of the royal ladies.

At the West Door of St George's, the cortège was greeted by the archbishops of Canterbury and York. As the massed bands that had accompanied the procession from the station fell silent, the only sounds were those of boatswains' whistles. 'As wild and weird as a seabird's plaint', they signalled the arrival of the gun-carriage at the foot of the broad stone steps.[21]

Within the Chapel, Edward's coffin was carried down the aisle to be laid before the altar. All eyes were fixed on Alexandra, who, in defiance of protocol, followed on the arm of the King. Stately and erect in her black gown and flowing veil, the blue sash of the Garter across her breast, she lent what Margot Asquith called a 'thrilling touch of beauty & pathos' to what had, until then, been a fairly shambolic scene. Throughout her married life, Alexandra's inexhaustible appeal to the hearts and imaginations of the British people had inspired love, and even adulation. Her last moments with her husband of almost half a century were to be her apotheosis. 'She has the finest carriage and walks better than any one of our time,' marvelled Margot, '& not only has grace, charm and real beauty, but all the atmosphere of a fascinating female queen for whom men & women die.'[22]

Faultlessly intoned by Archbishop Davidson, the ancient words of the Anglican Service for the Burial of the Dead echoed in the recesses of the hushed church. As the choir sang Handel's Funeral Anthem and the coffin began its descent into the Royal Vault, Alexandra dropped to her knees on her prie-dieu, her face hidden in her hands. There were stifled sobs along the Quire as the onlookers dissolved into sympathetic tears.

Moving to the foot of the grave, Sir Alfred Scott-Gatty, Garter Principal King of Arms, proclaimed the death of 'the Most High, Most Mighty, and Most Excellent Monarch Edward' and beseeched God to bestow 'long life, health, honour and all worldly happiness' on his successor, George. There was a final hymn, 'Now the Labourer's Task Is O'er', and the Archbishop pronounced a benediction. With that, *The Times* correspondent wrote, 'King Edward was at rest.'

To the strains of an organ recital by Sir Walter Parratt, the congregation quietly dispersed. For those who wanted it – and it turned out many did – lunch was served in the Waterloo Chamber at the Castle. Amid the throng, Schomberg McDonnell spied the hunched and scowling figure of the Home Secretary. Bolstered by the approval of his colleagues, he admonished him for his behaviour on the threshold of Westminster Hall the night before. Unabashed and unapologetic, Churchill insisted that he had had every right to be there. No, McDonnell retorted, he had had no right at all. Flabbergasted by such pugnacity, his opinion of Churchill sank lower than ever. 'Pity that success and promotion should have made him a ruffian,' he observed in disgust.[23]

As Queen Alexandra received her special guests in the Green Drawing Room, the King entertained his fellow crowned heads in the adjacent White Drawing Room. Even in 1910, it was rare to find so many reigning monarchs in one place, and the firm of W. & D. Downey had supplied a photographer to record the gathering for posterity. The resulting image has come to define not only the occasion and year, but an entire world order soon to be decimated by war and revolution.

Stiffly settled in a gilded armchair, George was flanked by his cousin-by-marriage, Alfonso of Spain, and his maternal uncle, Frederick of Denmark. Planted firmly behind his host was the Kaiser, with Haakon of Norway, Ferdinand of Bulgaria and Manuel of Portugal to his right and George of Greece and Albert of Belgium to his left. It was apparent that this was no mere family reunion. It was, in the words of Lionel Cust, 'the mustering of a profession'.[24]

As the representative of the ascendant superpower over the Atlantic, Theodore Roosevelt was button-holed by first one and then another of the kings and princes during his sojourn in London. A proud American who had little patience with questions of rank and protocol, he was underwhelmed by his exposure to the insular but backbiting royal fraternity. In a perceptive letter home, he summarised the impression it had made upon him:

In a way, although the comparison sounds odd, these sovereigns, in their relations among themselves and with others, reminded me of the officers and wives in one of our western army posts in the old days, when they were all shut up together and away from the rest of the world, were sundered by an impassable gulf from the enlisted men and the few scouts, hunters and settlers round about, and were knit together into one social whole, and nevertheless were riven asunder by bitter jealousies, rivalries and dislikes.[25]

It came as a relief to the former president when, in early June, he was able to escape the hothouse atmosphere of Europe to return to the fresh air and relative informality of the United States.

Roosevelt was not the only guest to set down his thoughts in writing. In the flurry of letters sent and received in the aftermath of Edward's funeral, a host of conflicting viewpoints emerged. The Dowager Empress missed her brother-in-law acutely. 'It is so unspeakably sad here now,' she told the Tsar. 'His absence is so deeply felt everywhere.'[26]

To Lord Esher, George V confessed that the final ceremony in St George's Chapel had been a 'terrible ordeal' during which he had struggled not to break down. He pledged to live up to his father's legacy: 'I know that God will give me strength to try to follow in his footsteps & to do my duty & to work for the welfare of my people & this great Empire.' He concluded by thanking Esher for all that he had done to make the funeral 'so perfect & so beautiful'.[27]

It was not an assessment Sir John Fortescue, the librarian at Windsor Castle, shared. Margot Asquith wrote to him in the hope he would be able to supply her with a copy of the Order of Service. In his reply, Fortescue's contempt dripped off the page. 'They were provided by the Earl Marshal's people who, as usual, made a mess of things & supplied not nearly copies enough to go round,' he fumed. 'I do not know whether you could obtain what you want by application to one or other of the Heralds. Personally, I would rather kick them than ask favours of them after their miserable mismanagement.'[28]

Perhaps the saddest letter of all was penned by Princess Victoria to the Countess of Derby. Demanding at the best of times, Alexandra had leaned heavily on her daughter in their bereavement. Victoria had supported her heroically through a harrowing sequence of events: the sickroom, the deathbed, the interminable religious services, the lyings-in-state at Buckingham Palace and Westminster Hall, the public processions through London and Windsor and the burial in St George's Chapel. Physically ailing and emotionally wrung-out, she faced an uncertain future as the unmarried and middle-aged sister of the King.

In a short but anguished note to her old friend, Victoria vented some of the misery she had suppressed for a fortnight:

My dearest Starling,

God bless you for your cheer.

Oh! It was an awful moment when he was taken out of the House.

I have been feeling wretched and the cough is cruel, shaking one to pieces.

Yes, indeed, the true sympathy and love (of some) does help one. But alas — he has <u>gone</u> — and <u>no</u> one can help there.

God bless you.

V[29]

13: 'I was looking for you everywhere, but, of course, it was quite impossible to find you'

A few weeks after Edward's funeral, Lord Esher dined at the Marlborough Club with Francis Knollys and the Marquis de Soveral. It was obvious that they, like him, were profoundly disoriented. 'At any rate to us, the King's death has made a great difference,' Esher wrote. 'And yet many of those to whom he was kindest seem only to be trying to find excuses for resuming at once their normal life of pleasure.'[1]

In truth, even the most heedless sybarites were struggling to adapt to the changed conditions of the new reign. The 'curious electric element' that had made the Edwardian Court the most dazzling in Europe had been supplanted by an atmosphere Esher described as 'very charming and wholesome and sweet'.[2] Gruff and undemonstrative, George V nevertheless derived comfort from the proximity of his immediate family. Devoted to his wife, he couldn't bear to spend time away from her. At lunch, the royal children romped around the table. At dinner, their governess was seated beside the King. Afterwards, Queen Mary knitted while a handful of guests made stilted conversation. Everybody retired at 10 p.m. The late-night bridge parties enlivened by the bright chatter of Mrs Arthur James were clearly a thing of the past.

So were the days of 'unknown Americans, of the *nouveaux riches*, and of the Hebrew persuasion', observed the *Tatler*, snobbishly.[3] Under the open-minded Edward, the perimeters of Society had been rolled back to accommodate his insatiable appetite for amusement. Now the arrivistes found themselves on the wrong side of the impenetrable 'wall of steel' surrounding the sovereign and his famously reserved consort. From hence, preference was to be given to representatives of the 'old families' of the British aristocracy, who prized lineage, dignity and discretion over wealth, wit and glamour. The shift was not lost on Max Beerbohm, who drew a group of Jewish financiers – among them Alfred and Leopold de Rothschild, Arthur Sassoon and Sir Ernest Cassel – creeping nervously along a corridor at Buckingham Palace. The caption read, 'Are we as welcome as ever?' Unwritten but tacitly acknowledged, the answer was 'No'.

At first, there had been apprehensions that George would dispense with the stud at Sandringham and the stables at Newmarket where the royal racehorses were trained. When, on 24 May, it was announced that both were to be retained, the *Sporting Life* called it 'an inexpressible relief to those of us who recognise what an important factor is the Turf to the prosperity of the Nation'. More than that: it was a welcome symbol of continuity between the reign that was over and the one that was just beginning. 'It is not too much to say that King George's decision to follow in the footsteps of his lamented father confers upon the Turf a new lease of life,' the paper crowed. 'The King is dead. Long live the King!'[4]

Viscount Churchill, the King's Representative at Ascot, had already informed the press that the annual race meeting would proceed that year as usual. 'The Royal Pavilion will be closed,' he said, 'but the other portions of the Royal Enclosure will be open. Ladies and gentlemen attending should wear mourning.'[5] As May turned to June, Society had one final tribute up its sleeve. Far from being forgotten, Edward was to be honoured with the most idiosyncratic act of remembrance of the twentieth century.

From the outset, the connection between Ascot and the Crown was symbiotic. The inaugural meeting had taken place in 1711, when it was attended by Queen Anne and a party of courtiers from nearby Windsor Castle. After a slow start, the fortunes of the new course improved in the second half of the eighteenth century as English racing entered a golden age. Revived between 1750 and 1753, the Jockey Club gradually developed into the sport's presiding authority. Racing calendars were published, racing colours were introduced, and the Derby was first run in 1780. By the Regency, Ascot had assumed the character of a country holiday for the urban elite at the height of the summer Season.

Following his accession in 1820, George IV, a lifelong devotee of the Turf, commanded John Nash to construct a new stand in the neoclassical style for the use of his invited guests. Surrounded by railings, its trim lawn was the first iteration of what would become the Royal Enclosure. Ever the showman, it was George who launched another Ascot tradition: the grand carriage procession up the course. Where royalty led, Society inevitably followed. 'Ascot may be deemed the rallying point for all the nobility and gentry . . . to pay homage to their beloved monarch,' wrote the journalist Pierce Egan in 1832.[6]

First as Prince of Wales, and then as King, Edward was the most celebrated royal race-goer of all. Making his first appearance at Ascot in 1863, his patronage boosted its fortunes to unprecedented heights. Indeed, his much-vaunted love of racing was to be an important factor in the phenomenal popularity he would eventually enjoy. In his passion for the Turf, the 'typical Englishman' could see himself reflected, the *Evening Mail* explained, and it earned him a reputation 'which cannot be fully attained except by one who shows himself to be in sympathy with that love of sport which is almost a passion with all ranks and classes in this country'.[7] The racecourses of the Victorian and Edwardian eras were at once intensely hierarchical and pleasingly egalitarian. On them, wrote one observer, the common labourer was bound 'with cap-touching loyalty to the aristocrat. There were those who would only back King Edward's, Lord Derby's or Lord Rosebery's horses. In winning, they felt for a brief moment a glow of unity with the greatest in the land.'[8]

During her long widowhood, Queen Victoria lost no opportunity to remonstrate with her son over his enthusiasm for racing. It made no difference, either to him or to those who blithely followed his lead. *Sui generis* in terms of elegance, Ascot became the Season's most unmissable fixture. Nearby country houses were hired at exorbitant rates, and hostesses convened parties that descended in fleets of varnished carriages. There were lavish luncheons in the marquees pitched by the smartest regiments and clubs: the Guards, the Cavalry and the Royal Artillery, as well as White's, the Bachelors' and the Grosvenor. Vast sums were expended on new toilettes, and social fortunes were made by those who, like the young Margot Tennant, caught Edward's approving eye. Not everybody relished the meeting's fabled extravagance. Racing, Arthur Ponsonby fulminated, 'degrades many who take part in it with sinister rapidity, it encourages fraud and deception, it is a canker of rottenness in public life, and it receives the highest sanction and patronage'.[9] But most, like Princess Daisy of Pless, found it delightful. At Ascot, she observed, 'One sees the racing in the most comfortable way, meets all one's friends (and enemies), makes – or loses – a little money, and all without any fatigue or bother.'[10]

Unable to attend Ascot in the first two years of his reign owing to mourning for his mother, and then to the bout of ill-health that led to the postponement of his Coronation, Edward never missed a meeting thereafter. 'The stimulus he gave to the social side was like unto a great awakening indeed,' wrote the *Tatler*.[11] Not even a steep hike in the cost of vouchers to the Royal Enclosure – from a pound in 1902 to four pounds in 1903 – could deter those who clamoured for entry. About the only wild card in what had become a pageant of opulence and exclusivity was the weather. In 1906, it was glorious from start to finish. In 1908, the opening day was bad, and the second was atrocious, with a sea of mud underfoot, and torrential rain ruining scores of feathered hats.

Even in the first week of May, there had been fears the Season of 1910 would be a flop. Edward's death introduced a potentially fatal element into an already dismal prospect. The observance of Court mourning necessitated the cancellation of innumerable functions. The social lives of the King and Queen were suspended for the duration, and so were those of their relations and Households. Those who, strictly speaking, were not compelled to go into mourning did so in a spirit of sympathy and solidarity.

For the more reluctant debutantes, it came as a relief. 'The death of the King saved me many festivities,' recalled Vita Sackville-West.[12] For those who depended on the activities of Society for their livelihoods – caterers, florists, musicians, waiters – it was a calamity. Mindful of the boredom inflicted on those at the top of the ladder, and of the economic distress of those lower down, George V requested the Earl Marshal to let it be known that, outside the circles immediately affected, a degree of discretion could be exercised. 'Quite well he knows that his people mourn,' wrote the *Sketch*, 'but he does not wish them to suffer. While as a matter of feeling we are in mourning, that mourning is not to be either dull or dowdy.'[13] Balls, concerts and 'other flamboyant entertainments' were prohibited, but, after a month or so of enforced inactivity, the younger members of the upper classes could attend 'their little dinners and theatre parties, their restaurant suppers and steam-launch outings, all the milder forms of amusement which can be indulged in without unseemliness'.[14]

Then there was Ascot. The fact that, as early as 10 May, George had instructed his Representative that the meeting should take place as planned was indicative of its importance. He would not attend, and the Royal Pavilion would, as Lord Churchill made clear, be closed. On the other hand, it would be business as usual in the Royal Enclosure. Society could look forward to the first large-scale social event in weeks.

The crucial proviso pertained to the dress code. After Edward's death, two separate but overlapping periods of mourning had been decreed. The first, to be observed for a calendar year, was Court mourning, which applied to the Royal Family and those in attendance upon it. The second, lasting for eight weeks, was general mourning, which was due to expire on 30 June. At Court, full mourning of unrelieved black would abate to half mourning on 7 November, after which white, grey and various shades of purple would be acceptable.

Those frequenting the Royal Enclosure were bound by the dictates of general mourning, with a similar transition occurring on Friday, 17 June. It would therefore be a 'Black Ascot'.

Such an event was not without precedent. In 1880, the death of the Empress of Russia had necessitated the wearing of mourning. In 1896, there was no carriage procession because Prince Henry of Battenberg had passed away that January. The Ascot of 1901 had occurred six months after the death of Queen Victoria. Moderate mourning had been observed on the course, with ladies appearing in sombre tones of lavender and mauve on the third and fourth days. But Victoria herself had not attended the meeting for decades and, in any case, the weather had been bad and the war in South Africa had cast a further pall of gloom.

Nine years on, the situation was quite different. Britain was at peace. After its unsettled start, the summer was proving to be fine, dry and warm. Poised to emerge from the first flush of grief, Society was about to pick up where it had left off in early May. Before it did so, it would pay homage to the memory of a monarch who had symbolised an entire era, in a setting he had known well and loved dearly. Black Ascot was to be a farewell from the elite as surely as the lying-in-state in Westminster Hall had been a farewell from the masses.

Superintending the proceedings was Victor Spencer, 1st Viscount Churchill. A member of Edward's innermost circle, he was thoroughly embedded in the ranks of the aristocracy. Descended from the 4th Duke of Marlborough, he was in many ways the *beau idéal* of the English gentleman: a casual Anglican, a committed Tory and a passionate rider to hounds. A godson of Queen Victoria, he was proudly unintellectual, and often claimed he never read a book.

Yet Churchill was no dolt. Unlike many of his peers, he had an impressive head for business, serving as Chairman of the Great Western Railway, President of the Overseas Bank and a director of the Peninsular & Orient steamship company. Outwardly self-assured, he ruthlessly divested himself of his ancestral estates, 'breaking away from Victorian stuffiness to lead an up-to-date fox-hunting life in Leicestershire with plenty of loose cash available'.[15] Forty-five years old, he was the product, his son believed, of an era in which 'the Englishman's tweeds had become a sort of contemporary version of the toga of ancient Rome, and a five-pound note was the best pass-port in any country'.[16]

When, at the time of his accession, Edward had abolished the ancient post of Master of the Buckhounds, Churchill, who had been its last incumbent, assumed the mantle of His Majesty's Representative at Ascot. It was his responsibility to assign vouchers for admission to the Royal Enclosure. Entry having been capped at 1,200, competition was fierce. Applications had to be submitted by a certain date, with no guarantee they would be successful. It was forbidden to transfer vouchers once allocated, and legal action was brought against those who attempted to sell them on the black market.

Divorced persons were not eligible for presentation at Court, and they were therefore barred from the Royal Enclosure as well. Under Churchill, the rule was rigorously enforced. He instituted a system whereby the partners of Withers & Co., the firm of London solici-tors, were invited to check the list of applications for the Enclosure against the Divorce Lists for each term. The practice was justified on the grounds that it was necessary 'to see that only those persons shall be admitted to whom objection could not be taken by His Majesty'.[17] Ironically, Churchill's own record was not unblemished. In 1909, his eccentric wife Verena had bolted from home, taking their three children with her. The family lawyer posted an anony-mous advertisement, offering a reward for information pertaining to their whereabouts. Word leaked out and the press took up the story. Averse to scandal, Edward had staged an intervention. In accordance with his wishes, the miserable marriage was preserved for the time being.

In 1910, the race-goers assembled in the Royal Enclosure personi-fied the composition and values of an elite forged over the course of the previous half-century. Rumours had circulated beforehand that the meeting would be a damp squib. It was said that almost a thou-sand vouchers had been sent back by those who had decided not to attend. Whatever truth there was in those reports, it turned out to have been exaggerated. While it was noted that on opening day, Tuesday, 14 June, attendance was sparse, it was only by comparison with former years, when it had been felt that the Enclosure had been uncomfortably crowded. 'It does not appear that there was any less general letting of the surrounding houses,' wrote the *Queen*. 'Indeed, there seems to have been a special demand for these, especially any situated on or close to the river.'[18]

Churchill prided himself on his ability to know the name and face of every man and woman in the Enclosure, and he would demand proof of identity from anybody he failed to recognise. The rigour he brought to the vetting process meant there was little danger of embarrassing encounters. Titled, landed and influential, the aristocracy was out in force. The 9th Duke of Devonshire, who presided over vast estates from his ancestral seat of Chatsworth, and the 4th Marquess of Cholmondeley, who until recently had served as Lord Great Chamberlain, were there, and so was the Marchioness of Londonderry, who was one of Society's most formidable political hostesses. Edward's approval had ensured the assimilation of the Dollar Princesses, and they too were well-represented. The former Cornelia Martin, now Countess of Craven, and the former Adele Grant, now Countess of Essex, were among the most conspicuous.

For some, the interest of Ascot lay firmly in the racing. Mrs Arthur James was one, and the Earl of Coventry was another. Scrutinising the course most closely was the former Prime Minister and three-times Derby winner Lord Rosebery, who shepherded a party in which blue blood and new money were seamlessly blended. Among his guests were the Arthur Sassoons and the Leopold de Rothschilds. Rosebery's connection with the latter was more than merely social. His late wife, Hannah, had been a Rothschild heiress. The vast fortune she had brought to their marriage in 1878 had left her grief-stricken widower a very rich man, effectively quashing whatever reservations the stuffier members of the aristocracy harboured over its Jewish origins. All four of Rosebery's children were with him at Ascot. His first daughter, Sybil, was married to Charles Grant, a distinguished army officer, while his second, Peggy, was the wife of the 1st Earl of Crewe, the Liberal leader of the House of Lords. His heir, Lord Dalmeny, had wed a granddaughter of the 1st Duke of Westminster in 1909.

Rosebery surely exchanged tips with the Countess of Derby, who was piloting her teenage daughter around the Enclosure. Lady Victoria Stanley was one of the debutantes whose first Season had been blighted by Edward's death. Her coming-out ball, which was to have been attended by the King and Queen, had been among the first to be cancelled. To many girls, it would have been a tragedy. To Victoria, it was more important that Ascot had gone ahead. No clan was more closely identified with English racing than the Stanleys. The 12th Earl of Derby had been instrumental in founding the race that bore his name. A century later, the 16th Earl had established a stud that would, under the auspices of his son, become one of the most successful in the world. It was to Victoria's father, one of his closest friends, that George V let the royal horses during the year of Court mourning for Edward VII.

From childhood, Victoria's devotion to the family sport was obvious. A passionate equestrienne, she filled her letters to her parents with tales of the exploits of her ponies. When, in 1899, she sat for John Singer Sargent, he painted her in a scarlet blazer reminiscent of a hunting coat, a riding crop clasped between her hands. In the event her small-talk failed her at Ascot, she could fall back, with precocious authority, on the form of the day's runners. On that subject, she could certainly hold the attention of Rosebery's younger son, the Honourable Neil Primrose. A rising star in the Liberal ranks, he had entered Parliament as the Member for Wisbech that January. Into Westminster, he carried an air of aristocratic insouciance, electioneering in tweeds and peppering his speeches with the idiom of the Turf. 'Politics is the most exciting game I have ever played,' he declared. 'It's fine sport as long as you keep your temper.'[19] Such flippant remarks masked considerable ability. Before she had left London for her Mediterranean cruise that spring, Queen Alexandra had done what no queen consort had done before when she visited the Commons to hear Primrose speak in favour of the motion to limit the power of the Lords.

Inevitably, the shadow of the conflict between the Houses hung heavy over an event where so many members of the ruling class were gathered. Those on opposing sides who wished to remain civil avoided the subject, concentrating instead on their immediate surroundings. On opening day, and on the three days that followed, Ascot had never looked lovelier. Refreshed by recent rain, the Heath rolled away to meet the yellow gorse and green treetops of Windsor Forest. Within the palings of the course, smooth lawns were studded with flowerbeds in which vivid rhododendrons rioted. Along so-called 'Luncheon Avenue', club marquees were festooned with geraniums and potted palms. Spilling out onto the grass beyond the gaily striped awnings, tables covered with crisp napery invited members to take their ease. The menu provided by the Marlborough Club, of which Edward had been a founder, was particularly extensive, and its cold curry and pigeon pie were voted 'fit for a king'.[20] Under the baton of Lieutenant George Miller, the band of the Portsmouth Division of the Royal Marines played for hours on end.

Wafting through the warm summer air, the popular melodies suited the theatrical aspect of the Royal Enclosure. Built of brick and wood, its viewing stand contained three tiers of seating. In the centre of the lowest level was a glazed loge from which descended a pair of curved staircases with elaborate wrought-iron balustrades. At the front, an open-air platform bore the Royal Cypher beneath a gilded crown. It was from this stage-like eyrie that Edward, Ascot's undisputed leading man, had surveyed his friends and acquaintances as they promenaded below.

Now the platform was vacant and the box shuttered. Trellised screens festooned with pink rambling roses had been erected, but they were hardly necessary to keep interlopers at bay. Governed by respect, or perhaps by superstition, race-goers kept as far away as possible, averting their eyes from what had, in former years, been even more of a cynosure than the finishing post.

On Monday, 13 June, Lord Churchill had issued a stern reminder that clothing of unrelieved black would be mandatory in the Royal Enclosure. For men, that entailed only minor modifications. During the nineteenth century, colour had drained away from the male wardrobe. Quality of materials and perfection of cut, the latter ensured by the expertise of the world-renowned tailors of Savile Row, conspired to create an appearance of immaculate but unobtrusive sobriety. In spite of his best efforts, Edward had been unable to arrest the decline of the traditional frock coat. That year, the majority of race-goers donned morning coats of black barathea, hopsack, or fine feather-weave worsted, which were, on younger and slimmer physiques at least, more flattering. Striped trousers were sported by some, but most wore black ones to match their black ties and single-breasted black waistcoats. The only relief came from the ubiquitous white shirts to which stiff collars were attached with tiny studs. Whether turndown or wing – both styles were deemed 'correct' – they were, without exception, starched to cracking point.

If gentlemen aspired to tasteful uniformity, ladies were encouraged, and indeed required, to display elegant individuality. At Ascot, Lady Duff Gordon explained, 'The most perfect types of the modes are worn, and here fashions are made positive instead of merely tentative; they are set, as it were, and of course it is a momentous time for fashionable women.'[21]

By 1910, the serpentine 'S-bend' or 'pouter pigeon' silhouette in vogue for much of Edward's reign had gone the way of the leg-of-mutton sleeves of the 1890s. From 1907, sweeping draperies had narrowed season by season until the notoriously restrictive 'tube' or 'hobble' skirt emerged. The press had a field day, filling its pages with caricatures of women unable to mount kerbs or board buses. The trend was so debilitating that even style reporters lost patience. Derided as 'truly ridiculous', the hobble skirts at Ascot gave rise to hilarity and outrage as their wearers teetered around the Enclosure. 'The whole breadth round the ankle (for these absurd frocks never went further) might be measured by inches instead of by yards, or even feet!' scoffed the correspondent of the *Queen*.[22]

Sensible race-goers eschewed such extremes. Edward's death having temporarily effaced every trace of colour, modistes had to resort to other means to introduce variety into their creations. With a branch of Lucile Ltd newly established in New York, Lady Duff Gordon had been promoting Ascot gowns made of textiles woven in American mills to the readers of the papers to which she contributed columns. It had been her intention that her designs should be executed in a floral palette of pinks, blues and mauves. Now that that was out of the question, she reassured clients that 'the present styles lend themselves most gracefully to mourning costumes' owing to the pliancy of their fabrics.[23] The supple laces and chiffons she advocated imbued countless ensembles with what was approvingly described as 'a lightness and indescribably cool finish'.[24] Considerable mileage was derived from filmy silk voile, but there was an abundance of ninon de soie, mousseline de soie, charmeuse and foulard too. 'One realised how exceedingly pretty and tasteful black can be made to look if used properly, and not too, too conscientiously,' marvelled the *Bystander*. 'So long as the outer material is black, it matters not how gossamer-like its transparency – and that is the whole point about it.'[25]

For both sexes, gloves were essential. The London Glove Company of New Bond Street and Cheapside had advertised 'gloves for national mourning' throughout May and June. Before Ascot, there had been a run on twenty-button gloves of black suede, which encased ladies' forearms from wrist to elbow. It had been thought the transition to half-mourning might see gentlemen exchange their black gloves for dark grey ones on the final day of the meeting, but the hope proved to be forlorn. 'I say, this is the Ascot of the black hand!' a veteran clubman dolefully remarked.[26]

No such regret accompanied the pretext afforded by Ascot for the wearing of an astounding quantity of jewels. Wealthy Edwardians were passionate about pearls, which, as luck would have it, were considered appropriate ornaments for periods of bereavement. The Duchess of Beaufort was festooned with ropes of them, while the Duchess of Newcastle tied her 'cable' necklace like a cravat. The Duchess of Roxburghe, one of the richest of the Dollar Princesses, sported pearls described simply as 'superb'. Alternatively, fresh flowers could be worn in lieu of gems. The Countess of Londesborough relieved her black crêpe-de-Chine with white carnations. Greatly daring, the Marchioness of Zetland tucked a corsage of mauve carnations into her bodice.

More than anything, it was the display of spectacular headgear that fascinated observers. No garment signified status more thoroughly than the top hat. To H. G. Wells, the acquisition of his first topper had signalled a definite step on his upward climb through the ranks of society. It was, he believed, 'the symbol of complete practical submission to a whole world of social conventions'.[27] At Ascot, a burnished black silk hat with a mourning band was an indispensable attribute of every gentleman in the Royal Enclosure, setting him apart from the straw-boatered hoi polloi beyond.

Ladies relied on the talents of their milliners even more than those of their couturiers. That summer, rumours were circulating that small hats were about to come in. For now, they were the exception to the well-dressed rule. Lady Crewe was one of the few who opted for a natty little toque of looped tulle.

Clementine Churchill, whom Edward had greatly liked, was progressive in a 'high-brimmed turban with gossamer garniture poised on the crown towards the back'.[28] The Home Secretary's wife was always experimental, and her look was judged by the cognoscenti to be 'more wonderful than beautiful'.[29]

The Marchioness Camden, in a shoulder-wide cartwheel ringed with black ostrich plumes, was more typical. Three years earlier, Lady Duff Gordon had dressed the London production of Franz Lehár's operetta *The Merry Widow*. Its success was unprecedented – an enchanted Lord Esher saw it at least twenty times – and its impact on fashion was profound. The black hat Lucile Ltd designed for the show's star, Lily Elsie, sparked a trend that enjoyed remarkable longevity. 'Every woman who wanted to be in the swim had to have a "*Merry Widow*" hat,' Lady Duff Gordon recalled, 'and we made thousands of pounds through the craze.'[30] By its very nature suited to mourning, the model was endlessly amplified and reinterpreted. As if to compensate for the newly narrow skirts, headgear mushroomed. Changed each day, the hats at Ascot were what one paper described as 'marvels of eccentricity and variety . . . Dolly Varden bonnets, flat discs of leghorn or Rajahs' turbans of black tulle filled with paradise plumage, egrets' tails or dyed peacocks' feathers'. Bucking the avian trend, one woman opted for a 'Bacchante's wreath of black grapes and leaves' instead.[31]

Before 1910, black had rarely been associated with high style. Thanks to that year's Ascot, its potential began to be realised. Far from submerging its wearers in a faceless mass, the obligatory black – chic, svelte, dramatic – had, paradoxically, a liberating effect. The correspondent of the *Bystander* was ecstatic. Black Ascot was, he believed, 'the Englishwoman's charter of emancipation from the belief that her beauty owes aught to clothes. The eye, having little sartorial to occupy it, fell upon faces, to discover, to its delighted astonishment, that we can put together decidedly more pretty women to one rood than most other countries can to a square mile.'[32] The patriotic note was sounded by many onlookers. National mourning had kept away foreign visitors and the members of the diplomatic corps. Black Ascot was therefore a peculiarly British affair. 'There is no doubt that Englishwomen seldom appear to greater advantage than when in sombre attire,' noted the *Tatler*. 'Their complexions being generally the most noticeable part of their renowned beauty, it certainly never shows itself off half so well as when framed in black or dark shades.'[33] In Paris, the world capital of couture, the leading designers sat up. '*Une mode noire*', it was predicted, would soon be forthcoming.

In the meantime, the advantages of uniformity were sheepishly conceded. 'I like black,' one race-goer confessed, 'because in it I can always say to anybody I don't want to be bothered with, "I was looking for you everywhere, but, of course, it was quite impossible to find you."'[34]

On Friday, 17 June, Ascot closed, as it had opened, in brilliant sunshine. Before the crowds dispersed, Lord Coventry invited Lady Fingall to join him in the Jockey Club Stand. Looking down, she marvelled at the incongruity of the black-clad figures eddying and swirling on the green grass below. Together, she thought, 'They looked like nothing so much as an immense flight of crows that had just settled!'[35]

In some ways, the meeting had surpassed expectations. The racing had been, as the *Tatler* put it, 'rattling' in its excellence. Ridden by the popular American jockey Danny Maher, Bayardo had swept to a spectacular, once-in-a-generation victory in the coveted Gold Cup, cementing his reputation as one of the great racehorses of the twentieth century. Lord Churchill, too, could congratulate himself on a job well done. At a moment when so much in England seemed to be in a state of conflict and change, the apparent unity represented by the Royal Enclosure, where everybody knew everybody else and common codes of dress, demeanour and *politesse* prevailed, had been reassuring.

Nothing, however, could compensate for the absence of the monarch who had provided Ascot, Society and the country at large with a shared sense of meaning. 'The dense black attire spread itself like an ocean of woe across stands, lawns and enclosures, and at what is usually the most brilliant moment of the Season,' wrote the *Sheffield Daily Telegraph*. 'The dense mourning recalled to all a sense of loss and tragedy.'[36]

In the paddock, one well-travelled gentleman struggled to articulate what the sight of so many black-clad figures reminded him of. Finally, he had it. 'It is like the *Jour des Morts*,' he exclaimed. And so it was, his companion agreed. Ascot resembled a French cemetery, 'with all the widows and orphans returning from decorating the graves'.[37] Undeniably elegant, the effect was variously described as 'dismal', 'fearful' and 'an overwhelming reminder of the nation's loss'. 'The Ascot of 1910 will be remembered for a good many years to come,' concluded the *Sketch*, 'and if it was enjoyed, no one wants another such experience'.[38]

14: 'Everyone agrees that the summer has been a mournful one'

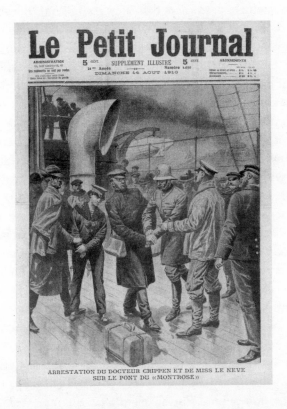

ARRESTATION DU DOCTEUR CRIPPEN ET DE MISS LE NEVE
SUR LE PONT DU «MONTROSE»

'I am unable to recall such an Ascot as this was as regards the setting of black,' wrote the *Tatler*'s racing correspondent in his summary of the meeting. 'It really began to get on one's nerves, and I expect many ladies who have not looked at their best for some time past will be glad now that the strict period of mourning has expired.'[1]

The effects of the relaxation into half-mourning were soon apparent. The Sunday after Ascot, the Thames at Boulter's Lock was busy with boating parties making the most of the hottest day of the summer so far. The river was a heaving mass of mauve muslins and lilac lawns worn with broad-brimmed straw hats decked with purple flowers and white feathers. There were some 'striking studies' in black and white, and many of the men wore ties of violet or up-to-the-minute 'aeroplane blue'.[2] Similar scenes were enacted in Hyde Park where 'beautiful and harmonious colour schemes of exquisite shades of mauve, purple and grey' were prevalent.[3] In anticipation of more wonderful weather, Wareing's, the umbrella manufacturer of Northampton, informed its female customers that they could send their black parasols to be recovered in shades suitable for half-mourning.

For the majority of the population, life returned to normal. There was much talk of Halley's Comet, which was clearly visible to the crowds that gathered each evening on Hampstead Heath. Building on the achievement of Louis Blériot, the Honourable Charles Rolls, the aviator son of Lord Llangattock, made the first non-stop double crossing of the English Channel, from Dover to Calais and back again, in ninety minutes. At White City, the Japan-British Exhibition was thronged with sightseers. The decision to open just two days later than planned had caused one Satori Kato, who feared the Japanese would be accused of a lack of respect, considerable unease. In its reply to his apologetic letter, *The Times* assured him that the instruction to proceed had come from the highest quarter. 'The determination not to postpone the opening – though it is to be shorn of all ceremony – has been taken in obedience to the expressed wish of King George, whose considerate motives are known,' it said. 'Mr Kato will understand that for Englishmen that wish is final.'[4] On 24 May, the honorary president of the Japanese Commission, Prince Fushimi Sadanaru, had paid a low-key visit with Prince Arthur of Connaught. His trip to London had served a dual purpose. Four days earlier, he had ridden in the procession behind Edward's coffin as the representative of the Emperor.

After a spike at the end of the nineteenth century, there had been a drop in the number and frequency of weddings between Dollar Princesses and British aristocrats. Blighted though it was by the King's death, the Season of 1910 witnessed something of a revival. On 8 June, the banking heiress Margaretta Drexel married Viscount Maidstone, heir to the 13th Earl of Winchilsea, at St Margaret's, Westminster. A fortnight later, Mildred Carter, the daughter of the

American Minister to Romania, married Viscount Acheson, heir to the 4th Earl of Gosford, at St George's, Hanover Square. The groom's cousin, Lady Victoria Stanley, was a bridesmaid in a Paquin gown with myrtle in her hair and a large bouquet of crimson roses. Two days before the wedding, the bride's parents hosted a reception at Dorchester House, the home of the American ambassador, Whitelaw Reid. Among the presents, which included a rope of pearls, a diamond tiara, a motor-car and a house in Chesham Place, was a scarf-pin sent by Queen Alexandra. Touchingly, it consisted of the intertwined initials 'E' and 'A'.

That summer, Virginia Stephen remained largely oblivious to events in the wider world. 'I stupidly made my head bad again, and have been doing nothing,' she had written to her friend Violet Dickinson in April.[5] After their holiday in Dorset, she and the Bells took another break in June, this time seeking relaxation in a rented house near Canterbury. The tone of Virginia's letters varied from the perfunctory to the verbose as her moods swung back and forth. 'It takes a long time to get one's faculties to work again,' she told Dickinson.[6]

At the end of the month, Vanessa was advised by her sister's doctor that Virginia should seek professional help in a nursing-home near Twickenham. It was not a prospect Virginia relished but she grudgingly acceded. Although the experience turned out to be even worse than she feared, she stuck with it in the belief that, by the autumn, she would be well again. 'I feel my brains, like a pear, to see if its ripe,' she joked. 'It will be exquisite by September.'[7] Vanessa sent her regular reports on life in London, where even Bloomsbury was less lively than usual. 'Everyone agrees that the summer has been a mournful one,' she wrote, 'whether on account of your disease or the King's death, does not seem to be certain.'[8]

Elsie Bowerman was also away from home. Her interest in the suffragette movement continued to grow, and her correspondence with her mother Edith Chibnall, who was a committed member of the WSPU, brimmed with references to the Conciliation Bill, which had been presented to the Commons on the same day, 14 June, Ascot had opened. The Bill, which would enfranchise a limited number of women, won a good deal of support, and the suffragettes were optimistic that progress might be made at last. The truce Mrs Pankhurst had declared at the end of January still held, and there had been few instances of violent protest in recent months. On the other hand, Lord Lytton, the Chairman of the Conciliation Committee, was far from sanguine about what might happen next. Should the Bill stall, or fail altogether, a return to militancy seemed guaranteed. 'I dread the future more than I can say,' he admitted to Winston Churchill.[9]

'Owing to the lamented death of the King', the WSPU had postponed a march from the Embankment to the Royal Albert Hall. Originally scheduled for the afternoon of 28 May, it finally took place on the evening of Saturday, 18 June. Its aim was two-fold: to reinforce support for the Conciliation Bill among those MPs who had already come out in favour of it, and to prove to those in opposition that further resistance would be futile. Less than a month earlier, Edward's coffin, followed by monarchs and princes, and watched by innumerable spectators clad in deepest black, had passed through the streets of the hushed capital. Now those same streets were filled again, only this time with tens of thousands of women moving to the sound of rousing music as colourful banners fluttered overhead.

Indeed, after so many weeks of unremitting mourning, it was to be the procession's colours that produced the strongest impression. Snaking all the way from Kensington to St James's Palace, it was a walking rainbow of teachers and secretaries, nurses and shop assistants, factory workers and civil servants. In the front ranks more than six hundred women carried silver wands, which symbolised the time they had spent in prison in the service of the cause. Behind them were the so-called 'pioneers': elderly campaigners – one riding in a wheelchair – who had been active in the movement from its earliest days. At the other end of the spectrum, *Votes for Women* observed a group of girls aged between thirteen and twenty who 'typified the devotion and thanks of the younger generation'.[10] There were delegations from every regional branch of the WSPU, from Scotland, Ireland and Wales, and from the Empire, the United States and many countries in Europe. The Actresses' Franchise League wore pink, white and green, and university graduates sported their academic robes and hoods of every hue. Almost everybody else was dressed in white trimmed with flowers, ribbons and rosettes of purple and green. When Mrs Pankhurst cried, 'Victory!' in the Royal Albert Hall, she was greeted with thunderous applause. The word was still ringing in the ears of Henry W. Nevinson when he filed a report for *Votes* on 24 June. 'From end to end of that glorious scene,' he wrote, 'we were conscious of Victory's presence. To imitate the famous phrase, we seemed to hear the fluttering of her wings.' Lest his readers be in any doubt of the stakes, he concluded on a warning note. 'If the Government should thwart or postpone that victory now, God help them in the times that are coming!'[11]

Elsie, who was staying with friends in Surrey, had not participated. Her hosts, 'red-hot Tory antis', expressed such horror when they heard that Frances Dove, the founder of Wycombe Abbey, had joined the march that she judged it prudent to lie low and say nothing. She did, however, beg her mother to procure a copy of *Votes* and keep it for her return: 'I don't think I will produce one here, they would be so frightfully shocked.'[12]

In July, she decamped to a *pension* in Tours, where she hoped to perfect her French. From there, she kept in constant touch with Edith, following the latest developments in Westminster with fascination. The atmosphere was febrile. The Conciliation Bill passed its second reading in the middle of the month, but the chance of it becoming law in 1910 seemed remote, particularly after MPs voted against sending it to a Grand Committee. The suffragettes' self-imposed truce hung by a thread. Even so, a feisty militant named Emily Davison managed to smash two windows in the Crown Office at the Houses of Parliament with lumps of chalk to which she had tied threatening messages addressed to the Prime Minister. There was a second march through London on 23 July, followed by a rally in Hyde Park. 'I do wish I were at home now,' Elsie told her mother. 'I do hate missing all this.'[13]

Between lessons and sightseeing, she worked assiduously to win over her fellow guests. 'I have made one of the Scotch girls quite keen & she has promised always to take *Votes* when she goes home,' she announced triumphantly on 16 July. 'I feel quite proud of myself!'[14] Edith plied her daughter with suffragette literature, which Elsie duly passed on to those she considered most in need. A male student from Oxford who was a disciple of Lloyd George and Churchill, both of whom had come out against the Bill, was judged particularly ripe for conversion. So was Mrs Ager, a professed 'anti', who was laid up with rheumatism. To Elsie, it was a golden opportunity. 'I thought she would probably have time for reflection,' she wrote, and delivered a copy of *Votes* to the invalid's bedroom. 'She thinks it is a splendid paper,' she reported in due course, '& is going to take it when she goes home.'[15]

News of the suffragettes took second place to the first really big story to break since Edward's death. On 30 June, the theatrical manager John Nash and his wife Lil Hawthorne paid a visit to their friend Superintendent Frank Froest at New Scotland Yard. The couple explained that they were concerned about their acquaintance Cora Crippen, who hadn't been seen since late January. Her husband, Dr Crippen, had let it be known that she had returned to her native America, and had died there in March. It was not a tale either Nash or Hawthorne could credit. Nor, when he had heard them out, could Froest. Summoning his colleague, Detective Chief Inspector Walter Dew, he asked him to investigate.

At first, Dew was inclined to give Dr Crippen the benefit of the doubt. The fact that cheques allegedly signed by Cora had been presented after the last sighting of her did not seem sufficient grounds for alarm. Indeed, Dew attributed it to 'the Bohemian character of the persons concerned'.[16] Even in theatre-loving 1910, a whiff of impropriety clung to those who had chosen to make the stage their profession. A failed music-hall artiste like Cora might be suspected of anything. However, once Dew had probed a little deeper, he too began to harbour doubts. When he discovered that Crippen had gone to Dieppe following his wife's supposed death, and that he had taken his young secretary Ethel Le Neve with him, he resolved to speak to Crippen in person.

On the morning of 8 July, Dew called unannounced at the Crippens' home, 39 Hilldrop Crescent. He was received by Le Neve who, clearly flustered, told him that her lover was out. Refusing her suggestion that he should come back later, Dew insisted that she take him and his companion, Detective Sergeant Arthur Mitchell, to Crippen at once.

At Crippen's office on New Oxford Street, Dew was confronted with 'an insignificant little man',[17] who immediately confessed that the version of events he had disseminated in the spring was untrue. In the course of the interview, Crippen described the collapse of his marriage. Cora had had dalliances with other men, while he himself had 'been intimate' with Le Neve for some time. On the evening of 31 January – the same day that Paul and Clara Martinetti had come to dine – they had had a flaming row. Before she made good on her oft-repeated threat to leave him once and for all, Cora had tasked him to cover up the circumstances of her departure as best he could. 'As far as I know,' Crippen said, 'she is still alive.'[18]

The statement was delivered calmly, yet Dew had a nagging suspicion it was far from the whole story. The house on Hilldrop Crescent was thoroughly searched, but nothing untoward presented itself. Cora was officially listed as a missing person.

What happened over the course of the following week transformed a tale of domestic dysfunction into the most sensational story of the year. The day after his 'confession' to Dew, Crippen, accompanied by Le Neve, bolted. They supplied no hint of their whereabouts, but a note Crippen left for his business partner announced his intention to 'escape trouble' by disappearing for a while. To Dew, this precipitate departure, which had apparently seen Le Neve disguise herself as a boy, suggested only one thing – guilt.

For forty-eight hours, the house and garden on Hilldrop Crescent were searched again and again. On 13 July, with Dew and his team close to exhaustion, there was a breakthrough of the grisliest kind. Drawn to the cellar by what he later described as a kind of sixth sense, Dew scrutinised its brick floor until he detected signs that it had recently been disturbed. Digging into the earth below, a sickening stench forced him and Mitchell to quit the confined space in search of air. When they had steeled themselves to return, they discovered a mass of human flesh mixed with scraps of clothing and covered with lime to aid decomposition. The ghastly scene was rendered even more appalling by the fact that there was no sign at all of the head, bones or sexual organs. Cora, or what little remained of her, had, it seemed, been found. On 16 July, a warrant for the arrest of Crippen and Le Neve was applied for. Physical descriptions of the fugitives were circulated throughout Europe and in the United States and Canada.

The British have always loved a good murder, and this one gave every appearance of being the best since the days of Jack the Ripper. Mild-mannered, unassuming and entirely unremarkable, Crippen was outwardly indistinguishable from any number of other middle-aged professionals. That he had killed and then dismembered his wife before absconding with a not unattractive younger woman with whom he had been conducting a clandestine affair beggared belief. Breaking at a point in the year when the news cycle was slowest, the unfolding drama gripped the nation. 'There never has been a hue and cry like that which went up throughout the country for Crippen and Miss Le Neve,' recalled Dew. 'It was the one big topic of conversation. On the trains and buses, one heard members of the public speculating and theorising as to where they were likely to be.'[19]

In a hotel in Italy, Max Beerbohm was agog. He pored over the papers, his 'great daily excitement', in the process incurring the disapproval of his wife, Florence. Then she too was 'gradually drawn into the vortex' of the universal fascination. Beerbohm was convinced their fellow guests suspected *them* of being the fugitives. 'Whatever we did,' he joked, 'seemed to lend colour to the suspicion. "They seemed animated and cheerful at meals" – "They kept themselves to themselves" – "They used to go out daily to buy the Paris edition of the *Daily Mail*" – etc etc.'[20]

The story was about to become more incredible still. Passing themselves off as father and adolescent son, Crippen and Le Neve fled to Belgium. In Antwerp, they boarded a small liner, the *Montrose*, which sailed for Québec on 20 July. That they were two of only twenty passengers booked into second class was their first misfortune. Their second was that the ship's well-informed and attentive captain, Henry Kendall, immediately smelt a rat. Their third and most consequential was that the *Montrose* was one of fewer than a hundred vessels to be equipped with a wireless set. Having conducted some discreet tests of his own devising – Crippen did not at first respond to his alias of 'Mr Robinson', he had marks on the bridge of his nose that indicated he usually wore spectacles, and he employed terms during a discussion of seasickness likely to have been known only to a medical practitioner – Kendall ordered a message to be sent to the shipping company to forward to Scotland Yard. 'Have strong suspicions that Crippen London Cellar Murderer and accomplice are amongst saloon passengers,' it read. 'Moustaches shaved off, growing beard. Accomplice dressed as boy, voice, manner and build undoubtedly a girl.'

Prior to the invention of wireless, ships at sea had been totally cut off from the outside world. Thanks to the new technology, all that had changed. In May, travellers aboard the larger liners had learnt of Edward's death before their families on land. Now, in late July, the police were alerted to the whereabouts of an already notorious murderer as he attempted to place thousands of miles between himself and the scene of his crime. The development heralded a new era in which nobody, given the necessary apparatus, would ever again be out of reach of justice.

In London, Dew made some swift calculations. He realised that if he embarked upon a faster ship, he could overtake the plodding *Montrose* in mid-ocean and so be able to apprehend Crippen and Le Neve as soon as they arrived in Québec. He therefore boarded the *Laurentic* in Liverpool on 23 July. Despite attempts to shroud his mission in secrecy, the press was with him every step of the way. Captain Kendall proved himself to be every bit as adept as a showman as he was as an amateur sleuth. The regular updates he wired to the papers created an atmosphere of almost unbearable suspense as Dew gave chase across the Atlantic. Nobody was immune. On 30 July, the Home Secretary, Winston Churchill, requested an update on his progress.

Aboard the *Montrose*, Crippen was unaware that he was the object of the world's avid attention. Kendall revealed nothing of his suspicions, so the murderer and his lover passed their time in pleasant, if uneventful, fashion. They enjoyed leisurely meals, read popular fiction and conversed amiably with the other passengers. Born in Michigan, Crippen assured them that the best place in England to procure American beverages was the brand-new Selfridges on Oxford Street. He was particularly intrigued by the ship's wireless. 'What a wonderful invention it is!' he exclaimed, ignorant of the fact that it had helped to seal his doom.[21] From the moment Kendall's original message had been despatched, Crippen and Le Neve had, as *The Times* put it, 'been encased in waves of wireless telegraphy as securely as if they had been within the four walls of a prison'.[22]

When it was made, the arrest was flawlessly executed. Disguised as a pilot whose responsibility it was to see the *Montrose* safely into port, Dew was rowed out to the ship in the St Lawrence River. Shinning up a rope ladder with two representatives of the Canadian police similarly attired, he found the suspects walking on deck. Remaining under cover just long enough to get a good look at them,

Dew pounced. Crippen, it was reported, 'turned the colour of death, and his voice gargled some unintelligible sound as he was hurried below'.[23] When he had recovered from his shock, he claimed to be relieved. The strain, he said, had been too much. He was glad it was over.

The news that Crippen had been caught, and that he would soon be on his way back to Britain to stand trial, prompted many to reflect on the inexorable march of technology. Hitherto, mused the *Daily News*, the average man had thought of wireless telegraphy 'as a luxury, a kind of scientific plaything, a toy to amuse the fortunate passengers on board a Cunarder.' Now he had learnt, in the most dramatic fashion, that it could be harnessed in daily life. It had 'been fitted into the machinery of civilisation and has become a thing to be reckoned with'.[24] The Crippen case would, *The Times* speculated, have beneficial side-effects. Thanks to the headlines it had generated, wireless telegraphy had ceased to be 'a very vague and intangible agency'.[25] A Bill was already in motion in Parliament to have wireless apparatus installed upon all ships leaving British ports, further minimising the possibility of mishaps at sea. Set within the broader context – of more and faster automobiles on the roads, of aeroplanes criss-crossing the Channel, and of allegedly unsinkable super-liners at that very moment under construction in Belfast – there was every reason to believe a brave new world was at hand.

It was not a world King George and Queen Mary had time to contemplate as they grappled with the difficulties incumbent upon their new positions. Eclipsed for most of his adult life by his venerable grandmother and gregarious father, George was, to most of his subjects, an unknown quantity. What *was* known – or rather supposed – was as embarrassing as it was untrue. The belief that he did not share the love of racing that had so endeared Edward to the masses had been swiftly scotched. Less easy to stem was the story that he was a drunkard. George's time in the Navy, combined with his loud voice and blotchy complexion, seemed to lend credence to the tittle-tattle, which circulated in Society drawing rooms and East End pubs alike. 'Everybody says G.V. is a knurd,' Venetia Stanley wrote to her friend Violet Asquith four days after Edward's death, using contemporary slang for an alcoholic.[26] In September, the Austrian ambassador, Count Mensdorff, despatched a report to Vienna. Things had got so bad, he claimed, that special prayers were being said for Queen Mary and the royal children at temperance meetings. Torn between amusement and annoyance, George, who was in fact the most abstemious of men, could only wait for the talk to die down of its own accord.

He was far less tolerant of a scurrilous tale, first documented in the early 1890s but resurrected upon his accession, that he was a bigamist. According to the journalist Edward Mylius, George had married the daughter of an English admiral in Malta two decades earlier. His subsequent marriage to Princess May of Teck was therefore invalid and their offspring were illegitimate. In years gone by, he had treated this patent falsehood as a joke. Now he responded to it with fury. Mylius was arrested on a charge of criminal libel that ultimately saw him consigned to gaol for twelve months.

While rumours buzzed, George struggled to bring himself up to speed on the many matters demanding his urgent attention. Diligent and methodical, he had endless face-to-face meetings with his ministers and courtiers. The King's determination to contribute to the smooth running of his father's lying-in-state and funeral was typical of his conscientious approach. That summer, he articulated his long-term objective. 'He means to do for the Empire what King Edward did for the peace of Europe,' Lord Esher noted, after a conversation at Balmoral in August. 'He proposes to attend himself the Indian Durbar in January 1911 and crown himself at Delhi. He means to visit every Dominion. These are bold projects.'[27] From the outset, George staked a claim to a sphere of influence quite distinct from that of his predecessor. 'In his political calculations,' wrote Ella Hepworth Dixon, 'King Edward was essentially a European; in his tastes, he was almost a Parisian.'[28] In spite of his mingled German and Danish blood, nobody could make a similar claim of his son. Unsophisticated, well-meaning and resolutely British, George was resolved to look far beyond the Continental courts in which his father had been so revered.*

★ The 'Indian Durbar' mentioned by Lord Esher took place in Delhi in the presence of King George and Queen Mary on 12 December 1911. They were the only British monarchs ever to attend such an event in person. With hindsight, it has come to be seen as the high-water mark of the British Empire.

In the meantime, the most pressing issue with which he had to contend was the deadlock between the Commons and the Lords. Edward had not discussed the brewing crisis with his heir, so George was largely ignorant of what his strategy had been. But there were grounds for hope. George was keen to reconcile the opposing camps, while Asquith was resolved, at least for now, to be gentle with the inexperienced sovereign. On the Prime Minister's suggestion, a constitutional conference between the senior figures in the Liberal and Conservative parties was set up to explore ways to ensure the primacy of the Commons without destroying the Lords. Asquith told Arthur Balfour that, while Edward's death had not altered the facts of the matter, it *had* changed the climate in which further discussions might unfold.

The conference, which opened on 17 June and included Lloyd George and Lord Crewe representing the Government, and Balfour and Lord Lansdowne representing the Opposition, got off to a good, or at least a civil, start. There were no fewer than twelve sessions before the end of July, when it seemed sufficient progress had been made for further meetings to be contemplated. When Parliament went into recess for the summer, it was proposed that they should relocate to Crewe's country house. Lansdowne dismissed the idea as frivolous – there was a risk, he maintained, that any agreement would be attributed to the excellence of their host's champagne – so there was a hiatus until the autumn, when it was hoped the talks would resume.

Although Queen Mary was spared first-hand involvement in the political strife that bedevilled the opening months of her husband's reign, she had troubles of her own. Not least among them was the question of her mother-in-law. For forty-seven years, Edward had been Alexandra's rock. With his passing, she felt herself to be untethered. Acutely deaf and with few inner resources, she struggled to adapt to widowhood. Upon the death of Queen Victoria, she had been extremely reluctant to move from Marlborough House to Buckingham Palace. Now she proved equally reluctant to move back. Sequestered with her sister, the Dowager Empress of Russia, she resisted all attempts to dislodge her. When the Kaiser took it upon himself to reason with his aunt, Alexandra stonewalled. 'Willy dear, you know that you always speak rather indistinctly,' she told him. 'I am afraid I have not heard a single word you were saying.'[29] In mid-June, the *Bystander* predicted she would not vacate the Palace until early 1911. 'The task of packing and removing Her Majesty's and Princess Victoria's personal possessions will be, by the way, no light one,' it reminded its readers. 'Room after room is filled with them, and all were arranged in their present positions by the Queen herself.'[30]

For Mary, this intransigence made it difficult, if not impossible, to plan ahead. 'Everything at this moment appears to me to be chaos & with my methodical mind I suffer in proportion,' she admitted.[31] Charming but evasive, Alexandra was more than ever oblivious to the needs of others. When the Dowager Empress at last departed in August, Victoria was compelled to cut short her own, much-needed, holiday in Harrogate to dance attendance on her mother at Sandringham.

Years earlier, when Mary was a newlywed, Lord Esher had derived a favourable impression of her abilities. 'She is educating herself carefully and with her exceptional memory and intelligence will be a woman of much importance one of these days,' he observed.[32] Calm, clear-headed and sensible, the Queen helped to keep the King on an even keel as he found his feet. Certainly, he came to rely heavily upon her for emotional support in the wake of Edward's death. In October, when they spent their first night apart since his accession, George sent his wife an unusually expressive letter:

> I want you to understand, that I am indeed grateful to you, for all you have done all these busy months for me & to thank you from the bottom of my heart for all your love & for the enormous help & comfort which you have been to me in my new position . . . God bless you my sweet Angel May, who I know will always stick to me as I need your love & help more than ever now.[33]

The passing of time made no difference to Edward's fox terrier, Caesar. Wandering restlessly from room to room at Buckingham Palace, he slept each night on the late King's bed. He couldn't count on much affection from Alexandra, who considered him smelly, spoiled and selfish. He was, she assured Margot Asquith, a 'horrid little dog' that had ignored Edward in his final hours. When Margot replied that the Prime Minister had seen him curled up beside the corpse, Alexandra merely scoffed, 'For warmth, my dear.'[34]

The sentimental public interpreted Caesar's behaviour in a different light. His starring role in the funeral procession had transformed him into the most famous dog in the world. All that summer, and well into the autumn, he was big business. The *Illustrated London News* commissioned the artist Maud Earl to paint Caesar with his head resting forlornly upon Edward's empty armchair. Entitled *Silent Sorrow*, copies were advertised for sale: five shillings for a photogravure plate, or ten shillings and sixpence for a limited-edition India proof. Itself a relatively recent addition to the Edwardian nursery, the teddy-bear temporarily took a back seat to the toy Caesars manufactured by the German firm of Steiff. Fashioned out of shaggy mohair with glass eyes, jointed legs and leather collars replete with embossed brass tags, the endearing animals were soon flying off the shelves.

Most popular of all was the anonymously authored *Where's Master?*, which narrated the events surrounding Edward's death from Caesar's perspective. Dedicated to Alexandra (who was called 'She' throughout) and published by Hodder & Stoughton, it was guaranteed to raise a lump in the most stoic throat:

> She says I can go if I am very good and follow close behind Master, and walk very slowly, and never move from the middle of the road. Oh, how glad and thankful I am. I wonder if Master knows, and is pleased that, after all, his little dog is going with him on his last journey.[35]

In spite of the disapproval of Queen Mary, who judged the whole enterprise to be in poor taste, the book went through numerous editions, and eventually became one of the year's bestsellers.

15: 'A time when all was a sizzle of excitement'

By the beginning of August, the subdued Season was winding down. Edward's love of sailing had been second only to his passion for racing, and his patronage had made Cowes Regatta, which opened on the first of the month, almost as unmissable as Ascot. On the lawn of the Royal Yacht Squadron, the members of Society – the men in navy blazers and white duck trousers, the ladies in broad-brimmed hats swathed with veils – gazed seaward as a brass band played and bunting snapped smartly overhead. There were any number of parties on shipboard but, in deference to Court mourning, there were no fire-works, and the annual Squadron dinner did not take place.

As the elite decamped from London to the German spas or the French resorts of Dinard and Deauville, tourists moved in. The Savoy and the Ritz were 'simply over-run' with Americans, and it seemed the losses incurred by the cancellation of so many bookings in May might well be recouped. On 8 August, King George and Queen Mary departed for Balmoral. Before they did so, George gave a sitting to the sculptor Bertram Mackennal, who was to design and model the coins and stamps of the new reign. In 1909, Mackennal had been the first Australian to be elected an associate of the Royal Academy. His latest commission was a sign of George's determination to forge bonds with the peoples of the far-flung Empire.

Even in the dog days of summer, important minds were focused on the question of a permanent memorial to Edward. In early July, Lord Esher had a meeting with the King. The Victoria Memorial was still not finished, and it was felt it would be unwise to solicit further donations while work continued. Esher conveyed this message to the Prime Minister, who responded by writing to the Lord Mayor of London on behalf of the Government. 'The object in view,' Asquith believed, 'would best be secured by local rather than national memorials.'[1] Might the Lord Mayor consider spearheading the initiative on behalf of the capital? Reading between the lines, the implication was clear. In the absence of centralised coordination, outlying towns and cities would be on their own.

To the outraged *Times*, the Prime Minister's letter amounted to a 'gratuitous renunciation' which saw him wash his hands of responsibility for the matter.[2] Nothing daunted, provincial corporations rose to the challenge with gusto. In Bath and Bradford, Bristol and Ipswich, Leicester and Nottingham, memorial committees were formed, and various schemes were soon afoot. Issued by the Mansion House, invitations to join the London Committee were accepted by a range of 'influential people' who represented the spheres in which Edward had been active. They included his son-in-law the Duke of Fife; the financial wizards Lord Rothschild and Sir Ernest Cassel; and the actor-manager Sir Herbert Beerbohm Tree. Suggestions from the public poured in. Some, like that of the joker who proposed a yearly banquet at the Guildhall as homage to Edward's legendary appetite, were dismissed at once. Others, such as increased funding for hospitals or the purchase of recreational space in the cramped East End, merited more serious consideration. Particularly vocal was the faction that favoured the remodelling of the East Front of Buckingham Palace. Dirty, undistinguished and in terrible condition, it was felt by many to be a national embarrassment. The sparkling white marble of the Victoria Memorial only highlighted its shortcomings. 'Grimmer and more repulsive than ever,' opined one journalist, the Palace 'strikes one as some ugly and gigantic chimney-sweep standing behind a spotless chorister'.[3] A new façade would be a fitting tribute to a monarch whose reign had seen London scale new heights of architectural magnificence.

On 27 August, Dr Crippen and Ethel Le Neve disembarked from the liner *Megantic* at Liverpool. They had made the voyage from Québec in the custody of Detective Chief Inspector Dew, who personally escorted the prisoners down the gangplank. Interest in the case had not diminished, and immense crowds had gathered to witness the arrival. There were similar scenes at Euston, where the train carrying Crippen was greeted with hoots and jeers, and outside Bow Street Police Station, where he was formally charged with his wife's murder.

For most in England, this was the first glimpse they had received of the accused. Crippen's countenance belied the savagery of the crime. His face, marvelled the journalist Frank Dilnot, 'carried the message of thoughtfulness, apprehension, sensitiveness. One would never have thought that he was a cold-blooded murderer . . . You could see the innate gentleness of the man as you looked at him.'[4] At his trial, which opened at the Old Bailey on 18 October, Crippen pleaded not guilty.

That same day, *Howards End* was published by the firm of Edward Arnold. Its critical and popular success elevated E. M. Forster to the uppermost literary circles. Hailed by R. A. Scott-James of the *Daily News* as the finest novel of the year, it was set in a thoroughly up-to-date London of motor-cars, discussion groups and class distinctions. The eponymous house was, Scott-James felt, 'a sort of symbol of everything in England, old and new, changeless, yet amid flux'.[5] Forster's epigraph, 'Only Connect', was a plea to readers who found themselves entangled in the conflicts – between men and women, rich and poor, conservative and progressive – that had defined Edward's reign, and escalated dramatically in the wake of his death.

Consensus was certainly in short supply during the weeks that marked the run of an art exhibition that opened at the Grafton Galleries in Mayfair the day after the Court transitioned to half-mourning on 7 November. It was the realisation of Roger Fry's scheme to display works by 'the newest French painters' he had mooted to Clive and Vanessa Bell in January. Throughout the summer and autumn, he had been braced for an outcry. He can't have anticipated the seismic shock of what was to prove one of the most seminal shows in the history of modern art in Britain.

From the outset, Bloomsbury had rallied to provide him with extremely able support. Clive was enlisted to help secure paintings, while Robert Dell, the Paris correspondent of the *Burlington Magazine*, facilitated introductions. Lady Ottoline Morrell, the blue-blooded but bohemian hostess, was generous with advice and encouragement. Most crucially, there was Desmond MacCarthy, the urbane critic, who was roped in as the exhibition's secretary. First in September, and then again in October, MacCarthy accompanied Fry to Paris to solicit loans from dealers and collectors. On the second occasion, Clive and Morrell went too.

Not all the painters they had in their sights were French. Some weren't even particularly new. Henri Matisse, André Derain and the Spaniard Pablo Picasso were very much alive, but Paul Cézanne had been dead since 1906, and Paul Gauguin since 1903. The Dutchman Vincent van Gogh had committed suicide in 1890. In addition to works by artists who have since become legends, there were scores of others by the likes of Rouault, Vallotton and Vlaminck. Édouard Manet was represented by eight paintings, chief among them *A Bar at the Folies-Bergère*, which he had completed the year before his death in 1883. He was the only Impressionist in the exhibition, but it was his name that featured in its official title, 'Manet and the Post-Impressionists', which was hastily decided upon by Fry as a logical catch-all.

The organisers were aware their selections would cause ructions. To cover themselves, they invited a number of prominent individuals to join an honorary committee. For its members, it entailed no responsibility, or even the obligation to endorse the works. Their sole purpose was to supply gravitas to a ground-breaking venture nobody was certain would succeed. By his own admission, Edward VII had cared little for art, but some of those he had known in a private or official capacity now lent their names. They included Lewis 'Loulou' Harcourt, Schomberg McDonnell's colleague at the Office of Works; Lionel Cust, who retained his position as Surveyor of the King's Pictures; Lord Ribblesdale, who had preceded Lord Churchill as Master of the Buckhounds; Sir Charles Holroyd, the director of the National Gallery; and the Duchess of Rutland, who was an artist and sculptress of no mean ability.

The British weren't entirely unacquainted with recent developments in European art. Back in 1905, the Grafton Galleries had staged an exhibition that included several works by Cézanne. That very June, Dell had organised a show in Brighton that presented paintings by Gauguin, Matisse and Dérain. Visitors were warned they might be 'tempted to laugh at them as mere eccentricities or denounce them as outrages'.[6] Yet, in the event, they produced scarcely a ripple, perhaps because they hung outside London, or possibly because the nation was still deep in mourning.

In any case, British painting was a distinctly parochial affair. The departure from the policy of 'Splendid Isolation' in the field of diplomacy had not, as yet, been mirrored in the world of art. Although they had been established in Paris for decades, the Impressionists received a lukewarm reception in London, where painters continued to labour under what Vanessa Bell described as a 'Victorian cloud', either tinkering with the effects of light or harking back to the Pre-Raphaelites.[7] Looming over all were the schools that stressed the importance of years of training. Spontaneity withered under their stultifying hands. Becalmed in a cultural backwater, the majority of British artists were content to conform to the same narrow standards.

'Manet and the Post-Impressionists' tore off the blinkers with a violence even those who were favourably disposed found quite bewildering. Hitherto, 'modern' pictures had been displayed piecemeal, or else had been glimpsed as inadequate reproductions in the pages of books with limited circulations. Now, on the walls of a prestigious gallery in the most fashionable part of the capital, hung a galaxy of works by artists whose names and techniques had, until then, been known to only the cosmopolitan few. London reeled.

Fry, who had been rearranging until the last possible moment, deemed it 'good for people to have their lives stirred'.[8] Yet he sincerely believed in the value of the paintings he had selected. With their vibrant colours, vigorous brushstrokes and apparent freedom from the teaching of hidebound academies, the Post-Impressionists seemed to him to be compatible with his earlier interest in Renaissance art. The Impressionists had, he maintained, been weak on 'structural design'. In Cézanne, Gauguin and Van Gogh, it had begun to reassert itself. The history of art was, to Fry's way of thinking, an unbroken continuum. Picasso might seem alien to the uninitiated but, in reality, he was only pushing things 'a little further' than preceding generations.

It was not a message London was primed to hear. Judging the works to be juvenile in execution and adolescent in their determination to shock, conservative critics fell over themselves to record their mystification and disgust. The show was, *The Times* asserted, nothing but a 'flagrant' exercise in reaction. Post-Impressionism 'throws away all that the long-developed skill of past artists had acquired and bequeathed. It begins all over again – and stops where a child would stop.'[9] To *Truth*, the overall effect was akin to the results of 'a child's miscellaneous handling of his first paint-box'. The colour schemes of Cézanne and Van Gogh contained 'a certain beastliness, which, on the whole, needs no rediscovery'. The canvases of Gauguin represented 'uncouthness at its best', while the vaunted 'primitiveness' of Matisse was so incomprehensible that, following the path to its logical conclusion, painters could soon be dispensed with altogether.[10]

The *Daily Telegraph* admitted that only time would tell whether Post-Impressionism had intrinsic merit. The exhibition, it said, 'must be seen and faced' as a reflection of an increasingly discordant and fragmented age. Discerning viewers might be appalled by what it termed 'the garishness and horror of it all', but it would be a mistake to shy away lest the painting of the future might emerge from the painful experiment.[11] The *Yorkshire Post* was less equivocal. The show was 'an orgy of ugliness', which marked the 'last word in artistic decadence'. What a relief it was to discover that the catalogue contained not a single English name.[12]

It wasn't just reporters who were aghast. Professor Henry Tonks of the Slade deplored the deleterious impact of Post-Impressionism on his students. Oscar Wilde's literary executor Robert Ross framed it in terms of degeneracy, criminality and lunacy. John Singer Sargent declared that he was 'absolutely sceptical' of the right of the paintings to have 'any claim whatever to being works of art'.* Sir Philip Burne-Jones, the son of the late Pre-Raphaelite, perceived only 'anarchy and degradation'.[13] He regretted that Sir Charles Holroyd should have permitted the use of his name in connection with the show. Once he had actually seen it, Holroyd withdrew from the honorary committee. So did the Duchess of Rutland, who explained that she was '*horrified*' to be linked in any way with 'such an *awful* exhibition of horrors'.[14]

In spite, or likely because, of the critical firestorm, public interest was intense. Throughout the autumn and winter, twenty-five thousand sensation-seekers poured through the doors. Wilfrid Scawen Blunt was among the most apoplectic. He discerned nothing in the works 'but that gross puerility which scrawls indecencies on the walls of a privy'. It was, he concluded, 'a pornographic show'.[15] Those who were not scandalised split their sides with laughter. H. E. Bateman drew a series of caricatures for the *Bystander*. In one, a hobble-skirted lady asks her companion, 'What on earth are those things, rabbits or snails?' 'Neither,' he replies, 'they're cats!' Elsewhere, a dapper gentleman seen arriving in a morning coat and silk hat departs in a state of disarray, a handkerchief clutched to his fevered brow. Along the bottom of the page, well-dressed gallery-goers double up, tears of merriment pouring down their cheeks.[16]

Once the initial chorus of outrage and incomprehension had subsided, the British began to realise the significance of what they were seeing. It was observed the exhibition was just as crowded when

---

* Fry had implied, in a letter published in the *Nation* on 24 December 1910, that Sargent was one of the luminaries to have endorsed the Post-Impressionists. A fortnight later, Sargent issued a firm rebuttal. Fry's existing prejudice was confirmed. His dismissal of Sargent's entire *oeuvre* would adversely affect the artist's reputation for years after his death in 1925. (Stanley Olson, *John Singer Sargent: His Portrait*, Barrie & Jenkins, 1989, pp. 234–6.)

it closed in January as it had been when it opened two months earlier. Somewhere along the way, derision was replaced by avid attention. 'Public taste in pictures is advancing faster than the critics',' noted the *Graphic*. 'The general attitude was one of admiration.'[17] Like it or loathe it, modern art seeped into the consciousness of even the best-insulated. On 25 November, Lady Edmund Talbot hosted a charity ball at the Grafton Galleries at which members of Edward's inner circle – the duchesses of Norfolk and Marlborough, the countesses of Strafford and Kenmare, and the wife of the American ambassador, Mrs Whitelaw Reid – waltzed and one-stepped in their tiaras beneath the vivid canvases.

The young, in particular, were transfixed. Vanessa Bell found it difficult to overstate the impact of the show on her peers. 'It is impossible, I think, that any other single exhibition can ever have had so much effect as did that on the rising generation,' she recalled. Post-Impressionism may have been 'primitive' but it was also profoundly liberating, releasing British artists from the straitjacket of stale convention. Taking a sledgehammer to the shibboleths of the academies, it opened up a world of possibility for self-expression. 'Freedom was given to be oneself,' she said. The encouragement to see and feel without inhibition was 'absolutely overwhelming'.[18] Writers, too, were affected. Katherine Mansfield was indelibly impressed by the brushwork of Van Gogh. It taught her something about her budding craft: 'a kind of freedom – or rather, a shaking free'.[19] Well might Vanessa remember the autumn of 1910 as 'a time when everything seemed springing to new life – a time when all was a sizzle of excitement.'[20] Prefiguring the language of the counter-cultural Sixties by two decades, Desmond MacCarthy would, in a retrospective penned in 1945, describe the exhibition as an 'Art-Quake'.

A gradual improvement in Virginia Stephen's health had seen her return to London by mid-October. In a letter to Violet Dickinson, she was mildly derisive about the show that was offending and electrifying in roughly equal measure. 'Why all the Duchesses are insulted by the Post-Impressionists, a modest sample set of painters, innocent even of indecency, I can't conceive,' she confessed. 'However, one mustn't say that they are like other pictures, only better, because that makes everybody angry.'[21]

Nevertheless, Virginia, like the rest of her set, was soon in thrall to the opportunities the exhibition afforded for old forms of mischief as well as new modes of representation. Back in February, she and her co-conspirators had donned fancy dress to deceive their way aboard the *Dreadnought*. Besides subverting the tropes of race and gender, the stunt had cocked a snook at three of the foundations – royalty, the military and the Empire – upon which the Edwardian edifice rested. Headlines had been generated, but meaningful change was neither intended nor effected.

Twelve months on, three of the *Dreadnought* hoaxers, Virginia, her brother Adrian and Duncan Grant, as well as Fry and the Bells, attended a costume ball in Chelsea. Once again, they assumed the trappings of 'exotic' otherness – flowers, beads and brilliant fabrics with 'very little on beneath the draperies' – in an approximation of figures by Gauguin.[22] The reference, which until recently would have been obscure as well as scandalous, was lost on nobody. When the party swept into the ballroom in triumph, the dancers stopped to applaud. The older guests shook their heads. Bloomsbury, which had set the revolution in motion, couldn't have cared less.

The exploit was a symptom of how far things had travelled. In the final weeks of 1910, Post-Impressionism had advanced from the fringe to the forefront of the collective imagination with astonishing rapidity. Already, Fry was mulling plans for a follow-up exhibition to include British and Russian as well as French painters. From hence, the divide was not to be between London and the Continent, but between those who resisted the forces of modernity and those who embraced them. One way or another, the art of the future would look very different from everything that had gone before.

That autumn, the tectonic plates of Edwardian England were shifting in every direction. The explosive impact of the show at the Grafton Galleries sprang from and fed back into the pent-up appetite for reform which had been suppressed during the summer of mourning for the King. Frank Rutter, the art critic of *The Sunday Times*, cast the Post-Impressionists as front-line warriors in a universal struggle in which painting and politics were indivisibly linked. Provocatively entitled *Revolution in Art*, his little book on Cézanne, Gauguin, Van Gogh 'and Other Modern Painters' was dedicated, in bold capitals, 'TO THE REBELS OF EITHER SEX ALL THE WORLD OVER

WHO IN ANY WAY ARE FIGHTING FOR FREEDOM OF ANY KIND'.[23]

Rutter knew of what he wrote. A founder member of the Men's League for Women's Suffrage and the Men's Political Union for Women's Enfranchisement, he was increasingly embroiled in the campaign for the vote that was about to erupt into violence of the most shocking kind.

Two days after the opening of 'Manet and the Post-Impressionists', the inter-party conference between the Liberals and the Conservatives, which had got off to such a promising start in June, collapsed. In the wake of the Parliament Bill passed by the Commons, the Lords had signalled willingness to reach some sort of compromise. Their counter-proposals were not deemed sufficiently far-reaching, so the Cabinet decided it had no choice but to request a dissolution to be followed, inevitably, by a general election.

The crisis that had caused Edward such anxiety in his final months was now thrust onto the shoulders of his successor. The Prime Minister, who was determined it must be brought to a decisive conclusion, demanded that the King provide a guarantee that he would, if necessary, create a sufficient number of peers to flood the Lords and so see the Bill through. To Edward, the very idea had been repugnant. It sat no more comfortably with George but, after an extremely tense meeting with Asquith and Lord Crewe on 16 November, he gave his begrudging consent. Almost as distasteful to the straight-dealing sovereign as the guarantee itself was the injunction that it should be kept secret. In the event, the election in December yielded almost exactly the same results as the one the previous January. Far from being settled, the war between the Commons and the Lords rolled over for its denouement into 1911.

Preoccupied as he was by these developments, Asquith, who had never been in favour of the Conciliation Bill, which had received its second reading in July, let it be known that there would be no time that year for further progress to be made. For the suffragettes, this unwelcome news was not entirely unexpected. In late October, Mrs Pankhurst had warned the WSPU that the vacillating Liberals would likely sink the Bill. 'We shall know how to respond to such a declaration of war,' she wrote menacingly. 'Our power as women is invincible, if we are united and determined.'[24] At a rally in the Royal Albert

Hall on 10 November, she 'threw down the gage of battle' when she announced her intention to petition the Prime Minister in person when Parliament reconvened. Hundreds of members pledged to go with her.

On Friday, 18 November, the suffragettes gathered in Caxton Hall. Situated a short distance from the Palace of Westminster, its walls and balconies were festooned with colourful banners. Their martial slogans – 'Deeds Not Words', 'Go On Pestering' and, most stirring of all, 'Arise! Go Forth and Conquer!' – left nobody in any doubt that a return to militancy after the ten-month truce was in the offing. The bulletin that arrived as the women took their seats detonated like a hand grenade in the already volatile atmosphere. Parliament was to be dissolved on 28 November. The Conciliation Bill on which so many hopes had rested was dead in the water.

The immediate reaction was one of fury. Annie Kenney compared it to 'a great storm-burst. All the clouds that had been gathering for weeks suddenly broke, and the downpour was terrific.'[25] Gathering her volunteers, Mrs Pankhurst set out on foot for the Commons. Delegations of more than a dozen were prohibited by law, so she was accompanied by only a handful. The rest would divide into groups of the same size to follow at two- or three-minute intervals throughout the afternoon.

To her delight, Edith Chibnall was one of those selected to go in the first party. At the age of forty-six, she brought the same conviction to the fight for the vote that she had to the question of her daughter's education. That day, she was in illustrious company. Her companions included the venerable Elizabeth Garrett Anderson; the Honourable Evelina Haverfield, one of the earliest and most committed of the militants; and Sophia Duleep Singh, an Indian princess who lived in a grace-and-favour apartment at Hampton Court Palace provided for her by the Crown.

The women were aware they were advancing into hostile territory. Even so, their reception in Westminster, which they reached around 1.20 p.m., was far uglier than anything they had encountered before. The ground had been prepared by a separate band of suffragettes who were marching up and down with banners. Attracted by the spectacle, a crowd had gathered to witness the arrivals from Caxton Hall. At the sight of Mrs Pankhurst, it surged forward. Somehow, the deputation was able to struggle through the jostling and jeering throng until it reached St Stephen's Entrance. Prevented from proceeding any further, Pankhurst and her followers watched in horror as successive groups of women were subjected to verbal, physical and sexual abuse.

In their coverage the next day, the papers played down the warfare that had erupted on the very threshold of Parliament. The police, claimed *The Times*, 'kept their tempers very well, but their method of shoving back the raiders lacked nothing in vigour'.[26] The *Daily Mirror* concurred. The men 'displayed great good temper and tact', but 'many of the suffragettes refused to be happy until they were arrested'.[27] The women had been inflamed by their leaders, it implied. They had come looking for trouble, and it was trouble they had found.

Such accounts belied the brutality that had, by evening, left many suffragettes bruised, battered and traumatised. In a letter published in *The Times* several months later, sixty-six-year-old Georgiana Solomon claimed that 'The methods applied to us were those used by the police to conquer the pugilistic antagonist, to fell the burglar, to maim the hooligan, or to reduce to inanity the semi-barbaric and dangerous rough.'[28] Bent double beneath the weight of one constable, her arms were almost wrenched from their sockets by several of his colleagues. Another woman was flung against a lamppost with such violence that her teeth were loosened. 'I will teach you a lesson. I will teach you not to come back any more. I will punish you, you —, you —,' snarled her assailant. The elisions in the official record denoted obscenities.[29]

One suffragette was pitched out of her wheelchair and beaten. Another was tossed into the road where she narrowly avoided being struck by a passing car. Nearly thirty women had their breasts grabbed and their long skirts lifted. The banners that had waved so bravely that morning were snatched and shredded. Within the Commons, the Prime Minister refused suggestions by appalled MPs that he should at least receive Mrs Pankhurst. When the House rose at 6 p.m., and the exhausted and bedraggled suffragettes staggered back to Caxton Hall to tend their wounded, there had been more than a hundred arrests. On the orders of the Home Secretary, Winston Churchill, all the prisoners were speedily discharged. No advantage would be gained by proceeding with the prosecution, he declared.

A defiant Edith fired off a telegram to her daughter to assure her of her safety. She followed up with a letter in which she described the fracas in detail. Her scorn for both police and politicians was withering. 'I must say that the behaviour of the Men + Members especially is not such that we women can be proud of and trust to,' she raged. Their actions would, she maintained, 'hold them up to the contempt of the whole civilised world for the way in which they allow their women to be treated when they make a just claim'.[30]

From Cambridge, Elsie, who was 'simply wild with excitement', congratulated her on bold new stationery emblazoned with the logo and colours of the WSPU. 'How glorious to have gone with Mrs Pankhurst,' she exclaimed. 'It makes me feel very envious.'[31] The dauntless Edith was not done yet. On Monday, 21 November, she was back in Westminster with senior suffragettes to request a meeting with the Prime Minister. This time there was no violence but, once again, they were denied entry.

Impressed as she was by her mother's tenacity, Elsie grew concerned for her well-being. 'I hope you won't go on any more raids,' she wrote on 23 November. 'I think you have done your share for one week.'[32] She was right to worry. Faced with the intransigence of the beleaguered Government, the WSPU grew more confrontational. Mrs Pankhurst led a delegation to Downing Street, where they attempted to storm Number 10. Although they were not able to gain access to the residence, they did manage to subject Asquith, who arrived unannounced, to some rough handling of their own. Bundled into a taxi, he was whisked away, but not before the cab window was smashed. Edith, who had so far evaded injury, was on that occasion left badly shaken and took to her bed for a period of recuperation. Glass was shattered at the homes of Churchill and Sir Edward Grey, as well as that of 'Loulou' Harcourt, who had recently left the Office of Works to become Secretary of State for the Colonies. The militant campaign was once again in full swing.

'Black Friday', 18 November 1910, became infamous in the annals of the WSPU. With hindsight, it was viewed as a watershed in the ongoing fight for the vote. On the one hand, the violence so indiscriminately meted out to peaceful campaigners frightened away those members reluctant to submit themselves to such treatment in future. On the other, conviction hardened that the time for conciliation had passed. The suffragettes would continue to stage rallies and choreographed marches, but from now on they were shadowed by a guerrilla programme of direct action that lurched ever further into the realm of extremism. If Black Ascot – dignified, decorous, well-ordered – had been the elegant epilogue to an era that had drawn to its close with the death of Edward VII, Black Friday presaged the discord and division of the one that was opening. The values, assumptions and hierarchies of the Edwardian age would not vanish overnight, but they found themselves increasingly at odds with the forces that were to define the century now hitting its stride. When, on 25 November, Christabel Pankhurst announced in *Votes for Women* that 'Negotiations are over. War is declared', she was more prescient than she knew.[33]

For the men and women who had been closest to Edward, the final weeks of 1910 were defined less by an awareness of new beginnings than by a sense that a curtain had been wrung down for good. Queen Alexandra vacated Buckingham Palace in early December. Even though she would be returning to Marlborough House, her marital home of almost forty years, she was in tears when she took her leave. Queen Mary, who moved into temporary quarters at the Palace a few days ahead of her husband, wrote him a plaintive letter. 'It is rather strange & lonely here without you & the children & I feel rather lost,' she admitted.[34] In his zealousness to create a *mise-en-scène* worthy of his theatrical conception of the Crown, her father-in-law had, Mary felt, gone a little too far. 'Many things were changed here and at Windsor much too quickly by our predecessors,' she observed crisply.[35] She wasted little time in drawing up plans for renovations of her own. While his wife settled in, George attended a men-only shoot at Elveden. 'In deference to His Majesty's well-known prejudice in favour of the comparatively simple life', Lord Iveagh toned down the luxury as well as the larkiness that had so endeared the place to Edward.[36]

In October, a revolution in Lisbon toppled the Portuguese monarchy. Of the nine sovereigns to have attended the funeral in May, King Manuel was the first to be swept from his throne. As Portuguese ambassador, the Marquis de Soveral – 'genial, merry, loquacious, discreet' – had been one of the most popular men in London Society.[37] Now he was compelled to resign his post.

Sir Ernest Cassel also took a step back. Mirthless but devoted, he had spent the months since Edward's death making endowments in his memory. In August, he set aside £200,000 to be used to assist struggling English workers in his native Germany and German workers in his adopted England. That was followed by a £5,000 contribution to the Lord Mayor's Fund of which he was a committee member. The plaudits he received for such conspicuous acts of philanthropy were no compensation for the absence of the royal favour in which he had basked for so long. Just before Christmas, he announced his retirement from the world of finance.

For Mrs Keppel, the process of recalibration had barely started. After a face-saving sojourn in Scotland, she dropped a bombshell on her daughters. Debutantes were expected to be fluent in French, and to possess a working knowledge of German and Italian too. Tamil figured nowhere on the list of ladylike accomplishments until the former favourite declared its rudiments to be indispensable. Violet and Sonia were duly whisked away to Sir Thomas Lipton's tea plantation in Ceylon. After several months, they were sent back to Europe: not to London, but to an international school in Munich while their mother travelled on to China. When at last she reappeared, Sonia failed to recognise her. Over the course of the preceding year, her hair had turned completely white.

16: 'On or about December 1910, human character changed'

On 16 May 1911, the Victoria Memorial was unveiled by George V. Orchestrated by Fritz Ponsonby, the ceremony went without a hitch. All the Queen's surviving children were there, and so were many of her grandchildren. Foremost among them was the Kaiser. During his visit to London for Edward's funeral, Wilhelm had mounted the scaffolding to inspect the work at close quarters. A year on, he reaffirmed his commitment to the cause of Anglo-German solidarity. In accordance with his uncle's wishes, his presence was sure, he said, to produce

'the happiest results in the relations between the two countries and the two sovereigns'.[1] Expatriate Germans turned out in force to enjoy the spectacle of the King and the Kaiser united in friendship as well as blood. The weather was perfect. Only later in the day did clouds gather ahead of what promised to be a terrific storm.

Ostensibly a commemoration of the reign of Queen Victoria, the Memorial inevitably called to mind thoughts of her successor. For almost a decade, Edward had watched its halting construction with what George, in his speech of dedication, described as 'tender interest and close attention'. Now his spectre was evoked as one of the most important links in 'a golden chain of personality, of memory and of love'.[2] The association was too painful for Queen Alexandra, who was conspicuous by her absence.

The unveiling marked the apotheosis of the Memorial's designer, Thomas Brock. In a gesture of uncharacteristic spontaneity, George knighted him on the spot. By then, the sculptor's connection with the Crown was indissoluble. Acting on behalf of a group of Edward's closest friends, Lord Esher had commissioned him to model a bust of the late King to be presented to George on the day of his Coronation. In 1913, copies were distributed to the friends themselves: not just to Esher, but to Lord Rosebery, Lord Crewe, the Marquis de Soveral, Sir Ernest Cassel and Arthur Sassoon too.

Reactions to Brock's greatest – at any rate, largest – achievement were mixed. Was the abundance of allegorical statuary a little too bombastic, the critics wondered, and was the gilded figure of Victory a little too blatant? On the whole, *The Times* decided it approved. Nevertheless, it couldn't let the occasion pass without echoing the sentiments of those who had, since the previous summer, lobbied for a remodelling of Buckingham Palace. Behind so much white marble and glittering gold leaf, the Mall-facing East Front looked dingier than ever. When, the paper demanded to know, was it to be rebuilt 'in a style and a material . . . worthy of the British Monarchy?'[3]

On the same day the Victoria Memorial was unveiled, the Parliament Bill, which had been reintroduced in late February, received its first reading in the House of Lords. After months of strife, the debate raged as fiercely as ever. The leader of the Opposition, Arthur Balfour, decried the Bill as 'an instrument of revolution',[4] while the Prime

Minister, Herbert Henry Asquith, retorted that the Lords had sealed their own doom when they rejected the Budget back in 1909.

In fact, a schism was developing in the second chamber. On the one hand were the 'Hedgers': peers who, however begrudgingly, recognised that it would be better to accede to the proposed reform, lest they be swamped by new creations who would pass the Bill anyway. On the other were the 'Ditchers': diehards who were prepared to hold out against any infraction of their hereditary rights until 'the last ditch'. During the summer of 1911, the conflicts – not just between the Commons and the Lords, but between the rival factions within the Lords – witnessed the almost complete collapse of working relations between the main political parties.

In mid-July, the Lords returned so many amendments to the Bill that an exasperated Asquith considered it no longer fit for purpose. The idea of a third election being unconscionable, he informed the King that he would, if pressed, advise him to exercise his Royal Prerogative to create a sufficient number of peers to ensure the Bill's passage. George agonised, but at last accepted that, as a constitutional monarch, he would have little choice but to agree. Once he had signalled his consent, he spent an unhappy hour with his dentist.

On 24 July, the Lords' proposed amendments went before the Commons. The atmosphere was so rancorous the Prime Minister couldn't make himself heard above the abuse hurled against him by the Opposition. The attack was led by Lord Hugh Cecil, the fire-brand son of the late Lord Salisbury, who was the ring-leader of a gang of boisterous Conservatives dubbed the 'Hughligans'. Considered by Asquith to be 'the best speaker in the House of Commons and indeed anywhere', Cecil was a dangerous enemy. In him, Winston Churchill recalled, 'I met for the first time a real Tory, a being out of the Seventeenth Century.'[5]

That day, Cecil and his followers accused the Prime Minister of treachery, and of having precipitated Edward's death by placing upon him an unbearable burden of stress (a charge, incidentally, with which the resentful Queen Alexandra concurred). For forty-five minutes, pandemonium reigned. At last, Asquith folded his speech and resumed his seat. 'I am not going to degrade myself or my office by attempting to say more in an Assembly that will not hear me,' he said.[6] The statement he had been unable to deliver was instead printed in the press.

It warned the House that the Lords were backing the Government into a corner from which, in spite of its reluctance, it would be compelled to invoke the Prerogative.

Faced with this dire prospect, more moderate peers resolved to facilitate the passage of the Bill by abstaining from the final vote. Lady Victoria Stanley's father, the Earl of Derby, was one of them. He had started off with the Ditchers, but now came over to the Hedgers. 'I should certainly have been with the Stalwarts if I thought I could have done any good by so doing,' he explained to the editor of the *National Review*. 'But as the action they take will neither defeat the Bill nor result in the insertion of our amendments but only on the contrary present the Government with a majority in the Upper House as well as in the Lower House, I can see no good to be gained by dying in the last ditch.'[7] Yet even with such tactical abstentions, the number of Conservative peers was so great the Ditchers could still unite to thwart the Bill. Clearly, some of the moderates would have to swallow their scruples and back legislation inimical to their own interests.

Spearheaded by Lord Curzon, the former Viceroy of India, a campaign was launched to talk around those deemed most susceptible to reason. The King himself waded into the fray when, over an intimate lunch at Buckingham Palace, he asked Lord Rosebery to vote with the Liberals. Put on the spot, Rosebery at first refused. The following day, swayed by a mixture of loyalty and pragmatism, he agreed to abide by his sovereign's wishes.

The climactic battle of the epic struggle was fought on Thursday, 10 August, when the tension within the Lords was almost as unbearable as the furnace-like heat on the streets outside. Until the last moment, it was touch and go. Ultimately, the machinations of the Hedgers paid off. The Archbishop of Canterbury voted in favour, bringing a dozen bishops with him. So did Rosebery, who accounted for the conversion of around twenty of his fellow members. The Bill was passed by 131 to 114. For George, who was spared the 'odious necessity' of a mass creation of peers, the relief was incalculable. 'If they had been made, I should never have been the same again, the humiliation would have been so great,' he told Queen Mary.[8]

It had been a summer of extraordinary political drama and equally extraordinary social splendour. Even as it contemplated the destruction of its privileges in Parliament, the aristocracy had massed in velvet and ermine at the Coronation on 22 June. Weeks of balls, dinners and garden parties had ensued as the thermometer nudged 100°F in the shade. At the Savoy, guests were sprayed with cooling ozone as they tapped their toes to the raucous strains of the ragtime that had just swept in from America.[9]

To compensate for the ubiquitous black of the previous year, the palette of that Season ran rainbow-riot. The Post-Impressionists had been partly responsible for awakening London to the potential of flamboyant colour contrasts. The refined vernacular of the eighteenth century suddenly seemed insipid, if not downright precious. 'I believe elegance is becoming rather tiresome,' remarked Vanessa Bell after viewing a set of rooms decorated by Robert Adam. In revolt against everything pastel-tinted and proper, she sallied forth to Debenham & Freebody to buy stockings of green and red.[10]

However, it was the Russian Ballet, recently arrived at Covent Garden, that effected the greatest transformation. The combined talents of Sergei Diaghilev and Michel Fokine, Alexandre Benois and Léon Bakst, Vaslav Nijinsky and Tamara Karsavina launched what *The Times* called 'an aesthetic revolution . . . a positively new art'. The Russians 'extended the realm of beauty for us, discovered a new continent, revealed new faculties and means of salvation in ourselves.'[11] Society and Bloomsbury were enthralled.

From 1911, the Orientalism of Rimsky-Korsakov's *Scheherazade*, Stravinsky's *Firebird* and Strauss's *Joseph* carried all before it. Lady Duff Gordon's French rival, Paul Poiret, challenged the sweet-pea shades of the Edwardian era with strident scarlets, jades, purples and oranges. Not to be outdone, Lucile Ltd responded with *têtes de couleurs*: wigs of blue or pink to be worn while dancing the tango, which was all the rage from 1912. The fashionable silhouette remained narrow, but skirts were slit, draped and tiered, overlaid with wired 'lampshade' tunics, and surmounted by lamé turbans crowned with bristling aigrettes. In June 1914, 'Eve', writing in the *Tatler*, could describe the 'absolute screams in the way of frocks being got ready for Ascot'. The more bizarre the ensembles, the more 'fearfully right' they were likely to be.[12]

By then, the suffragettes' militant campaign was at fever-pitch. The previous year, Emily Davison had been fatally injured at the Epsom

Derby when she threw herself beneath the hoofs of the King's horse in full view of thousands of stunned spectators. Now, the police took no chances. Even in the Royal Enclosure, female race-goers were subjected to body-searches, lest their swirling capes should conceal hammers or bombs. It was a far cry from the subdued decorum of Black Ascot. Edward VII would have wondered what the world was coming to.

In an essay on literature published in 1924, Virginia Stephen – since her marriage in 1912, Virginia Woolf – looked back over the preceding quarter-century to pinpoint December 1910 as its point of departure. It was then, she maintained, that 'human character' had changed, and with it very much else.[13]

In making such a bold assertion, she took pains to protect herself. She admitted that her choice of date was somewhat arbitrary, and so open to dispute. She also explained that the transformation, although profound, had been neither so sudden nor so definite as a hen laying an egg or a rose bursting into bloom. Still, having traced the developments of that tumultuous year, it is hard not to believe she had a point.

1910 had opened with a minor sensation (the *Dreadnought* hoax) and concluded with a major one (the Post-Impressionist exhibition). Between had come the summer of mourning for the King. Although her essay made no reference to any of those events, Virginia surely recognised that each had, to some degree, marked a further step away from the Victorian era and its all-too-brief Edwardian coda. That journey, which continued unchecked until 1914, and accelerated dramatically with the outbreak of the First World War, fostered the social, cultural and political conditions that were to define the rest of the century.

Hailed in his lifetime as 'the Peacemaker', Edward VII was spared the destruction of the European order of courts and crowned cousins in which he had been the dominant figure. Both of his imperial nephews, Tsar Nicholas of Russia and Kaiser Wilhelm of Germany, were brought low. Along with his wife and all of their children, Nicholas was butchered by the Bolsheviks in the summer of 1918. The year before, George V, worried about his own position, had resisted the suggestion that they should be given refuge in Britain. Once the news of their murders had been confirmed, he despatched a battleship to the Crimea to rescue his aunt, the Dowager Empress Marie, as well as a large party of her relations and retainers. Grand Duke Michael Alexandrovich, who had represented Nicholas at Edward's funeral, was not among them. The first of the Romanovs to die, he had been taken into a forest in the Urals and shot a month before his elder brother. In the chaos that enveloped Russia during that terrible period, another, more improbable, victim met his end. Minoru, the royal racehorse which had swept to victory in the Epsom Derby of 1909, had subsequently been sold to a stud near Kharkiv for £20,000. He was last seen struggling to draw a cart on the 900-mile evacuation from Moscow to the Black Sea.

Swept from his throne just before the Armistice in November 1918, the Kaiser was fortunate to escape with his life. He passed the remainder of his days in comfortable but ignominious exile in the Netherlands, never ceasing to rage against the legacy of his hated uncle, whose machinations had, he insisted, contributed to his downfall. 'It is he who is the corpse and I who live on, but it is he who is the victor,' Wilhelm snarled shortly before his death in 1941.[14]

Schomburg McDonnell, the organisational genius who had masterminded Edward's lying-in-state in Westminster Hall, had expressed a desire to be spared such elaborate obsequies. His wish was granted. In November 1915, at the age of fifty-four, he died of wounds sustained at Ypres: just one of almost nine hundred thousand British soldiers to perish in the war. Interred in a military cemetery in Belgium, McDonnell would have been amazed, and possibly aghast, had he learnt that Winston Churchill, whom he had routed on the threshold of the Hall on the eve of the funeral, would half a century later lie in state in precisely the same spot as the King.

In the spring of 1915, Lady Victoria Stanley, who, but for Edward's death, would have been one of the star debutantes of 1910, married the Honourable Neil Primrose at St Margaret's, Westminster. Their wedding was attended by everyone from Queen Alexandra and Margot Asquith to the Marquis de Soveral and an assortment of Sassoons. In November 1917, Neil was killed as he fought against the Turks outside Jerusalem. His grief-stricken father Lord Rosebery was inundated with so many messages of condolence that he was unable to reply to them all. Instead, he arranged for a letter of appreciation to be printed in all the leading papers.

A widow at twenty-five, Victoria accompanied her father to Paris when he was appointed British ambassador in early 1918. Notwithstanding German air-raids and the ravages of Spanish flu, they were enthusiastically embraced by their hosts. An ebullient sportsman, Lord Derby was viewed as the spiritual successor of Edward VII. When Britain and France emerged from the war as victorious allies, it was felt that the Entente Cordiale had attained its 'historic and fateful fulfilment'.[15] Returning home in triumph, Lord Derby's cup of joy overflowed when, in 1924, he won the race to bear his name with his horse Sansovino.

In Paris, which she considered to be 'the most wonderful place in the world', Victoria plunged headlong into the Jazz Age. Casting off the corsets and ankle-length dresses of her youth, she relished the new short skirts in which she could show off her thin silk stockings. She confessed to her mother that in the salons of Chanel and Patou she had 'entirely lost my head . . . & have bought masses'.[16] In June 1919, she married Captain Malcolm Bullock, an attaché at the British Embassy. The congregation included many of the leading statesmen who had convened for the Peace Conference that concluded with the signing of the Treaty of Versailles.

In 1923, Bullock was elected Conservative MP for the constituency of Waterloo near Liverpool. When she wasn't campaigning on his behalf, Victoria immersed herself in the equestrian pursuits she had adored since childhood. While hunting with the Quorn in the autumn of 1927, she was knocked unconscious by a low bridge, and died of her injuries soon afterwards. Lord Derby was devastated. 'No year in future can be a happy one – except the one in which I re-join her,' he wrote to his son-in-law.[17] Victoria and Malcolm's only daughter, Priscilla, inherited her mother's passion for racing. In 1977, she was one of the first women to be elected a member of the Jockey Club. Priscilla's granddaughter is the well-known sports presenter Clare Balding.

The strides in technology that had defined Edward's reign continued at a dizzying pace. Less than eighteen years after he had crossed the Channel, Louis Blériot was on hand to greet Charles Lindburgh when he landed in France after his flight across the Atlantic. Just as

H. G. Wells had predicted, aeroplanes had by then been deployed as lethal weapons. The primitive air raids of the First World War would be reprised on an infinitely more devastating scale across Europe and Japan between 1939 and 1945.

The sensational pursuit and capture of Dr Crippen had demonstrated the efficacy of wireless to those who had yet to be convinced. Crippen himself was dead before the year was out. Throughout his trial, he had continued to protest his innocence. The jury, which took less than half an hour to reach its verdict, believed otherwise. Convicted on the back of what seemed an overwhelming body of evidence, he was hanged at Pentonville Prison on 23 November 1910. Charged with being an accessory after the fact, Ethel Le Neve was acquitted. Changing her name, she married, had two children and died in obscurity in 1967. To this day, question marks hang over the crime. The exact method Crippen used to murder Cora is a matter of conjecture. It is generally believed he administered poison, then slit her throat before draining her blood and dismembering her corpse with surgical precision. The case, which became one of the most notorious of the century, was acknowledged by Alfred Hitchcock as an inspiration for his 1954 film, *Rear Window*.

In April 1912, the optimism engendered by the apparently unstoppable march of technology was shattered in the most dramatic circumstances. Vaunted as unsinkable, the super-liner *Titanic*, which had been under construction in Belfast since 1909, sank after collision with an iceberg while on her maiden voyage from Southampton to New York. In spite of her glittering luxury, she carried lifeboats for only a fraction of her passengers and crew. More than fifteen hundred souls were lost in the worst-ever disaster at sea. Britain and the United States were rocked to their foundations by the most shocking event in living memory.

Before she foundered, the *Titanic* was able to summon help by wireless. Among the pitifully few survivors rescued by the *Carpathia* were Edith Chibnall and Elsie Bowerman, who had been on their way to visit suffragette sympathisers in the Midwest. Remarkably unperturbed by their ordeal, they saw no reason to change their plans. Landing in America, they proceeded to Indianapolis, Chicago and Niagara. Heading northward into Canada, they were persuaded by some cousins to embark on a cruise to Alaska. Even the doughty Elsie confessed that that late addition to their schedule was, hard on the heels of the *Titanic*, 'somewhat nerve-wracking'.[18]

At home, mother and daughter retained their involvement with the WSPU as its militant campaign intensified up to the summer of 1914. In the event, it was the contribution women made to the war effort that saw the franchise awarded to female property owners over the age of thirty in 1918. Another ten years were to elapse before women would enjoy electoral equality with men. In 1930, a statue of Emmeline Pankhurst was unveiled in Westminster, not far from the spot where, two decades earlier, she and Edith had watched the violent assault of the delegations from Caxton Hall.

Elsie's wartime exploits were more exciting than most. In 1916, she was invited by Evelina Haverfield, who had marched with her mother on 'Black Friday', to accompany her to Serbia to support the work of the Scottish Women's Hospitals. Over the next few months, she journeyed from Archangel to Odessa, and from there to the Romanian front. In her spare time, she had many adventures. Galloping across the moonlit snow with a group of Cossacks and attending an opera gala in the presence of the Tsar's aunt, Grand Duchess Vladimir, were among the more memorable. In 1917, she was in Petrograd (as St Petersburg had been rechristened at the outbreak of war) to witness at close and sometimes perilous quarters the outbreak of the Russian Revolution. At the time, her belief in progress caused her to view it as a 'perfectly wonderful experience'. The uprising was 'amazingly well-organised & the self-control of the people was beyond all praise. They certainly deserve to succeed.'[19]

Elsie's enthusiasm for the far-left did not endure. Upon her return to England, she became increasingly conservative, campaigning against Communism and trade unionism as well as the dark new creed of Fascism. In 1924, in a step symbolic of the advancement of her sex, she was called to the Bar, becoming one of the first female barristers to appear at the Old Bailey. Until her death in 1973, she remained devoted to her alma mater, Wycombe Abbey. The embodiment of the principles of self-reliance and public service expounded by Frances Dove, her memory is cherished at the school to this day.

Among the other survivors of the *Titanic* was Lady Duff Gordon. Her husband Sir Cosmo made a gift of five pounds to each of the crewmen in their lifeboat, which, like many others, left the sinking liner with unfilled spaces. His well-meaning gesture was misconstrued by a sensationalist press looking for scapegoats. Amid baseless allegations of cowardice and bribery, the Duff Gordons were summoned to testify before the British Inquiry into the disaster. In a display of solidarity and support, London Society packed the galleries to hear the couple speak. When she took the stand, Lucy, in a faint echo of Black Ascot, was attired in mourning for the *Titanic*'s victims. In its front-page coverage, the *Daily News & Leader* described 'the sweep of a large black picture hat, shading her eyes to the left, and dropping with a hint of tears over the left shoulder'.[20]

Exonerated of the charges brought against him, Sir Cosmo was forever grieved by the aspersions cast upon his honour as a gentleman. Nothing daunted, Lucy immersed herself in work in her flourishing salons in New York, Paris and, latterly, even Chicago. During the First World War, she grew richer and more famous than ever, designing ultra-feminine gowns for such celebrities as the ballroom dancer Irene Castle and the movie goddess Mary Pickford, as well as lavish costumes for the star-studded *Ziegfeld Follies*. But the glory years were not to last. In the early Twenties, financial reverses caused the once-mighty Lucile empire to falter. In spite of the reduction in her circumstances, Lady Duff Gordon continued to create almost until her death in 1935. For a time, her legacy was overshadowed by those of her French competitors. She is now acknowledged to have been one of the most innovative and influential couturières of her era.

Sir Ernest Cassel's devotion to the memory of the late King never waned. In 1911, he presented land to the town of Newmarket upon which the King Edward VII Memorial Hall was erected a stone's throw from the Jockey Club. As a tribute to a monarch who had loved racing, it was peculiarly apt. Eager to dissociate himself from his German origins, Cassel made lavish donations to the British Red Cross and other charities throughout the war. His philanthropy made little dent in his colossal fortune. When he died in 1921, his estate was valued at over seven million pounds. The following year, his granddaughter Edwina, who as a child had shared the royal holidays in Biarritz, married Edward's great-nephew, Lord Louis Mountbatten. In due course, the couple would become the last viceroy and vicereine of India. Mountbatten was also the maternal uncle of Prince Philip, Duke of Edinburgh.

Alice Keppel's withdrawal in the wake of the King's death was a smart move. When at last she reappeared, Society welcomed her with open arms. Establishing herself in a new house on Grosvenor Street, where she could indulge what Osbert Sitwell described as her 'instinct for splendour',[21] the former favourite was admired and respected by almost all. She never forsook her policy of discretion and, unlike many of her contemporaries, she never published her memoirs. Her view of the Abdication Crisis, when Edward's grandson Edward VIII gave up his throne for the love of Wallis Simpson, was revealing. 'Things were done much better in my day,' she sighed.[22]

In 1920, Mrs Keppel's younger daughter, Sonia, made a suitable marriage to Lord Ashcombe's son, the Honourable Roland Cubitt. In 1947, Sonia's granddaughter, Camilla Shand, was born two months before Alice's death. Married to Andrew Parker Bowles in 1973, Camilla was divorced in 1995. Today, she is Queen Consort to Edward's great-great-grandson, King Charles III.

Violet Keppel, later Trefusis, courted scandal when, in 1918, she embarked upon a passionate affair with her friend Vita Sackville-West, who had been one of the most reluctant debutantes of 1910. By 1921, the liaison had run its shattering course. Violet settled down to a career as a social and literary figure of some renown. Vita achieved an excellent understanding with her husband, Harold Nicolson, and together they established a legendary garden at Sissinghurst in Kent. In the mid-Twenties, she began a relationship with Virginia Woolf, who, as the author of *Mrs Dalloway* and *To the Lighthouse*, was one of the most celebrated writers of her generation. In 1928, Virginia was inspired by Vita's illustrious lineage to pen her gender-shifting fantasy *Orlando*.

During the same period, Vita worked on her own novel, *The Edwardians*. Into it, she poured her recollections of life in the lost world of her aristocratic youth: the country houses, the clothes, the food and the infidelities. 'I find that these things are a great deal more vivid to me than many things which have occurred since, but will they convey anything whatever to anyone else?' she wrote doubtfully to Virginia.[23]

The answer was yes. Published in 1930, *The Edwardians* capitalised on renewed interest in the stately era before the war. In its first six months, it sold 30,000 copies. 'No character in this book is wholly fictitious,' announced Vita, provocatively, and readers had fun assigning real-life identities to its colourful cast. The Jewish financier Sir Adam is clearly modelled on Sir Ernest Cassel, while sexy Romola Cheyne is obviously Mrs Keppel. Looming just off-stage is the benevolent bulk of Edward VII himself. 'I always felt that he kept things together somehow,' remarks a disconsolate duchess after his death in the final pages. 'Oh dear, how things are breaking up.'[24]

The Bloomsbury Group continued to weave its complicated web of literary, artistic and sexual relations. In 1911, Roger Fry began an affair with Vanessa Bell. Vanessa eventually transferred her affections to one of the *Dreadnought* hoaxers, Duncan Grant, who was predominantly gay, but who fathered a daughter by her in 1918. The child, Angelica, was raised by Vanessa's husband, Clive, as his own. In 1916, Vanessa and Grant acquired a Sussex farmhouse, Charleston, which they shared with Grant's lover, David Garnett, whom Angelica married in 1942. By then, Vanessa's younger sister, Virginia, was dead. Plagued with bouts of mental illness throughout her life – 1910 was a particularly bad year – she had drowned herself in the River Ouse in 1941.

After her pitch-perfect performance at the time of her husband's death, Queen Alexandra lost her way. The First World War cast her still further adrift. In 1915, after a German submarine torpedoed the *Lusitania*, killing almost twelve hundred of her passengers and crew, she beseeched George V to haul down 'those hateful German banners in our sacred Church, St George's at Windsor', and particularly that of the Kaiser, whom she now had reason to loathe more than ever.[25]

Old age, which Alexandra had defied for so long, caught up with her at last. Her deafness became almost total. Unable to reconcile herself to the loss of her fabled good looks, she secluded herself at Sandringham, where she repined her own decrepitude. 'Ugly old woman,' she said. 'Nobody likes me any more.'[26] King George and Queen Mary were unfailingly kind and attentive, but they were greatly saddened by her deterioration. 'It is so hard to see that beautiful woman come to this,' Mary said.[27] On 19 November 1925, Alexandra had a heart attack. Her son and daughter-in-law were with her when she died the following day. With her passing, a crucial link with the Edwardian era was severed. 'The Kingdom is plunged in grief, no one had any idea how loved the old Queen was,' noted the diarist Henry 'Chips' Channon. 'People are weeping in the streets.'[28]

After decades of subservience, Princess Victoria was able to make a life of her own. She had always been close to George, who had granted her a set of apartments in Kensington Palace in 1922. Now she acquired a country house, Coppins in Buckinghamshire, where she lived, unmarried, until her death in 1935. 'How I shall miss her & our daily talks on the telephone,' the King wrote.[29]

Against a backdrop of wars and revolutions, jazz and talking pictures, the General Strike and the rise of Hitler, George V and Queen Mary reigned for a quarter of a century. In 1913, Buckingham Palace was at last remodelled using funds left over from the Victoria Memorial. The new façade – architecturally uninspired but dignified – was a symbol of a particular vision of the monarchy. Mary, for whom the word 'majestic' might have been coined, wore a barely modified version of Edwardian dress well into the 1940s. Even when there were no guests, she invariably donned a tiara for dinner. The King wore his orders and decorations.

George never shared his father's affinity with Europe. Their choice of recuperative resorts was telling. Where Edward had relished Biarritz, his son preferred Bognor. Edward had travelled abroad for a combined total of three months during 1907 and 1908. By contrast, in the sixteen years from 1919, George was absent from Britain for seven weeks.

In 1935, the nation came together to celebrate the Silver Jubilee of a sovereign who, in spite of his lack of glamour, was a reassuring symbol of stability in a world that grew more precarious with each passing year. In London, Selfridges was adorned with a gigantic figure of Britannia. St James's Street was thronged with members of Society admiring the flags and bunting. 'It was like Ascot on Cup Day,' observed Chips Channon.[30] After a service of thanksgiving at St Paul's Cathedral, the King and Queen appeared on the balcony at Buckingham Palace to be cheered by their adoring subjects. Alongside them was their nine-year-old granddaughter, Princess Elizabeth of York.

When George died in January 1936, grief was widespread and sincere, but there was no repetition of the mass mourning of 1910. Court mourning was reduced to nine months, and general mourning was laid aside immediately after the funeral. When George VI died in February 1952, Court mourning was further reduced to ten weeks, and there was no general mourning at all.[31] By that stage, Queen Mary had lived to witness the passing of four successive monarchs. At her son's lying-in-state in Westminster Hall, she was photographed in all the trappings of Edwardian bereavement: black cap, black veil, black gloves and a floor-length black dress. To her left was her daughter-in-law, the widowed Queen Elizabeth. To her right, sorrow etched clearly on her face, was Queen Elizabeth II.

On 20 July 1921, George V, watched by his wife and mother, unveiled a statue of Edward VII on Waterloo Place. The outcome of the Memorial Committee convened eleven years earlier, its dedication had been delayed by the First World War. That day, dignitaries of every stripe assembled to acknowledge their 'debt of deep gratitude and devotion . . . to a great and august Sovereign whose memory the capital city of the Empire will ever cherish and preserve'.[32]

By then, the appellation 'Peacemaker' rang somewhat hollow. Nevertheless, the press paid tribute to the legacy of a king who had defied the low expectations that had accompanied his accession. Edward's passion for racing – which, *The Times* acknowledged, 'endeared him to people of all classes because it was so typically English' – had masked 'a depth of purpose and a human and statesmanlike devotion to the welfare of his people that no English sovereign before him had possessed in fuller measure'.[32] It was those latter qualities, not the fabled love of fun, that were evoked by Bertram Mackennal in his statue of a slimmed-down Edward on horseback, a field marshal's baton clasped in his hand and his gaze trained serenely on the Athenaeum.

Also sculpted by Mackennal was the full-length effigy that surmounts Edward's tomb on the south side of St George's Chapel at Windsor. At first, it had been kept covered with the Royal Standard while the coffin, which had been brought up from the Royal Vault, rested in the adjacent Albert Memorial Chapel. Upon the passing of Queen Alexandra, her remains, and those of Edward, were interred beside each other in the tomb, which was finally revealed in a low-key ceremony in the autumn of 1927. Of white Carrara marble, the recumbent figures of the King and Queen appear timeless in their inscrutable dignity. Alexandra wears a diadem, while Edward nurses his sceptre. Both are clad in flowing robes. Only upon closer inspection does a personal touch reveal itself. Nestled at Edward's feet is a representation of his terrier, Caesar, who had moved the nation to tears during the funeral procession through the streets of London in May 1910. Inseparable from his master in life, he is now bonded to him in death: forlorn but tranquil, and faithful to the end.

EPILOGUE: 'The motionless frieze of ladies like magpies against a white drop'

In November 1918, with the ink barely dry on the Armistice, *The Times* reported that house agents around Ascot were already receiving enquiries about the availability of properties for rent the following summer. Suspended for the duration of the First World War, the annual race meeting would resume in the Season of 1919.

Until his death in 1934, Lord Churchill ran the Royal Enclosure with a rod of iron. The changes sweeping across Britain scarcely registered with a man who continued to uphold the most rigorous standards of exclusivity. Sifting through the deluge of applications for vouchers of admission, he sorted them into three baskets labelled 'Certainly', 'Perhaps' and 'Certainly Not'. It was a task he relished. 'There!' he said, with satisfaction, as he put the finishing touches to his master list for another year. 'Now I am the best-hated and the best-loved man in the country.'[1]

Among those he snubbed was Esther 'Etty' Beaton. The wife of a well-to-do timber merchant, her overtures were repeatedly rebuffed. The 'slap in the face' was especially galling for her ambitious son, Cecil, who yearned for definitive proof that he and his family were 'In Society'.[2]

In the event, it was Cecil Beaton's stellar achievements as a photographer and designer that propelled him into the uppermost echelons of wealth, fashion and celebrity. Blessed with energy, determination and a rapier-sharp eye, he became one of the twentieth century's most formidable arbiters of style. He certainly had his revenge on Lord Churchill. Once deemed unworthy of entry to the Royal Enclosure, he single-handedly redefined the iconography of the Crown. Taken at Buckingham Palace in the summer of 1939, Beaton's ultra-romantic portraits of Queen Elizabeth cemented a relationship that would find its finest expression when he was appointed photographer for the Coronation of Queen Elizabeth II in 1953.

Beaton's fascination with royalty went way back. In 1924, he had glimpsed the aged Queen Alexandra at a flower show at Sandringham. Even then, she retained sufficient glamour to leave an indelible impression. When, six years later, Beaton compiled his *Book of Beauty*, he included as his frontispiece his own sketch of the then Princess of Wales in her late Victorian heyday.*

For Beaton, Alexandra was an avatar of the kind of elegance to which his imagination continually returned. He dated his lifelong obsession with the Edwardian era to the morning upon which, playing on his mother's bed as a tiny boy, he had seen a postcard bearing a picture of the original *Merry Widow*, the 'drenchingly lovely' Lily Elsie. 'The beauty of it caused my heart to leap,' he recalled.[3] In due course, he acquired another postcard of the star, this time wearing the giant black hat designed for her by Lucile Ltd. It was swiftly augmented by innumerable other images of actresses and Society beauties posing for the cameras of Lallie Charles and Rita Martin.

During the irreverent and iconoclastic Jazz Age, Beaton's passion for the period of his childhood was expressed flamboyantly, and

---

* Among the host of Society women and celebrities profiled by Beaton in his *Book of Beauty* was Virginia Woolf. Having previously declined to be photographed by him, she was incensed by what she considered to be his presumption.

occasionally mischievously. Around 1926, he donned full drag in an outrageous imitation of an Edwardian matron. As late as 1939 – the same year he deified Queen Elizabeth – he authored *My Royal Past*, a spoof of the volumes of memoirs by superannuated members of the aristocracy then flooding the market. Illustrated with photographs of his male friends camping it up in tiaras, orders and decorations, it was a wicked subversion of the signed presentation portraits that littered the tables at Marlborough House and Windsor Castle.

With maturity, Beaton's already pronounced nostalgia deepened. In a radically reshaped world menaced by the threat of nuclear annihilation, the Edwardian era seemed infinitely alluring. Sensing that the bombed and rationed audiences of 1945 were 'starved for bright colours, rich silks, artificial flowers',[4] he contributed lavish sets and even more lavish costumes to John Gielgud's revival of Oscar Wilde's play *Lady Windermere's Fan*. Maintaining that the theatre 'at its finest should be an opulent cornucopia showering the spectator with golden illusions',[5] he honed a signature style that, while firmly rooted in the past, was, if anything, even more glamorous and seductive.

In 1954, the now middle-aged Beaton chronicled the evolution of taste over the previous half-century in *The Glass of Fashion*. Part memoir, part survey, it is at once lyrical and acute. Peppered with brisk but incisive sketches, it reads as a manifesto of his entire aesthetic, with a particular emphasis on the formative influence of the years preceding 1914. To Beaton, they were the missing link 'between Victorian bourgeois security and the febrile modernity that was to follow it'.[6] The opening chapter swoons with references to Edwardian luxury: to 'the spangled chiffon, filigree-embroidered tulle, veils, billowing ostrich-feather boas, and, trimmed with clover, honey-suckle, or paradise feathers, the ubiquitous cartwheel hats'[7] worn by his mother and her contemporaries. Lady Duff Gordon comes in for a particularly loving encomium.

With the death of Edward VII, Beaton, who was six at the time, felt that the cover of 'the book of opulence' had been closed. It was the 'first suggestion of the profound organic break-up which many of the component parts of Western European society and culture were to undergo in the next three or four decades'. He homed in on Black Ascot as a sad but ineffably chic manifestation of the national mourning 'for a glory that was gone forever'. His accompanying illustrations, of female race-goers 'like strange giant crows or morbid birds of paradise strutting at some Gothic entertainment', were derived from the photographs that abounded in the press during the summer of 1910.[8]

Two years after *The Glass of Fashion*, Beaton was enlisted to design the costumes for Alan Jay Lerner and Fritz Loewe's musical adaptation of George Bernard Shaw's play *Pygmalion*, which they rechristened *My Fair Lady*. The pair had been adamant that Beaton should come aboard – as Lerner put it, 'His very look is such that it is difficult to know whether he designed the Edwardian era or the Edwardian era designed him'[9] – but they had initially believed the production should be set around 1904. Beaton was 'frantic' in his plea that the action should be brought forward to the period immediately before the First World War.[10] He was so persuasive that the producer, Herman Levin, and the director, Moss Hart, relented. Beaton was thrilled. 'Never had any theatre assignment given me so much pleasure,' he recalled. 'Suddenly, a myriad of childhood's impressions were paying dividends: haphazard pieces of the jig-saw puzzle of memory suddenly started sorting themselves into place.'[11]

Beaton's designs distilled the essence of the forces at work within Edwardian Britain. The opera-goers at Covent Garden were dressed in the peacock hues of Paul Poiret, the Russian Ballet and the Post-Impressionists, while the guests at the Embassy Ball wore the sorbet shades with which Lady Duff Gordon had made her name. However, it was the scene set at Ascot that really brought the house down. Directly inspired by Black Ascot, it had incurred doubt when Beaton outlined his scheme. 'You're sure it won't look like a comic strip?' asked Hart.[12] The misgivings were groundless. *My Fair Lady*, which premiered on Broadway in the spring of 1956, was a smash-hit. When the curtain rose on the patrician race-goers frozen against a stylised representation of the Royal Enclosure, audiences were in raptures. What Beaton described as 'the motionless frieze of ladies like magpies against a white drop' incurred ecstatic applause throughout a record-breaking run.[13] The critics were united in a chorus of praise. Such was the show's popularity that contemporary retailers drew upon Beaton's costumes to incorporate Edwardian elements into their merchandise.

In 1958, *My Fair Lady* opened to rave reviews in London. Four years later, Beaton began work on a movie adaptation in Hollywood. It was to prove a gruelling ordeal. He did not get on with the director, George Cukor; the all-American extras did not remotely resemble Edwardian aristocrats; and there were any number of logistical issues and personality clashes. On the other hand, he adored Audrey Hepburn, who was cast as Eliza Doolittle. Better still, he had responsibility for the sets as well as the costumes, which gave him further scope to realise the visions of his childhood.

The resources at his disposal were extraordinary. When it came to research, Beaton was exceptionally diligent, and many of his designs had their origins in the pages of old issues of the *Tatler*, the *Sketch* and the *Illustrated London News*. In addition, he was granted access to an extensive archive of vintage dresses by the likes of Lucile, Poiret, Chéruit and the Callot Soeurs. Handling them was akin to a Proustian experience. (That was as nothing, however, to a letter he had received back in 1959. The sender, one Mrs Haering, had seen the London production of *My Fair Lady* twice. As Laura Mabel Francatelli, she had been Lady Duff Gordon's personal secretary, and in fact had escaped the *Titanic* in the same lifeboat. She had greatly admired the Ascot scene and had been particularly struck by a costume that recalled the wedding gown made for her by her employer. Would he care to acquire the original? she wondered.)

Fraught though it was, the production telescoped Sixties' present and Edwardian past in surprising and piquant ways. Beaton's commitments prevented him from attending the wedding of Edward VII's great-granddaughter, Princess Alexandra, but he ensured the engraved invitation was prominently displayed in his office. Lady Diana Cooper, who at the time of Edward's death had swathed herself in black chiffon, wrote to him with a description of what her mother the Duchess of Rutland – the same one who had resigned from the honorary committee of 'Manet and the Post-Impressionists' – would have worn at Ascot. On his inspiration board, Beaton pinned portraits of Lily Elsie in *The Merry Widow* alongside snapshots of Queen Elizabeth II, Greta Garbo and Jacqueline Kennedy dancing the Twist.

Ever the perfectionist, Beaton was unable to eliminate every anachronism in what was to prove his most celebrated movie project.

Whatever shortfalls he detected in the finished picture were lost on practically everybody else. The Ascot scene was as much of a sensation on screen as it had been on stage. A friend assured him that his costumes 'are without doubt the most breathtakingly beautiful, exquisite creations ever wrought by man'.[14] Even Cukor, who was not usually forthcoming, pronounced them to be 'thrilling'. During a two-day shoot, which yielded over three hundred exposures, Hepburn was photographed by Beaton in her own black-and-white ensemble, as well as many of those worn by the extras. The images, which were printed in American *Vogue*, have since become iconic. The self-deprecating Hepburn was beside herself with delight over their sparkling wit and glamour.

Beaton's work earned him a brace of Oscars. The impact of the Ascot scene in particular was so profound that it has often been revisited by those hoping to achieve a similar style. The palette of Truman Capote's star-studded Black and White Ball in November 1966 was partly inspired by the musical. More recently, designers as diverse as Ralph Lauren and Christian Lacroix have referenced and reinterpreted it. It is probable that, thanks to Beaton, *My Fair Lady* is the main, and perhaps even sole, reference to the annual meeting at Ascot possessed by successive generations of movie lovers.

Yet what is often overlooked is that it was one specific Ascot that Beaton drew upon when he conceived his graphic scheme. Dressed in deepest mourning to honour the memory of a departed king, the race-goers of 1910 would likely be astonished that their sombre apparel has made such an enduring contribution to the notion of Edwardian England as an almost mythically elegant place. Black Ascot certainly *was* elegant, but it was enacted in a climate of unprecedented political, social and cultural ferment. With the benefit of hindsight, the obsequies that accompanied the passing of Edward VII can be viewed as an elegy for an entire way of life.

The same note of sadness, but also of foreboding, was sounded to poignant effect in *Upstairs, Downstairs*. Produced by London Weekend Television for ITV and broadcast between 1971 and 1975, the show brought the main events of the Edwardian era, from the suffragettes to the sinking of the *Titanic*, to millions of British and American viewers. Accompanied by Mrs Keppel, the King himself puts in a memorable appearance when he dines at 165 Eaton Place with Richard and Lady Marjorie Bellamy.

But it is in the finale of the second season that Edward's offstage presence looms largest. On 6 May 1910, the Bellamys assemble to celebrate Lady Marjorie's birthday. Given the complicated dynamics between the family and their servants, it is a tense occasion, further overshadowed by news of the King's illness. In the evening, the party drifts onto the balcony to listen to the distant murmur of the crowds outside Buckingham Palace. The mood is subdued. 'Nine years isn't very long for a reign,' remarks one character.

'Quite a decade,' replies another.

Elizabeth, the daughter of the house, is ruminative. 'I wonder what the next ten years will be like?' she wonders.

Suddenly chilled, Lady Marjorie shivers.[15]

Acknowledgements

The germ of this book lies in an Instagram post. I had long been seeking a suitable subject for a full-length work of social history. Voicing my frustration to Nicholas Morgan over dinner one evening in the summer of 2019, he suggested that I might wish to explore the famous Black Ascot of 1910 which I had referenced in a caption some weeks earlier. Within minutes, it became clear that I had at last found an event around which I could weave a sustained and illuminating narrative. I am indebted to Nico for planting the seed which has come to fruition in these pages – and for much else, as well he knows.

To my agent Ed Wilson of Johnson & Alcock, I tender my thanks for his cheerful encouragement and robust common sense as I further developed my preliminary proposal into one considerably broader and deeper than I envisaged at the outset. Ed's nurturing of a nervous and frequently self-doubting first-time author has been surpassed only by that of my editor Tom Perrin, whose commitment to this project has required him to demonstrate almost superhuman reserves of kindness, wisdom and, above all, patience, all of which he has administered with the lightest and most graceful of touches.

Faced with the Herculean task of whittling down my longlist of preferred images to the two-dozen contained in this book, Jane Smith was a model of unflappable efficiency, resourcefulness and good humour. Throughout successive rounds of edits, Hazel Orme's eagle-eyed professionalism enabled me to burnish my rough-hewn manuscript to a mirror-like shine. My heartfelt thanks to both for their contributions, and also to Zakirah Alam for her hard work behind the scenes.

For her gracious permission to reproduce extracts from Sonia Keppel's memoir *Edwardian Daughter*, I express my sincere gratitude to Her Majesty the Queen Consort. I also wish to thank: Copyright © the Trustees of the Asquith Bonham Carter Papers at the Bodleian Library, Oxford; the Literary Executor of the late Sir Cecil Beaton; the Estate of Sir Max Beerbohm courtesy of Berlin Associates Ltd; Julian Bell and the Society of Authors as representatives of the Estate of Clive Bell; the Estate of Vanessa Bell; the Trustees of the Duff and Diana Cooper Archive; the Provost and Scholars of King's College, Cambridge and the Society of Authors as the E. M. Forster Estate; the Harold Nicolson Estate; and the Vita Sackville-West Estate.

Extracts from *The Letters of Virginia Woolf, Volumes I–VI* by Virginia Woolf published by Chatto & Windus, copyright © Quentin Bell and Angelica Garnett, 1910, are reproduced by permission of The Random House Group Limited. Extracts from *The Essays of Virginia Woolf, Volumes I–V* by Virginia Woolf published by Chatto & Windus, copyright © Quentin Bell and Angelica Garnett, 1924, are reproduced by permission of The Random House Group Limited.

On a personal level, I am grateful to Artemis Cooper, Juliet Nicolson, Sophie Partridge, Mark Pottle and Hugo Vickers, the last of whom kindly consented to read sections of my work in draft. To receive Hugo's affirmative feedback at a crucial stage was a considerable boost to my confidence.

Various individuals and archives across Great Britain opened themselves up to me during my research. The Earl of Derby and Dr Stephen Lloyd welcomed me warmly to Knowsley Hall, where I spent a pleasurable day immersed in the fascinating albums of Lord Derby's great-grandfather. From their pages, Lady Victoria Stanley and her first husband, the Honourable Neil Primrose, sprang to vivid life. The postcard and letter written to the Countess of Derby by her friend Princess Victoria in May 1910 were transcribed from originals held by the Borthwick Institute for Archives at the University of York, as was the letter written by Lady Victoria to her mother from Paris in 1918.

Fania Wetherby hosted me at Wycombe Abbey, where Elsie Bowerman is fondly remembered to this day. I enjoyed reading Elsie's fragmentary memoir, 'Reflections of a Square', as well as perusing her photographs and academic reports. My thanks to the school for making those resources available to me. A further collection of Elsie's papers is held by the Women's Library at the London School of

Economics. I am indebted to the librarians for their assistance, as well as to Elsie's god-daughter Maggie Cawkwell for her permission to quote from unpublished letters and diaries.

The diaries of Margot Asquith, which contain a vivid account of the death and funeral of Edward VII, are housed in the Bodleian Library in Oxford. I am grateful to Christopher Osborn for permission to reproduce excerpts in this book. Equally evocative is the handwritten journal of Sir Schomberg McDonnell who oversaw the King's lying-in-state in Westminster Hall. For permission to quote from it, I am indebted to the Deputy Keeper of the Records at the Public Record Office of Northern Ireland with the kind permission of the Earl of Antrim.

I have been fortunate to be able to draw upon the insights of experts across many diverse fields. Richard Ormond and Stephanie Herdrich were generous with their time and engagement when it came to John Singer Sargent. Simon Martin contributed feedback on Bloomsbury and the staging of the Post-Impressionist exhibition. Randy Bryan Bigham read the sections on Lady Duff Gordon and provided essential information on the career and achievements of that talented and courageous designer. Nicholas Nicholson and Sophie Law were characteristically affirmative in their comments on the chapters pertaining to the Romanovs and Imperial Russia. Keith Levett of Henry Poole & Co. was a fountain of specialist knowledge when it came to Edwardian menswear. The same can be said of Toby Pennington, James Rawlins and George Sandeman at The Armoury of St James's, who between them answered my questions pertaining to matters military and ceremonial. Tim Cox read my paragraphs on English racing and made invaluable input for which I am grateful. Dr Kate Strasdin read the entire text in draft and was able to provide reassurance that my assessment of Queen Alexandra was not too wide of the mark. To each and every one, I extend my appreciation. Remaining errors of nomenclature, fact and interpretation are my own.

Innumerable friends buoyed me with their interest and enthusiasm during an intensely solipsistic and isolated writing process. For that, and for their inspiration, encouragement, support and hospitality over many years, I wish to thank Laura Archer, Brian Brennan, Ruthie Burgess, Lyn Calzia, Edward Cole, Theodore Crispino, Sean Crowley,

Lynn Dennis, Katherine Field, Mary Holzman, Daniela Mascetti, Alexandra Morgan, Sarah Muir, Michael Shane Neal, William and Catherine Norris, Robert O'Byrne, Kim Parker, Christian Ravina, Barbara Lennard Scott and Robin Woodhead. The perspectives – and occasionally the sympathies – of fellow writers have proved particularly precious. Thank you, Stephen Calloway, Sarah Langford, Susan Owens and Anna Thomasson.

The Suffolk contingent is almost too large to list by name. I must, however, express my gratitude to Lord and Lady Deben, Lord Gardiner, Giles Richardson and Tom and Leonora Faggionato. Tom's insistence that I should waste no more time, and that the book I'd talked about for so long wasn't going to write itself, was the decisive push I required at a timely juncture.

To my godsons and nephews – Alec, William, Rory and Luca – I apologise for the birthdays missed while I've been immersed in the world of 1910. I hope you'll let me make it up to you.

To my parents, I owe one of the greatest debts of all: not just for their unstinting moral and financial support over the past eighteen months, but for their boundless love and understanding throughout all the years before. There must have been many moments during my childhood and adolescence when they asked themselves quite how they'd managed to beget such a son. My hope is that, when they read this, they'll appreciate I've done my best to make them proud.

Last but in no sense least is Beau. He has put up with a great deal during the writing of this book: preoccupation, frustration, bad temper, anxiety and stress. I'm certain there have been several occasions when, for him, the end couldn't come soon enough. If he doesn't already know how vital to the process he has been, or how much his forbearance has been appreciated, this is my opportunity to tell him.

Thank you, Beau. This is for you.

Picture Credits

Page 4, bottom: Photos / Alamy Stock Photo

Page 4, bottom right: Underwood & Underwood / CORBIS / Corbis via Getty Images

Page 5, top: W. & D. Downey / Hulton Archive / Getty Images

Page 5, bottom right: Illustrated London News Ltd / Mary Evans

Page 6, top left: Reginald Haines / Hulton Archive / Getty Images

Page 6, top right: Glasshouse Images / Alamy Stock Photo

Page 6, bottom: W. & D. Downey / Hulton Archive / Getty Images

Page 7, top left: Hulton Archive / Getty Images

Page 7, bottom right: Illustrated London News Ltd / Mary Evans

Page 8, top right: Estate of H M Bateman / ILN / Mary Evans Picture Library

Page 8, bottom left: Rapp Halour / Alamy Stock Photo

Sources

Prologue: 'How sad it is!'

1 The *Queen*, 18 June 1910, p.37
2 Violet Bonham Carter, *Winston Churchill As I Knew Him*, Eyre & Spottiswood and Collins, 1965, p.133
3 G. K. Chesterton, 'The Late King: An Appreciation', the *Illustrated London News*, 14 May 1910, p.7
4 Princess Daisy of Pless, *Princess Daisy of Pless by Herself*, John Murray, 1928, p.211

1: 'He went everywhere, saw everyone, and *listened*'

1 Sir Sidney Lee, *King Edward VII: A Biography*, vol. II, Macmillan and Co., 1927, p.8
2 Leon Edel (ed.), *Henry James Letters: Vol. IV, 1895-1916*, The Belknap Press of Harvard University Press, 1984, p.181
3 Ibid., p.184
4 Ibid.
5 *The Times*, 23 January 1901, p.11
6 Philip Whitwell Wilson (ed.), *The Greville Diary*, vol. II, William Heinemann, 1927, p.455
7 Philip Magnus, *King Edward the Seventh*, The History Book Club, 1964, pp.77-8
8 Ibid., p.236
9 Jane Ridley, *Bertie: A Life of Edward VII*, Vintage, 2013, p.45
10 Magnus, p.136
11 Ibid., p.321
12 Ridley, *Bertie*, p.68
13 Magnus, p.62
14 A. L. Kennedy (ed.), *My Dear Duchess*, John Murray, 1956, p.214
15 Georgina Battiscombe, *Queen Alexandra*, Sphere, 1972, pp.55-6
16 Magnus, p.74
17 Ibid., p.73

18 Battiscombe, p.100
19 Ralph Nevill (ed.), *Leaves from the Note-Books of Lady Dorothy Nevill*, Macmillan and Co., 1907, p.33
20 *The Times*, 22 November 1909, p.13
21 Richard W. Davis, '"We are all Americans now!": Anglo-American Marriages in the Later Nineteenth Century', *Proceedings of the American Philosophical Society*, vol. 135, No. 2 (June 1991), p.164
22 Consuelo Vanderbilt Balsan, *The Glitter and the Gold*, George Mann, 1973, p.132
23 Henry Charles Bainbridge, *Peter Carl Fabergé*, Spring Books, 1966, p.83
24 Sir Sidney Lee, vol. II, p.62
25 The Countess of Warwick, *Afterthoughts*, Cassell and Company, 1931, p.40
26 A Foreign Resident, *Society in the New Reign*, T. Fisher Unwin, 1904, p.191
27 Ibid., p.196
28 Sir Sidney Lee, vol. II, p.64
29 Lord Redesdale, *King Edward VII: A Memory*, The Ballantyne Press, 1915, p.19
30 T. H. S. Escott, *King Edward and His Court*, T. Fisher Unwin, 1903, p.23
31 Pless, p.180
32 Simon Heffer, *Power and Place: The Political Consequences of King Edward VII*, Weidenfeld & Nicolson, 1998, p.259

2: 'A perfect master of his métier!'

1 Hannah Pakula, *An Uncommon Woman*, Phoenix Press, 1997, p.41
2 Anita Leslie, *Edwardians in Love*, Hutchinson & Co, 1972, p.43
3 Allen Andrews, *The Follies of King Edward VII*, Lexington Press, 1975, p.174
4 Gordon Brook-Shepherd, *Uncle of Europe: The Social and Diplomatic Life of Edward VII*, Book Club Associates, 1975, p.71
5 Ibid., p.69
6 Ibid., p.161
7 Ibid., p.162
8 Sir Sidney Lee, vol. II, p.237
9 Magnus, p.312
10 Brook-Shepherd, p.197
11 Magnus, p.312
12 The *Illustrated London News*, 9 May 1903, p.2
13 *Journal des débats* quoted in the *Daily News*, 2 May 1910, p.7
14 Magnus, p.314
15 Wilfrid Scawen Blunt, *My Diaries, Part II: 1900–1914*, Martin Secker, 1920, p.68
16 Sir Lionel Cust, *King Edward VII and His Court: Some Reminiscences*, John Murray, 1930, p.212

17 Hugh Montgomery-Massingberd and David Watkin, *The London Ritz: A Social and Architectural History*, Aurum Press, 1980, p.58

18 Ibid., p.67

19 Ibid., p.63

20 Luke Barr, *Ritz & Escoffier*, Clarkson Potter, 2018, pp.108–9

21 Montgomery-Massingberd and Watkin, p.22

22 Magnus, p.32

23 Ridley, *Bertie*, p.44

24 Magnus, p.92

25 Harold Nicolson, 'The Edwardian Weekend' in *The Age of Extravagance: An Edwardian Reader*, Mary Edes and Dudley Frasier (eds), Weidenfeld & Nicolson, 1955, p.247

26 Ibid., pp.248–9

27 Jehanne Wake, *Princess Louise: Queen Victoria's Unconventional Daughter*, Collins, 1988, p.354

28 Balsan, p.85

29 Ibid., p.83

30 Vita Sackville-West, *The Edwardians*, The Hogarth Press, 1930, p.43

31 Barr, pp.262–4

32 Ridley, *Bertie*, p.365

33 Barr, p.271

3: 'For the peace of the world'

1 *Novosti* quoted in *The Times*, 8 May 1903, p.3

2 Frances Welch, *The Imperial Party*, Short Books, 2018, p.23

3 Brook-Shepherd, p.74

4 Andrei Maylunas and Sergei Mironenko, *A Lifelong Passion*, Weidenfeld & Nicolson, 1999, p.99

5 Magnus, p.247

6 Maylunas and Mironenko, p.204

7 Hugh Walpole, *The Secret City*, Macmillan, 1919, p.134

8 Vladimir Nabokov, *Speak, Memory*, Penguin Modern Classics, 2000, p.53

9 The *Daily Telegraph*, 28 October 1904, p.9

10 Mark Bonham Carter and Mark Pottle (eds), *Lantern Slides: The Diaries and Letters of Violet Bonham Carter, 1904–1914*, Phoenix Giant, 1997, p.23

11 The *Daily Mirror*, 23 January 1905, p.3

12 Magnus, p.362

13 E. Nesbit, *The Railway Children*, Wells Gardner, Darton & Co., 1906, p.114

14 Lord Hardinge of Penshurst, *Old Diplomacy*, John Murray, 1947, p.133

15 Welch, pp.108–9

16 Heffer, *Power and Place*, p.176

17 The *Daily Telegraph*, 5 June 1908, p.10

18 Welch, p.128
19 Ibid., p.132
20 Sir Sidney Lee, vol. II, p.592
21 The *Tatler*, 17 June 1908, p.2
22 Magnus, p.389
23 Sir Sidney Lee, vol. I, p.646
24 James Lees-Milne, *The Enigmatic Edwardian*, Sidgwick & Jackson, 1986, p.127
25 Magnus, p.272
26 Pless, p.111
27 Magnus, p.339
28 Sir Sidney Lee, vol. II, p.544
29 Robert Graves, *Goodbye to All That*, Cassell & Company, 1957, pp.34-5
30 Blunt, p.218
31 The *Daily Telegraph*, 28 October 1908, p.11
32 Eric Dorn Brose, *The Kaiser's Army: The Politics of Military Technology in Germany during the Machine Age*, Oxford University Press, 2001, p.134
33 Margot Asquith Diary, November 1908, Bodleian Library, MS. Eng. d. 3206
34 Pless, pp.176-7
35 Magnus, p.419
36 Leslie, p.337

4: 'Conditions so altered'

1 Simon Heffer, *The Age of Decadence: Britain 1880–1914*, Random House, 2017, p.606
2 'Old Bloomsbury' by Virginia Woolf quoted by Peter Stansky in *On or About December 1910: Early Bloomsbury and Its Intimate World*, Harvard University Press, 1997, p.10
3 Clive Bell, *Old Friends*, Chatto & Windus, 1956, p.31
4 Leonard Woolf, *Beginning Again: An Autobiography of the Years 1911–1918*, The Hogarth Press, 1964, p.35
5 An analysis of Virginia's late-life recollection of her involvement in the *Dreadnought* Hoax is supplied by Georgia Johnston in her article 'Virginia Woolf's Talk on the *Dreadnought* Hoax' published in *Woolf Studies Annual*, vol. 15 (2009), pp.1-7, 9-45.
6 Adrian Stephen, *The 'Dreadnought' Hoax*, Chatto & Windus/The Hogarth Press, 1983, p.31
7 Martyn Downer, *The Sultan of Zanzibar: The Bizarre World and Spectacular Hoaxes of Horace de Vere Cole*, Black Spring Press, 2010, p.104
8 Johnston, p.13
9 Stephen, p.32
10 Downer, p.105
11 Stephen, pp.35-7

12 Johnston, p.24
13 *The Daily Mirror*, 16 February 1910, p.1
14 The *Globe*, 1 March 1910, p.1
15 Johnston, p.28
16 Downer, p.127
17 Stephen, p.22
18 'Report of the Opening of the Royal Edward Institute (for the Study, Preventions and Cure of Tuberculosis) by His Majesty King Edward VII (by cable) on Thursday, October the twenty-first, Nineteen-Hundred-and-Nine', Montreal, 1909, p.28
19 The *Daily Telegraph*, 22 October 1909, p.11
20 The *Leicester Chronicle and Leicestershire Mercury*, 29 January 1910, p.2
21 Lady Cynthia Asquith, *Remember and Be Glad*, James Barrie, 1952, p.16
22 Osbert Sitwell, *Great Morning*, Macmillan & Co., 1948, p.234
23 A Foreign Resident, p.113
24 John Malcolm Brinnin, *The Sway of the Grand Saloon*, Barnes & Noble, 2000, p.306
25 John Maxtone-Graham, *The Only Way to Cross*, Patrick Stephens, 1983, p.62
26 Johnston, p.21
27 'The Triumph of Wireless', the *Outlook*, 6 February 1909, p.297
28 S. J. Taylor, *The Great Outsiders*, Weidenfeld & Nicolson, 1996, p.120
29 *The Times*, 27 July 1909, p.12
30 Ibid.
31 *Le Siècle* quoted in the *Standard*, 26 July 1909, p.7
32 The *Tatler*, 5 January 1910, p.2
33 Brook-Shepherd, p.351
34 E. M. Forster, *Howards End*, Edward Arnold, 1910, p.105
35 Marie Corelli, *The Devil's Motor*, Hodder & Stoughton, 1910, p.3
36 Ibid., p.5
37 P. H. Ditchfield and Fred Roe, *Vanishing England*, Studio Editions, 1993, p.2
38 David Cecil, *Max: A Biography*, Constable, 1964, p.178

5: 'We shall all be in our graves before it is finished!'

1 Jerry White, *Zeppelin Nights: London in the First World War*, The Bodley Head, 2014, p.2
2 Stephen McKenna, *While I Remember*, Thornton Butterworth, 1921, p.79
3 Forster, p.44
4 Ibid., p.105
5 Viscount Esher (Reginald), *To-Day and To-Morrow and Other Essays*, John Murray, 1910, p.158
6 Magnus, p.101
7 Ibid., p.102

8 Cust, p.28

9 The Duke of Windsor, *A King's Story: The Memoirs of the Duke of Windsor*, G. P. Putnam's Sons, 1951, p.47

10 Cust, p.34

11 Ibid., p.35

12 Ibid., p.91

13 Viscount Esher (Oliver), *Journals and Letters of Reginald, Viscount Esher: Volume III, 1910–1915*, Ivor Nicholson & Watson, 1938, p.15

14 Battiscombe, p.263

15 Downer, p.51

16 Nicholas Connell, *Doctor Crippen: The Infamous London Cellar Murder of 1910*, Amberley, 2014, p.16

17 Ibid., p.21

18 Elsie Bowerman, *Stands There a School: Memories of Dame Frances Dove*, Wycombe Abbey School Seniors, 1965, p.16

19 Prior to her death in 1973, Elsie Bowerman was at work on a memoir provisionally entitled 'Reflections of a Square'. Although fragmentary and unfinished, the manuscript, which is held among her papers in the archive at Wycombe Abbey, provides an invaluable insight into her extraordinarily rich and varied life.

20 Diane Atkinson, *Rise Up, Women!*, Bloomsbury, 2018, p.61

21 Roger Fulford, *Votes for Women*, Faber & Faber, 1957, p.140

22 Ibid., p.143

23 Ridley, *Bertie*, p.404

24 Magnus, p.390

25 Margot Asquith Diary, November 1908

26 The Countess of Fingall, *Seventy Years Young*, Collins, 1937, p.305

27 Atkinson, p.126

28 Margot Asquith Diary, November 1908

29 Atkinson, p.167

30 John Wilson, *CB: A Life of Sir Henry Campbell-Bannerman*, Constable, 1973, p.511

31 Atkinson, p.190

32 Annie Kenney, *Memories of a Militant*, Edward Arnold, 1924, p.163

6: The Camel and the Needle's Eye

1 Arthur Ponsonby, *The Camel and the Needle's Eye*, A. C. Fifield, 1910, p.10

2 Ibid., p.21

3 Ibid., pp.11–12

4 Lady Cynthia Asquith, *Hap'ly I May Remember*, James Barrie, 1950, p.140

5 Violet Bonham Carter, *Winston Churchill As I Knew Him*, Eyre & Spottiswoode and Collins, 1965, p.134

6 Arthur Ponsonby, pp.24-5

7 Balsan, p.68

8 Barbara Tuchman, *The Proud Tower*, Hamish Hamilton, 1966, p.12

9 Bonham Carter, p.141

10 Sydney H. Zebel, *Balfour: A Political Biography*, Cambridge University Press, 1973, p.143

11 Magnus, p.348

12 Bonham Carter, p.161

13 Magnus, p.354

14 J. Mordaunt Crook, *The Rise of the Nouveaux Riches*, John Murray, 2000, p.239

15 Magnus, p.354

16 Ibid., p.357

17 Ibid., p.76

18 Max Egremont, *The Cousins*, Collins, 1977, p.34

19 Lord Ribblesdale, *Impressions and Memories*, Cassell & Company, 1927, pp.207-8

20 David Cannadine, *The Decline and Fall of the British Aristocracy*, Penguin Books, 2005, p.46

21 Ibid.

22 Ridley, *Bertie*, p.417

23 Bonham Carter, p.166

24 Ibid., p.167

25 Frank Dilnot, *Lloyd George: The Man and His Story*, Harper & Brothers, 1917, p.79

26 Cannadine, p.48

27 Bonham Carter, p.182

28 The *Eastern Evening News*, 27 July 1909, p.4

29 *The Times*, 31 July 1909, p.9

30 Magnus, p.431

31 Heffer, *Power and Place*, p.282

32 Lady Frances Balfour, *A Memoir of Lord Balfour of Burleigh*, Hodder & Stoughton, 1925, p.111

33 *London Evening Standard*, 3 December 1909, p.4

7: 'We shall have some very bad luck this year'

1 Battiscombe, p.257

2 Cust, p.234

3 Sir Sidney Lee, vol. II, pp.685-6

4 James Pope-Hennessy, *The Quest for Queen Mary*, Zuleika and Hodder & Stoughton, 2018, p.85

5 Windsor, p.52

6 Christopher Hibbert, *Edward VII*, Allen Lane, 1976, p.285
7 Mordaunt Crook, p.223
8 Ibid., p.57
9 The *Tatler*, 28 September 1910, p.4
10 Fingall, p.305
11 Ibid., pp.305-6
12 Ibid., p.306
13 The *Brighton Gazette, Hove Post, Sussex & Surrey Telegraph*, 12 January 1910, p.8
14 *The Times*, 13 January 1910, p.11
15 Nigel Nicolson (ed.), *The Flight of the Mind: The Letters of Virginia Woolf, Vol. I: 1888–1912*, The Hogarth Press, 1975, p.421
16 Ibid.
17 Ibid., p.422
18 Clive Bell, p.64
19 Vanessa Bell, *Sketches in Pen and Ink*, Pimlico, 1998, p.118
20 Ibid., pp.118-19
21 Ibid., p.119
22 Ibid., p.121
23 Stansky, p.98
24 Ibid.
25 Clive Bell, p.80
26 The *Tatler*, 23 February 1910, p.34
27 Ibid.
28 Lady Duff Gordon, *Discretions and Indiscretions*, Jarrolds, 1932, pp.123-4
29 The *Daily Express*, 23 February 1910, p.5
30 The *Queen*, 12 March 1910, p.34
31 The *Tatler*, 9 March 1910, p.2
32 Redesdale, p.33

8: 'That horrid Biarritz'

1 Magnus, p.438
2 Bonham Carter and Pottle, p.201
3 The *Daily Telegraph*, 22 February 1910, p.11
4 Ibid.
5 Sir Sidney Lee, vol. II, pp.510-11
6 Ibid., p.578
7 Ibid., pp.511
8 The *Tatler*, 30 March 1910, p.30
9 Ibid.
10 Sir Sidney Lee, vol. II, p.511
11 Sonia Keppel, *Edwardian Daughter*, Hamish Hamilton, 1958, p.4

12 Ibid. p.13

13 Celia Lee, *Jean, Lady Hamilton, 1861–1941: Diaries of a Soldier's Wife*, Pen & Sword Military, 2020, p.57

14 Keppel, p.28

15 Magnus, p.260

16 Diana Souhami, *Mrs Keppel and Her Daughter*, Harper Collins, 1996, p.61

17 Celia Lee, p.212

18 Keppel, p.13

19 Battiscombe, p.268

20 Keppel, p.42

21 Ibid.

22 Ibid., p.44

23 Janet Morgan, *Edwina Mountbatten: A Life of Her Own*, Harper Collins, 1991, p.28

24 C. W. Stamper, *What I Know*, Mills & Boon, 1913, p.73

25 Fingall, p.299

26 Keppel, p.45

27 Blunt, p.243

28 Magnus, p.450

29 *The Times*, 12 May 1910, p.8

30 The *Sheffield Daily Telegraph*, 14 March 1910, p.7

31 Brook-Shepherd, p.350

32 Michaela Reid, *Ask Sir James*, Hodder & Stoughton, 1987, p.239

33 *The Times*, 12 May 1910, p.8

34 The *Globe*, 19 March 1910, p.6

35 Sir Frederick Ponsonby, *Recollections of Three Reigns*, Eyre & Spottiswood, 1957, p.267

36 Brook-Shepherd, p.351

37 The *Tatler*, 27 April 1910, p.2

38 Ibid., 30 March 1910, p.30

39 Sir Sidney Lee, vol. II, p.709

9: 'In case I don't see you again, goodbye'

1 Battiscombe, p.138

2 Cust, pp.33–34

3 Maurice Brett (ed.), *Journals and Letters of Reginald, Viscount Esher, Volume I: 1870–1903*, Nicholson & Watson, 1934, p.373

4 Battiscombe, p.240

5 Ibid., p.121

6 Ridley, *Bertie*, p.308

7 Hibbert, p.180

8 Battiscombe, p.268

9   Sir Sidney Lee, vol. II, p.705
10 Ridley, p.452
11 Ibid., p.451
12 Ibid., p.452
13 Blunt, p.313
14 The *Tatler*, 20 April 1910, p.6
15 Ibid., 27 April 1910, p.2
16 Margot Asquith, *Autobiography*, vol. II, Penguin, 1936, p.100
17 *The Times*, 29 April 1910, p.13
18 Barbara Dayer Gallati with Erica E. Hirshler and Richard Ormond, *Great Expectations: John Singer Sargent Painting Children*, Brooklyn Museum in association with Bulfinch Press, 2005, p.176
19 Charles Merrill Mount, *John Singer Sargent: A Biography*, Cresset Press, 1957, p.238
20 Ibid., p.239
21 *The Times*, 30 April 1910, p.10
22 Redesdale, p.34
23 Sir Frederick Ponsonby, p.267
24 Reid, p.240
25 Ibid.
26 Sir Sidney Lee, vol. II, p.715
27 Reid, p.240
28 Sir Sidney Lee, vol. II, p.715
29 Margot Asquith Diary, May 1910, Bodleian Library, MS. Eng. d. 3208/9
30 Herbert Henry Asquith, *Fifty Years of Parliament*, vol. II, Cassell & Company, 1926, p.86
31 Princess Victoria to the Countess of Derby, 5 May 1910. Transcribed from an original held at the Borthwick Institute for Archives, University of York
32 Sir Frederick Ponsonby, p.270
33 The *Sketch*, 11 May 1910, p.2
34 Margot Asquith Diary, May 1910
35 Sir Sidney Lee, vol. II, p.716
36 Ibid., p.717
37 Ridley, *Bertie*, p.457
38 Ibid., p.458
39 Lees-Milne, *The Enigmatic Edwardian*, p.206
40 Margot Asquith Diary, May 1910
41 The *Tatler*, 18 May 1910, p.2
42 Margot Asquith Diary, May 1910
43 Ibid.
44 Herbert Henry Asquith, vol. II, p.87

10: 'The meaning of everything seems gone for the moment'

1 Lees-Milne, *Harold Nicolson: Volume II, 1930–1968*, Hamish Hamilton, 1988, p.234

2 Lees-Milne, *The Enigmatic Edwardian*, p.205

3 Jane Ridley, *George V: Never a Dull Moment*, Chatto & Windus, 2021, p.151

4 Celia Lee, p.108

5 Cust, p.257

6 *The Times*, 7 May 1910, p.11

7 Sir Sidney Lee, vol. II, p.739

8 William Scovell Adams, *Edwardian Heritage*, Frederick Muller, 1949, p.17

9 Viscount Esher (Reginald), *The Influence of King Edward and Essays on Other Subjects*, John Murray, 1915, p.44

10 Magnus, p.368

11 The *Illustrated London News*, 14 May 1910, p.7

12 Bonham Carter and Pottle, p.206

13 Jeanne Mackenzie, *The Children of The Souls*, Chatto & Windus, 1986, p.109

14 Ibid.

15 Montgomery-Massingberd and Watkin, p.69

16 *Votes for Women*, 13 May 1910, p.539

17 Anthony Masters, *Rosa Lewis: An Exceptional Edwardian*, Weidenfeld & Nicolson, 1977, p.86

18 The *Illustrated London News*, 14 May 1910, p.21

19 *The Times*, 12 May 1910, p.8

20 Wake, p.375

21 Philip Zeigler, *Diana Cooper*, Penguin, 1983, p.44

22 Margot Asquith Diary, May 1910

23 Celia Lee, p.108

24 Souhami, p.92

25 Keppel, pp.53–4

26 Brook-Shepherd, p.359

27 Sir Frederick Ponsonby, p.271

28 Esher, vol. III, p.1

29 Public Record Office of Northern Ireland, Schomberg McDonnell Papers, D/4091/A/6/6/1, 'Schomberg McDonnell's Journal of Death and Funeral of King Edward VII', May 1910, p.13

30 Viscount Esher, vol. III, p.1

31 The *Illustrated London News*, 21 May 1910, p.5

32 Esher, vol. III, p.2

33 *The Times*, 11 May 1910, p.8

34 Celia Lee, p.109

35 Reid, p.243

36 Peter Gordon (ed.), *Politics and Society: The Journals of Lady Knightley of Fawsley, 1885 to 1913*, Routledge, 2005, p.465

37 *The Times*, 13 May 1910, p.6
38 Bowerman, 'Reflections of a Square'

11: 'They're giving him to us now'

1 Brett, vol. I, p.276
2 McDonnell, p.6
3 Ibid., p.5
4 Ibid., p.6
5 Ibid., p.27
6 Ibid., p.30
7 Ibid., p.31
8 *The Times*, 18 May 1910, p.8
9 Ibid., p.6
10 Ibid., p.8
11 Lieutenant-Colonel John Mackenzie-Rogan, *Fifty Years of Army Music*, Methuen & Co., 1926, p.168
12 Ibid., p.167
13 Ibid., p.170
14 Ibid., p.167
15 Ibid., p.169
16 Cust, p.247
17 McDonnell, p.22
18 Hibbert, p.313
19 *The Times*, 18 May 1910, p.6
20 McDonnell, p.26
21 *The Times*, 20 May 1910, p.6
22 Hibbert, p.313
23 Margot Asquith, *Autobiography*, vol. II, p.104
24 Blunt, p.318
25 McDonnell, p.36
26 Bonham Carter and Pottle, p.211
27 McDonnell, p.37
28 Norman and Jeanne MacKenzie (eds), *The Diary of Beatrice Webb, Volume III: 1905-1925*, Virago in association with London School of Economics, p.139
29 Stansky, p.130
30 McDonnell, pp.39-41
31 Ibid., pp.42-44

12: 'But alas – he has *gone* – and *no* one can help there'

1 Sir Sidney Lee, vol. II, p.626
2 Lees-Milne, *The Enigmatic Edwardian*, p.210

3 Maylunas and Mironenko, p.332
4 *The Times*, 9 May 1910, p.9
5 Cust, p.249
6 *The Times*, 21 May 1910, p.5
7 The *Graphic*, 24 May 1910, p.16
8 The *Sketch*, 25 May 1910, p.39
9 Margot Asquith Diary, May 1910
10 Cust, p.252
11 Margot Asquith Diary, May 1910
12 Ibid.
13 Pless, p.212
14 Theodore Roosevelt, *The Letters of Theodore Roosevelt*, vol. VII, Cambridge, Massachusetts, 1951–4, pp.412–13
15 McDonnell, pp.45–6
16 Ibid., p.50
17 Souhami, p.93
18 *The Times*, 21 May 1910, p.7
19 Kennedy, p.213
20 Margot Asquith Diary, May 1910
21 *The Times*, 21 May 1910, p.7
22 Margot Asquith Diary, May 1910
23 McDonnell, p.50
24 Cust, p.255
25 Roosevelt, p.367
26 Coryne Hall, *Little Mother of Russia*, Shepheard-Walwyn, 1999, p.232
27 Lees-Milne, *The Enigmatic Edwardian*, p.212
28 Margot Asquith Diary, May 1910
29 Princess Victoria to the Countess of Derby, 20 May 1910

13: 'I was looking for you everywhere, but, of course, it was quite impossible to find you'

1 Esher, vol. III, p.8
2 Ibid., p.15
3 The *Tatler*, 8 June 1910, p.23
4 The *Sporting Life*, 25 May 1910, p.4
5 The *Times*, 10 May 1910, p.9
6 Sean Magee with Sally Aird, *Ascot: The History*, Methuen, 2002, p.57
7 The *Evening Mail*, 5 June 1896, p.4
8 Juliet Gardiner, *The Edwardian Country House*, Channel 4 Books, 2002, p.235
9 Arthur Ponsonby, p.67
10 Pless, p.186
11 The *Tatler*, 18 May 1910, p.30

12 Nigel Nicolson, *Portrait of a Marriage: Illustrated Edition*, Guild Publishing, 1990, p.40
13 The *Sketch*, 18 May 1910, p.48
14 Ibid., 25 May 1910, p.39
15 Viscount Churchill, *All My Sins Remembered*, Heinemann, 1964, p.45
16 Ibid. p.52
17 Magee and Aird, p.139
18 The *Queen*, 25 June 1910, p.32
19 Quoted from an undated clipping from the weekly paper *The Passing Show* pasted in an album compiled by the 17th Earl of Derby in 1917
20 The *Bystander*, 22 June 1910, p.8
21 The *Chicago Examiner*, 22 May 1910, p.4
22 The *Queen*, 25 June 1910, p.32
23 The *Chicago Examiner*, 22 May 1910, p.4
24 The *Queen*, 25 June 1910, p.32
25 The *Bystander*, 22 June 1910, p.8
26 The *Illustrated Sporting and Dramatic News*, 25 June 1910, p.36
27 H. G. Wells, *Experiment in Autobiography*, Macmillan & Co., 1934, p.233
28 The *Sheffield Evening Telegraph*, 17 June 1910, p.3
29 The *Bystander*, 22 June 1910, p.8
30 Duff Gordon, p.101
31 The *Sheffield Evening Telegraph*, 15 June 1910, p.7
32 The *Bystander*, 22 June 1910, pp.7-8
33 The *Tatler*, 22 June 1910, p.3
34 Ibid., 22 June 1910, p.7
35 Fingall, pp.331-2
36 The *Sheffield Daily Telegraph*, 15 June 1910, p.7
37 The *Sporting Times*, 18 June 1910, p.2
38 The *Sketch*, 22 June 1910, p.56

14: 'Everyone agrees the summer has been a mournful one'

1 The *Tatler*, 22 June 1910, p.8
2 The *Windsor and Eton Express*, 25 June 1910, p.6
3 The *Sphere*, 25 June 1910, p.8
4 *The Times*, 14 May 1910, p.10
5 Nicolson, *The Flight of the Mind*, p.424
6 Ibid., p.428
7 Stansky, p.58
8 Ibid., p.59
9 Atkinson, p.204
10 *Votes for Women*, 24 June 1910, p.4
11 Ibid., p.5

12 Elsie Bowerman to Edith Chibnall, 20 June 1910. Transcribed from an original among Elsie Bowerman's papers held by The Women's Library at London School of Economics, 7ELB, Boxes 395-6

13 Ibid., 15 July 1910

14 Ibid., 16 July 1910

15 Ibid., 28 July 1910

16 Connell, p.15

17 Ibid. p.25

18 Ibid.

19 Ibid. p.50

20 Cecil, p.306

21 Connell, p.56

22 *The Times*, 1 August 1910, p.7

23 Ibid.

24 The *Daily News*, 1 August 1910, p.4

25 *The Times*, 1 August 1910, p.10

26 Bonham Carter and Pottle, p.210

27 Esher, vol. III, p.17

28 The *Sketch*, 25 May 1910, p.39

29 Battiscombe, p.274

30 The *Bystander*, 15 June 1910, p.7

31 James Pope-Hennessy, *Queen Mary*, George Allen and Unwin, 1959, p.422

32 Lees-Milne, *The Enigmatic Edwardian*, p.119

33 Ibid. p.426

34 Ridley, *Bertie*, p.467

35 Anon., *Where's Master?* Hodder & Stoughton, 1910, p.49

15: 'A time when all was a sizzle of excitement'

1 *The Times*, 3 August 1910, p.8

2 Ibid. p.9

3 The *Eastern Daily Press*, 6 January 1910, p.5

4 Frank Dilnot, *The Adventures of a Newspaper Man*, Smith, Elder & Co, 1913, pp.130-131

5 The *Daily News*, 7 November 1910, p.4

6 The *South of England Advertiser*, 16 June 1910, p.3

7 Vanessa Bell, p.128

8 Stansky, p.210

9 *The Times*, 7 November 1910, p.12

10 *Truth*, 23 November 1910, p.38

11 The *Daily Telegraph*, 11 November 1910, p.5

12 The *Yorkshire Post*, 8 November 1910, p.6

13 *The Times*, 17 November 1910, p.4
14 Stansky, p.189
15 Blunt, pp.343-4
16 The *Bystander*, 23 November 1910, p.11
17 Stansky, p.227
18 Vanessa Bell, pp.129-30
19 Jeffery Meyers, *Katherine Mansfield: A Darker View*, Cooper Square Press, 2002, p.59
20 Vanessa Bell, p.126
21 Nicolson, *The Flight of the Mind*, p.440
22 Vanessa Bell, p.134
23 Frank Rutter, *Revolution in Art*, Art News Press, 1910, p.iv
24 Atkinson, p.215
25 Kenney, p.166
26 *The Times*, 19 November 1910, p.10
27 The *Daily Mirror*, 19 November 1910, p.4
28 *The Times*, 3 March 1911, p.10
29 Atkinson, p.224
30 Edith Chibnall to Elsie Bowerman, 19 November 1910
31 Elsie Bowerman to Edith Chibnall, 20 November 1910
32 Ibid., 23 November 1910
33 *Votes for Women*, 25 November 1910, p.10
34 Pope-Hennessy, *Queen Mary*, p.432
35 John Martin Robinson, *Buckingham Palace: The Official Illustrated History*, The Royal Collection, 2000, p.128
36 The *Tatler*, 14 December 1910, p.4
37 *The Times*, 6 October 1922, p.12

16: 'On or about December 1910, human character changed'

1 *The Times*, 16 May 1911, p.8
2 Ibid., p.9
3 *The Times*, 17 May 1911, p.12
4 Heffer, *The Age of Decadence*, p.635
5 Tuchman, *The Proud Tower*, p.397
6 *The Times*, 25 July 1911, p.8
7 Randolph S. Churchill, *Lord Derby, 'King of Lancashire'*, Heinemann, 1959, pp.125-6
8 Ridley, *George V*, p.179
9 Juliet Nicolson, *The Perfect Summer*, John Murray, 2006, p.170
10 Frances Spalding, *The Bloomsbury Group*, National Portrait Gallery Publications, 2013, p.46
11 *The Times*, 5 August 1911, p.9
12 The *Tatler*, 10 June 1914, p.5

13 Virginia Woolf, *Mr Bennett and Mrs Brown*, second impression, The Hogarth Press, 1928, pp.4-5

14 Lamar Cecil, 'History as Family Chronicle: Kaiser Wilhelm II and the dynastic roots of the Anglo-German Antagonism' in *Kaiser Wilhelm II: New Interpretations* by John C. G. Röhl and Nicolaus Stombart, Cambridge University Press, 1982

15 The *Morning Post*, 29 November 1918. Quoted from a clipping pasted in an album compiled by the 17th Earl of Derby

16 Lady Victoria Primrose, née Stanley, to the Countess of Derby, 30 October 1918

17 Randolph Churchill, *Lord Derby*, p.579

18 Bowerman, 'Reflections of a Square'

19 Elsie Bowerman to Stella [surname indecipherable], 20 March 1917

20 The *Daily News & Leader*, 21 May 1912, p.1

21 Sitwell, p.218

22 Souhami, p.4

23 Louise DeSalvo and Mitchell A. Leaska (eds), *The Letters of Vita Sackville-West to Virginia Woolf*, Hutchinson, 1984, p.358

24 Sackville-West, p.307

25 Battiscombe, p.285

26 Ibid., p.296

27 Pope-Hennessy, *Queen Mary*, p.537

28 Simon Heffer (ed.), *Henry 'Chips' Channon: The Diaries, 1918-38*, Hutchinson, 2021, p.191

29 Ridley, *George V*, p.410

30 Heffer, *Chips*, p.424

31 Lou Taylor, *Mourning Dress: A Costume and Social History*, George Allen and Unwin, 1983, p.280

32 *The Times*, 21 July 1921, p.11

33 Ibid., 20 July 1921, p.13

Epilogue: 'The motionless frieze of ladies like magpies against a white drop'

1 Dorothy Laird, *Royal Ascot*, Hodder & Stoughton, 1976, p.156

2 Hugo Vickers (ed.), *Beaton in the Sixties*, Phoenix Paperback, 2003, p.198

3 Cecil Beaton, *Photobiography*, Odhams Press, 1951, p.13

4 Charles Spencer, *Cecil Beaton: Stage and Film Designs*, Academy Editions, 1975, p.34

5 Ibid., p.110

6 Cecil Beaton, *The Glass of Fashion*, Doubleday, 1954, p.24

7 Ibid., p.25

8 Ibid., pp.84-5

9 Hugo Vickers, *Cecil Beaton*, Phoenix, 2003, p.387

10 Cecil Beaton, *Cecil Beaton's Fair Lady*, Henry Holt and Company, 1964, p.7
11 Ibid.
12 Ibid.
13 Vickers, *Cecil Beaton*, p.387
14 Ibid. p.472
15 The thirteenth and final episode of the second season of *Upstairs, Downstairs*, 'A Family Gathering' was written by the series co-creator Eileen Atkins and Alfred Shaughnessy and directed by Raymond Menmuir. Its first UK transmission was on 19 January 1973. For further information about the cast and production, readers are referred to *Inside Updown* by Richard Marson, Kaleidoscope Publishing, 2001.

Bibliography

The Edwardians were a prodigiously literate people, which explains the vast – indeed, overwhelming – volume of commentary on the events of the era in the form of letters, diaries, articles and memoirs. This bibliography, which I have endeavoured to make as comprehensive as possible, reflects something of the breadth and diversity of the sources consulted.

A Foreign Resident, *Society in the New Reign* (T. Fisher Unwin, 1904)

Adams, William Scovell, *Edwardian Heritage* (Frederick Muller, 1949)

Allfrey, Anthony, *Edward VII and His Jewish Court* (Weidenfeld & Nicolson, 1991)

Andrews, Allen, *The Follies of King Edward VII* (Lexington Press, 1975)

Anon., *Where's Master?* (Hodder & Stoughton, 1910)

Aslet, Clive, *The Last Country Houses* (Yale University Press, 1982)

Asquith, Lady Cynthia, *Hap'ly I May Remember* (James Barrie, 1950)

Asquith, Lady Cynthia, *Remember and Be Glad* (James Barrie, 1952)

Asquith, Herbert Henry, *Fifty Years of Parliament* (Cassell and Company, 1926)

Asquith, Margot, *Autobiography* (Penguin, 1936)

Atkinson, Diana, *Rise Up, Women!* (Bloomsbury, 2018)

Bainbridge, Henry Charles, *Peter Carl Fabergé* (Spring Books, 1966)

Balfour, Lady Frances, *A Memoir of Lord Balfour of Burleigh* (Hodder & Stoughton, 1925)

Balsan, Consuelo Vanderbilt, *The Glitter and the Gold* (George Mann, 1973)

Barr, Luke, *Ritz & Escoffier* (Clarkson Potter, 2018)

Battiscombe, Georgina, *Queen Alexandra* (Sphere, 1972)

Beaton, Cecil, *Cecil Beaton's Fair Lady* (Henry Holt and Company, 1964)

Beaton, Cecil, *The Glass of Fashion* (Doubleday, 1954)

Beaton, Cecil, *Photobiography* (Odhams Press, 1951)

Bell, Clive, *Old Friends* (Chatto & Windus, 1956)

Bell, Vanessa, *Sketches in Pen and Ink* (Pimlico, 1998)

Blunt, Wilfrid Scawen, *My Diaries, Part Two: 1900–1914* (Martin Secker, 1920)

Bonham Carter, Mark, and Pottle, Mark (eds), *Lantern Slides: The Diaries and Letters of Violet Bonham Carter, 1904–1914* (Phoenix Giant, 1997)

Bonham Carter, Violet, *Winston Churchill As I Knew Him* (Eyre & Spottiswoode and Collins, 1965)

Bowerman, Elsie, *Stands There a School: Memories of Dame Frances Dove* (Wycombe Abbey School Seniors, 1965)

Brett, Maurice, and Esher, Viscount (Oliver) (eds), *Journals and Letters of Reginald, Viscount Esher* (Ivor Nicholson & Watson, 1934-8)

Brinnin, John Malcolm, *The Sway of the Grand Saloon* (Barnes & Noble, 2000)

Brook-Shepherd, Gordon, *Uncle of Europe: The Social and Diplomatic Life of Edward VII* (Book Club Associates, 1975)

Brose, Eric Dorn, *The Kaiser's Army: The Politics of Military Technology in Germany during the Machine Age* (Oxford University Press, 2001)

Cannadine, David, *The Decline and Fall of the British Aristocracy* (Penguin Books, 2005)

Cecil, David, *Max: A Biography* (Constable, 1964)

Churchill, Randolph S., *Lord Derby, 'King of Lancashire'* (Heinemann, 1959)

Churchill, Viscount, *All My Sins Remembered* (Heinemann, 1964)

Connell, Nicholas, *Doctor Crippen: The Infamous London Cellar Murder of 1910* (Amberley, 2014)

Cooper, Diana, *The Rainbow Comes and Goes* (Rupert Hart-Davis, 1959)

Corelli, Marie, *The Devil's Motor* (Hodder & Stoughton, 1910)

Cust, Sir Lionel, *King Edward VII and His Court: Some Reminiscences* (John Murray, 1930)

DeSalvo, Louise and Leaska, Mitchell A. (eds), *The Letters of Vita Sackville-West to Virginia Woolf* (Hutchinson, 1984)

Dilnot, Frank, *The Adventures of a Newspaper Man* (Smith, Elder & Co, 1913)

Dilnot, Frank, *Lloyd George: The Man and His Story* (Harper & Brothers, 1917)

Downer, Martyn, *The Sultan of Zanzibar: The Bizarre World and Spectacular Hoaxes of Horace de Vere Cole* (Black Spring Press, 2010)

Duff Gordon, Lady, *Discretions and Indiscretions* (Jarrolds, 1932)

Edel, Leon (ed.), *Henry James Letters: Volume IV, 1895-1916* (The Belknap Press of Harvard University Press, 1984)

Edes, Mary, and Frasier, Dudley, *The Age of Extravagance: An Edwardian Reader* (Weidenfeld & Nicolson, 1955)

Egremont, Max, *The Cousins* (Collins, 1977)

Escott, T. H. S., *King Edward and His Court* (T. Fisher Unwin, 1903)

Esher, Viscount, *To-Day and To-Morrow and Other Essays* (John Murray, 1910)

Esher, Viscount, *The Influence of King Edward and Essays on Other Subjects* (John Murray, 1915)

Etherington-Smith, Meredith, and Pilcher, Jeremy, *The 'It' Girls* (Harcourt Brace Jovanovich, 1986)

Fingall, The Countess of, *Seventy Years Young* (Collins, 1937)

Forster, E. M., *Howards End* (Edward Arnold, 1910)

Fulford, Roger, *Votes for Women* (Faber & Faber, 1957)

Gallati, Barbara Dayer, with Hirshler, Erica E., and Ormond, Richard, *Great Expectations: John Singer Sargent Painting Children* (Brooklyn Museum in association with Bulfinch Press, 2005)

Gardiner, Juliet, *The Edwardian Country House* (Channel 4 Books, 2002)

Gordon, Peter (ed.), *Politics and Society: The Journals of Lady Knightley of Fawsley, 1885 to 1913* (Routledge, 2005)

Graves, Robert, *Goodbye to All That* (Cassell & Company, 1957)

Hall, Coryne, *Little Mother of Russia* (Shepheard-Walwyn, 1999)

Hardinge of Penshurst, Lord, *Old Diplomacy* (John Murray, 1947)

Hattersley, Roy, *The Edwardians* (Little, Brown, 2004)

Heffer, Simon, *Power and Place: The Political Consequences of King Edward VII* (Weidenfeld & Nicolson, 1998)

Heffer, Simon, *The Age of Decadence: Britain 1880–1914* (Random House, 2017)

Heffer, Simon (ed.), *Henry 'Chips' Channon: The Diaries, 1918–38* (Hutchinson, 2021)

Hibbert, Christopher, *Edward VII* (Allen Lane, 1976)

Kaplan, Joel H., and Stowell, Sheila, *Theatre and Fashion: Oscar Wilde to the Suffragettes* (Cambridge University Press, 1994)

Kennedy, A. L. (ed.), *My Dear Duchess* (John Murray, 1956)

Kenney, Annie, *Memories of a Militant* (Edward Arnold, 1924)

Keppel, Sonia, *Edwardian Daughter* (Hamish Hamilton, 1958)

Laird, Dorothy, *Royal Ascot* (Hodder & Stoughton, 1976)

Lee, Celia, *Jean, Lady Hamilton, 1861–1941: Diaries of a Soldier's Wife* (Pen & Sword Military, 2020)

Lee, Sir Sidney, *King Edward VII: A Biography* (Macmillan & Co., 1925 and 1927)

Lees-Milne, James, *The Enigmatic Edwardian* (Sidgwick & Jackson, 1986)

Lees-Milne, James, *Harold Nicolson: Volume Two, 1930–1968* (Hamish Hamilton, 1988)

Leslie, Anita, *Edwardians in Love* (Hutchinson & Co, 1972)

MacColl, Gail, and Wallace, Carol McD., *To Marry an English Lord* (Workman Publishing, 2012)

MacKenzie, Jeanne, *The Children of the Souls* (Chatto & Windus, 1986)

MacKenzie, Norman and Jeanne (eds), *The Diary of Beatrice Webb, Volume III: 1905-1924* (Virago in association with London School of Economics, 1984)

Mackenzie-Rogan, Lieut.-Col. J., *Fifty Years of Army Music* (Methuen & Co., 1926)

Magee, Sean, with Aird, Sally, *Ascot: The History* (Methuen, 2002)

Magnus, Philip, *King Edward the Seventh* (The History Book Club, 1965)

Marson, Richard, *Inside Updown: The Story of Upstairs, Downstairs* (Kaleidoscope Publishing, 2001)

Masters, Anthony, *Rosa Lewis: An Exceptional Edwardian* (Weidenfeld & Nicolson, 1977)

Maxtone-Graham, John, *The Only Way to Cross* (Patrick Stephens, 1983)

Maylunas, Andrei, and Mironenko, Sergei, *A Lifelong Passion* (Weidenfeld & Nicolson, 1996)

McGrath, Christopher, *Mr Darley's Arabian* (John Murray, 2016)

McKenna, Stephen, *While I Remember* (Thornton Butterworth, 1921)

Mendes, Valerie D., and de la Haye, Amy, *Lucile Ltd* (V&A Publishing, 2009)

Meyers, Jeffery, *Katherine Mansfield: A Darker View* (Cooper Square Press, 2002)

Montgomery-Massingberd, Hugh, and Watkin, David, *The London Ritz: A Social and Architectural History* (Aurum Press, 1980)

Mordaunt Crook, J., *The Rise of the Nouveaux Riches* (John Murray, 1999)

Morgan, Janet, *Edwina Mountbatten: A Life of Her Own* (Harper Collins, 1991)

Mount, Charles Merrill, *John Singer Sargent: A Biography* (Cresset Press, 1957)

Nabokov, Vladimir, *Speak, Memory* (Penguin Modern Classics, 2000)

Nesbit, E., *The Railway Children* (Wells Gardner, Darton & Co., 1906)

Nevill, Ralph (ed.), *Leaves from the Note-Books of Lady Dorothy Nevill* (Macmillan & Co., 1907)

Nicolson, Juliet, *The Perfect Summer* (John Murray, 2006)

Nicolson, Nigel, *Portrait of a Marriage: Illustrated Edition* (Guild Publishing, 1990)

Nicolson, Nigel (ed.), *The Flight of the Mind: The Letters of Virginia Woolf, Volume I: 1888–1912* (The Hogarth Press, 1975)

Olson, Stanley, *John Singer Sargent: His Portrait* (Barrie & Jenkins, 1989)

Ormond, Richard, *John Singer Sargent: Portraits in Charcoal* (The Morgan Library & Museum, 2019)

Pakula, Hannah, *An Uncommon Woman* (Phoenix Press, 1997)

Pless, Princess Daisy of, *Princess Daisy of Pless by Herself* (John Murray, 1928)

Plumptre, George, *The Fast Set: The World of Edwardian Racing* (André Deutsch, 1985)

Ponsonby, Arthur, *The Camel and the Needle's Eye* (A. C. Fifield, 1910)

Ponsonby, Sir Frederick, *Recollections of Three Reigns* (Eyre & Spottiswood, 1957)

Pope-Hennessy, James, *Queen Mary* (George Allen & Unwin, 1959)

Pope-Hennessy, James, *The Quest for Queen Mary* (Zuleika and Hodder & Stoughton, 2018)

Rappaport, Helen, *Caught in the Revolution* (St Martin's Press, 2017)

Redesdale, Lord, *King Edward VII: A Memory* (The Ballantyne Press, 1915)

Reid, Michaela, *Ask Sir James* (Hodder & Stoughton, 1987)

Ribblesdale, Lord, *Impressions and Memories* (Cassell & Company, 1927)

Ridley, Jane, *Bertie: A Life of Edward VII* (Vintage, 2013)

Ridley, Jane, *George V: Never a Dull Moment* (Chatto & Windus, 2021)

Robinson, John Martin, *Buckingham Palace: The Official Illustrated History* (The Royal Collection, 2000)

Röhl, John C. G. and Sombart, Nicolaus (eds), *Kaiser Wilhelm II: New Interpretations* (Cambridge University Press, 1982)

Roosevelt, Theodore, *The Letters of Theodore Roosevelt: Vols I–VIII* (Cambridge, Massachusetts, 1951–4)

Rutter, Frank, *Revolution in Art* (Art News Press, 1910)

Sackville-West, Vita, *The Edwardians* (The Hogarth Press, 1930)

Service, Alastair, *Edwardian Architecture* (Thames and Hudson, 1977)

Seymour, Miranda, *Noble Endeavours* (Simon & Schuster, 2014)

Sitwell, Osbert, *Great Morning* (Macmillan & Co., 1948)

Souhami, Diana, *Mrs Keppel and Her Daughter* (Harper Collins, 1996)

Spalding, Frances, *The Bloomsbury Group* (National Portrait Gallery Publications, 2013)

Spencer, Charles, *Cecil Beaton: Stage and Film Designs* (Academy Editions, 1975)

Stamper, C. W., *What I Know* (Mills & Boon, 1913)

Stansky, Peter, *On or About December 1910: Early Bloomsbury and Its Intimate World* (Harvard University Press, 1997)

Stephen, Adrian, *The 'Dreadnought' Hoax* (Chatto & Windus/The Hogarth Press, 1983)

Strasdin, Kate, *Inside the Royal Wardrobe: A Dress History of Queen Alexandra* (Bloomsbury, 2017)

Taylor, Lou, *Mourning Dress: A Costume and Social History* (George Allen & Unwin, 1983)

Taylor, S. J., *The Great Outsiders: Northcliffe, Rothermere and the Daily Mail* (Weidenfeld & Nicolson, 1996)

Tuchman, Barbara, *The Proud Tower* (Hamish Hamilton, 1966)

Vickers, Hugo (ed.), *Beaton in the Sixties* (Phoenix Paperback, 2003)

Vickers, Hugo, *Cecil Beaton* (Weidenfeld & Nicolson, 1985)

Warwick, The Countess of, *Afterthoughts* (Cassell & Company, 1931)

Wake, Jehanne, *Princess Louise: Queen Victoria's Unconventional Daughter* (Collins, 1988)

Walpole, Hugh, *The Secret City* (Macmillan and Co., 1919)

Welch, Frances, *The Imperial Tea Party* (Short Books, 2018)

Wells, H. G., *Experiment in Autobiography* (Macmillan & Co., 1934)

White, Jerry, *Zeppelin Nights: London in the First World War* (The Bodley Head, 2014)

Wilson, John, *CB: A Life of Sir Henry Campbell-Bannerman* (Constable, 1973)

Wilson, Philip Whitwell (ed.), *The Greville Diary* (William Heinemann, 1927)

Windsor, The Duke of, *A King's Story: The Memoirs of the Duke of Windsor* (G. P. Putnam's Sons, 1951)

Woolf, Leonard, *Beginning Again: An Autobiography of the Years 1911–1918* (The Hogarth Press, 1964)

Woolf, Virginia, *Mr Bennett and Mrs Brown*, second impression (The Hogarth Press, 1928)

Zebel, Sydney H., *Balfour: A Political Biography* (Cambridge University Press, 1973)

Ziegler, Philip, *Diana Cooper* (Penguin, 1983)

Index